Hist

The Heir Apparent

THE
Heir Apparent
Robert Kennedy
and the Struggle for Power

BY

William V. Shannon

NEW YORK / *The Macmillan Company*

LONDON / *Collier-Macmillan Limited*

The Macmillan Company, New York
Collier-Macmillan Canada Ltd., Toronto, Ontario
Printed in the United States of America

To Elizabeth,
with Love

Contents

The Heir Apparent

CHAPTER ONE

Destiny Unfulfilled

> "*There are millions of people all across this country who feel as Robert F. Kennedy does; for them the name of Kennedy is magic, as was the name Stuart under the Hanoverian reign of the Georges; and wherever old or young devotants of the Kennedy loyalty gather, the Bonny Prince Charlie of the faith is Robert F. Kennedy. Like the Jacobites, they await the Restoration.*"
> —THEODORE H. WHITE, The Making of the President, 1964
> (*Atheneum, New York, 1965*) p. 260.

"Let the word go forth from this time and place, to friend and foe alike," John Kennedy said on that cold, brilliantly sunlit Inaugural Day, "that the torch has been passed to a new generation of Americans—born in this century, tempered by war, disciplined by a hard and bitter peace, proud of our ancient heritage."

Of all his brother's words, these have had the deepest personal meaning for Robert Kennedy. Never for a moment did he believe that with his brother's assassination the torch had passed to Lyndon Johnson. Mr. Johnson had inherited the office of the Presidency, but Robert Kennedy feels a personal responsibility to carry the torch.

The difficulty is that one cannot be the nation's leader if one is not also President. Inescapably, in the months after his brother's death Robert Kennedy came to believe that the White House was to be his destiny. Like the oldest son of a royal family, his future status has been fixed by fate. He is the heir apparent. (True, John Kennedy had only spoken of power passing to "a new generation," but his brother naturally could not see any other forty-year-old worthy of that heritage. If there was a generation, he would have to do the epitomizing.)

Only a family of *nouveau riche* background and aspirations could so boldly stake out this royal claim and so confidently expect to carry it off. Historians have sought for precedents in American history for a family like the Kennedys and found none quite satisfactory. The Adamses, for all their family pride, are too prim and self-contained; the Roosevelts, for all their lustiness and ambition, are a divided clan and twenty-four years separated the presidential tenure of the two members of their family.

The true parallel is with the Bonapartes. JFK was, like Napoleon, a man of destiny, a man of brilliant practical intelligence and soaring ambition, who slashed his way to power through prior claims and strong opposition, and who, with the help of a beautiful wife, organized a glittering court and imposed a personal style. There are small coincidences: Napoleon, too, had an older brother named Joseph, and a next younger brother who was his political manager when he first acquired national power, and several vivacious sisters in whose foibles, quarrels, children, and love affairs he took a lively interest and whose husbands he appointed to high offices of government. The careers of Napoleon and Kennedy both ended at age forty-six: the one in exile and the other in death. The difference is that Kennedy did not live to dictate his memoirs and elaborate his legend. Those tasks have fallen to his widow, his brothers, and his courtiers.

The Kennedys share with the Bonapartes the qualities of character, talent, and temperament usually found in the first generation or two of dynasties. They have the same awesome energy and unshakable nerves, the voracious appetite for positions and honors, the imperious and sometimes rude temper, the rough, serviceable wit coupled with a humorlessness about their own egotism and ambition, the overpowering sense of family, the shrewd, effective intelligence and the bravura charm. Their methods may sometimes be gross, but their taste in people and things is good and their ideals are aristocratic, for like most *arrivistes*, they take on the standards of the class into which they have moved. The old heartiness and force are there, and sometimes a strain of coarseness, but so are the finer perceptions and the heightened sense of control; if this seems paradoxical, they are, it must be remembered, exceptional people. Not many families are capable of founding a dynasty. It requires the *élan* of a revolutionary, the "guts of a burglar,"* the acquisitive passion of the newly propertied, and the historic sense of a conservative.

The assassination of President Kennedy was as if Napoleon had been cut down immediately after the Peace of Tilsit. The great triumphs of Marengo, Jena, and Austerlitz were behind him and only the dubious victory of the Battle of Wagram lay ahead. A historian looking back can see that at Tilsit in 1807 Napoleon was at high noon; although many adventures lay ahead, few would be successful and the shadows would rapidly lengthen.

For all we know, the same might have proved true for Kennedy. Even if he had held office for another half-dozen years as he fully expected to do, it is conceivable, even likely, that his place in history would still rest largely on the accomplishments of his first three years—the successful confrontation with the Soviet Union concerning Cuba in 1962, the Nuclear Test Ban Treaty, the Alliance for Progress, and the comprehensive domestic programs already set forth in messages to Congress.

Napoleon and his family and admirers scarcely foresaw the disappointments and defeats to come. Neither could

---

* Robert Kennedy's admiring phrase when his brother appointed him as Attorney General.

the Kennedys and their supporters be reasonably expected to think of President Kennedy's unfulfilled future as anything but a golden age that had not been reached. The greatest triumphs must surely have lain ahead not behind. A lunatic's bullet had wrenched history from its appointed course. It is their duty to restore it to its appointed way. And here the Kennedys have showed their Bonapartist force. If Napoleon had been struck down when the French Empire stretched across half of Europe and two of his brothers occupied lesser thrones, the Bonapartes would not have yielded up such a heritage without a struggle. The Kennedys have proved themselves no less resourceful and determined.

Jacqueline Kennedy acted first and impressively. She arranged for her husband a state funeral modeled upon that of the martyred Lincoln. She bore herself through three days of ceremonies with such an unerring sense of what she wanted for her husband that she made the funeral a rare union of official solemnity and touching personal sentiment. In Alexander Pope's line, "She moves a goddess, and she looks a queen."

She and her advisers made the brilliantly right decision to bury her husband, not in some suburb of Boston, but on a hillside of Arlington overlooking the nation's capital, and there to memorialize him with a simple stone and a perpetual flame. It was thus delicately suggested that he was worthy of perpetual veneration. And for the foreseeable future, at least, he will receive it since his burial place has already joined the Washington Monument and the Lincoln Memorial as one of the capital's foremost tourist attractions.

As the dead President's body was borne away and Mrs. Kennedy stood, dry-eyed and beautiful, and her small son saluted, a hardened newsman stepped back and said, "God, I wish we were a monarchy and the kid was taking over and that woman was the regent."

Many other Americans shared this sentiment during that tragic weekend. The Kennedys may have, too, but as realists, they recognized that this royal drama would be played out in a republican setting. There would be no regency and no direct succession. Mrs. Kennedy and her attractive children soon faded into the background. She is much admired from a distance and intensely gossiped and speculated about but is not an active figure. Her principal remaining role is a passive one: it is up to her not to ruin the Kennedy prestige by a bad remarriage or reckless misbehavior. She also feels an obligation not to confer that prestige on any political figure who is not a member of the family or one of its intimates. True to that role, she has not returned to the White House since she left it. The Johnsons have beseeched her with repeated invitations but she did not yield even when they dedicated the rose garden that she had personally planned. Like Josephine gazing sadly from Malmaison toward the Paris of Louis XVIII, this dowager empress has no intention of conferring her approval upon these Texas Bourbons.

The real agent of the restoration, the bearer of the family's hopes, is Robert Kennedy. If Lucien Bonaparte, as President of the Council of the Five Hundred, had been instrumental in the success of the *coup d'etat* that overthrew the Directory and installed his brother Napoleon as a Consul, Robert Kennedy had played an equally important part in his brother's swift rise to the Presidency. He acted as his manager in the critical campaign against Henry Cabot Lodge for the U.S. Senate in 1952 and again through all the primaries and the election campaign of 1960. During their years in power, he had functioned as President Kennedy's alter ego. As Attorney General, he had not only commanded one of the most important and sensitive departments of the federal government, but he had also superintended overseas intelligence operations, advised on foreign policy, carried out confidential diplomatic missions, disposed of many kinds of patronage from post-masterships to sub-Cabinet jobs, and dealt with state party chairmen and political bosses around the country. No one was better situated to pick up the reins of authority.

There was idle speculation for a time after the assassination that the family's new presidential candidate would be the youngest brother, Edward Moore "Teddy" Kennedy. He had already been elected to the Senate from Massachusetts in 1962 and demonstrated an agreeable, plausible political personality. "The best natural politician in the family," the late President had said of him. His colleagues in the Senate liked him as an affable colleague in a way that few liked the often curt and abrasive Robert. But there was never any chance that the family would advance Teddy and drop Robert to his old role as manager. The royal rule of primogeniture was against it. Even when the Kennedys were still an obscure Boston family scarcely heard of on the national scene, John Kennedy was explaining to people that one reason he had entered politics was that he wanted to take up where his brother Joe had left off. "And if anything happens to me, Bobby will take over and if anything happens to him, it will be Teddy."

Although Robert had the advantages of experience, political acquaintance, and personal ability, he had weaknesses as a potential presidential candidate. His popular reputation was that of the "tough little brother," the President's hatchet man, a one-time McCarthyite. Probably the best-known single quote about him was his father's remark: "Bobby is like me. He hates the way I do."

His best resource in overcoming these adverse aspects of his own reputation was his dead brother's already developing legend. The potential strength of that legend first became clear less than two months after the assassination. In January 1964, at President Johnson's request, Kennedy went to Japan to try to work out a cease-fire between Indonesia and Malaysia, whose quarrel seemed about

to burst into serious warfare. The trip, which lasted thirteen days, was only a temporary diplomatic success since
the understanding he patched up between the adversaries
did not last. But it was an immense personal triumph. On
this brief Asian journey, which included stops in Korea
and the Philippines, Robert Kennedy's status as a world
figure was confirmed. He was not greeted merely as the
attractive young man and Very Important Person that he
had been in the past because of his brother's office. He was
now the political heir of a martyr and a probable future
President himself.

He began to define the meaning of the Kennedy legend.
After eight years of the political conservatism and intellectual sluggishness of the Eisenhower administration,
the Kennedy administration obviously represented a welcome infusion of energy, ideas, and canny political competence, but what it stood for in terms of philosophy and
programs was not easy to say. The "new frontier" was a
phrase without specific meaning. Once the 1960 campaign was over, President Kennedy never again used the
expression. Robert Kennedy, however, had used it, particularly when traveling abroad. On a previous trip to
Asia in 1962, he frequently spoke of the men of the
younger generation taking office in Washington and urged
his listeners to turn away from the past toward the "new
frontiers of education, science and technology."

In January 1964, he visited Waseda University in Japan
where a minority of Communist students had vigorously
heckled him two years earlier and disrupted his meeting.
This time, he was heard in deeply respectful silence and,
at his conclusion, with intense applause. He told the
Japanese students:

"There was a special feeling between President Kennedy
and young people. He was more than just the President of
a country. He was the leader of young people everywhere.
What he was trying to do was to fight for peace and also

to fight against hunger, disease and poverty around the world. You and I as young people have a special responsibility to carry on this fight!"

Robert Kennedy thus defined his brother's heritage as, first, a generational appeal to the young and, second, a commitment to peaceful economic development, using almost the same words ("fight against hunger, disease and poverty") as General Marshall had used in setting forth the Marshall Plan in 1947.

Meanwhile, the mythmakers were at work. Episodes, true or at least half true, were written up in the popular press in sympathetic ways which depicted Kennedy bravely carying on in his brother's behalf. Thus, Peter Maas wrote in the *Saturday Evening Post:* "In Manila, he spoke to another student group—one that John Kennedy would have addressed if he had lived to tour the Far East this past winter. After the Attorney General had finished speaking, the cheering students mobbed him. When he finally got into his car, his eyes welled with tears. 'It wasn't really for me,' he said. 'It was for him.' A friend seated beside him quietly replied, 'You've got to do it for him now.' For perhaps thirty seconds Bob Kennedy sat there lost in thought. Then he slowly nodded his head." [1]

Through the spring and early summer of 1964, Robert Kennedy brooded over alternative plans for his future. He spoke at times of withdrawing from Washington and becoming a teacher for a year or two, but there was never any real doubt that he would remain in politics. Shortly before the assassination, he and his brother had discussed the possibility that after the 1964 election, Secretary of State Dean Rusk would be eased out and replaced by Defense Secretary Robert McNamara with Robert Kennedy taking charge of Latin America in the dual post of Assistant Secretary of State and head of the Alliance for Progress. But President Johnson had confidence in his own skill in dealing with Latins and had already filled that post with a personal protégé, Thomas C. Mann.

The governorship of Massachusetts was a possibility, but Kennedy decided against it. It would mean competing with brother Teddy on their home terrain. The Senate seat held by Republican Kenneth Keating of New York was another possibility, but Kennedy, a man of executive temper and restless energies, looked askance at the droning routines of the Senate. In an impulsive moment, he scrawled a handwritten note to President Johnson volunteering to accept the ambassadorship to South Vietnam. But Johnson rejected this notion on grounds that he would not want to risk the life of a member of the Kennedy family, which had already lost two sons, by appointing him to a position of hardship and danger.

Although all these possibilities flickered fitfully for varying periods of time, Kennedy gradually fixed his ambition on the vice-presidential nomination. He recognized that it is inherently an empty office: "There isn't anything you can do in the Vice-Presidency . . . not one damn thing . . . that you are not told to do." It also galled him to accept second place under Lyndon Johnson, whom he personally disliked. But in the nuclear age, the importance of the second place has increased because no man who is only one heartbeat away from control of the H-bomb can be counted insignificant. Moreover, since Johnson has suffered a coronary and other illnesses, the statistical chances of succeeding to the Presidency in the next four years were better than normal. To become Vice-President would consolidate Kennedy's position as the second most powerful man in the Democratic Party and the heir apparent. To allow any other man to get that position would complicate his struggle to succeed Johnson later.

The Kennedy activists were divided as to how best to seek the second place on the ticket. Kenny O'Donnell, who had been John Kennedy's appointment secretary in the White House and one of Robert's closest friends since college days, proposed a frontal attack. If Kennedy marshaled his strength among party leaders in the North and openly avowed his candidacy, he could overawe Johnson and force his way on to the ticket. But others pointed out that since naming his running mate was a traditional prerogative of a presidential nominee, Johnson could cut the ground under this strategy by simply announcing that he would decide the matter himself.

Boldness appeals to Kennedy. He is much more given to direct, bold approaches toward men and issues than was his brother, the President, who preferred to have as many balls in the air at one time as possible. In this instance, Robert rejected boldness and emulated his brother. He decided to campaign for the Vice-Presidency through the press, through friendly politicians, and by demonstrating his crowd-pleasing powers—abroad. He thus pressured Johnson but did not directly challenge his right of decision.

In an interview with Ben Bradlee, then the Washington bureau chief of *Newsweek,* he assessed his vice-presidential prospects with his usual flat realism: "Actually, I should think I'd be the last man in the world he (Johnson) would want . . . because my name is Kennedy, because he wants a Johnson Administration with no Kennedys in it, because we travel different paths, because I suppose some businessmen would object, and because I'd cost them a few votes in the South . . . I don't think as many as some say, but some."

Why might Johnson put him on the ticket?

"Because most of the major political leaders in the North want me. All of them, really. And that's about all I've got going for me."

In that same interview, he added a third element to the family legend. The Kennedys now stood not only as symbols of youth and of the fight against hunger, disease, and poverty but also as proof against mediocrity in government.

"I'd like to harness all the energy and effort and incentive and imagination that was attracted to government by President Kennedy. I don't want any of that to die. It's important that the striving for excellence continue, that there be an end to mediocrity."

President Johnson might take it amiss that his own entry into the White House necessarily meant a precipitous decline from excellence to mediocrity, but from Kennedy's viewpoint, Johnson was only holding office on sufferance anyway.

"The torch really has passed to a new generation," he continued. "People are still looking for all that idealism. It permeated young people all over the globe. And I became sort of a symbol, not just as an individual. If I could figure out some course for me that would keep all that alive and utilize it for the country, that's what I'd do." [2]

A few days before the interview appeared in print, Kennedy, on invitation from the West Berlin government, dedicated a plaque in the square now renamed "John F. Kennedy Platz," where his brother had spoken one year earlier. He repeated to the West Berliners the theme that Kennedy stood for an end of mediocrity.

There was a plausible reason for his trip to Germany, but none for the visit to Poland that followed. There the government had most definitely not invited him; it curtained his trip with silence. No advance announcement of his arrival was made in the newspapers or on the state-controlled radio network. But since many Poles listen to Western broadcasts, gossip soon spread the word. Kennedy arrived in Warsaw late one Saturday. The next morning, he and Mrs. Kennedy and their three oldest children started from their hotel to St. John's Cathedral for Mass.

As they walked, passersby recognized him and began to shake his hand, ask for autographs, trail after him. By the time he had walked a few blocks there were hundreds; by the time he left the cathedral an hour later, there were thousands. Singing, waving, shouting, the enthusiastic Poles thronged about the car that had been sent to pick him up. The short trip back to the hotel took an hour.

"This is the way we always come home from Mass," Kennedy said delightedly.

Similar demonstrations occurred in the next several days as he visited in Warsaw, Cracow, Czestochowa. Everywhere, Kennedy demonstrated his increasingly sure touch with crowds. He joked with them and blarneyed them. He introduced members of his family and then invited all those in the crowd who had relatives in America to "drop in on us" when they visited the United States. He led the singing of what he assured listeners was a very popular song back home, "When Polish Eyes Are Smiling."

In Cracow, where he met with local officials of the government and the Communist Party, he answered candidly and seriously a broad sweep of questions, including one about his brother's assassination. When he finished, the mayor of Cracow asked if he were planning to run for President of the United States because, if so, it would be a great honor if he announced his candidacy in Cracow.

Kennedy pondered the question, then replied: "No, I don't think I'll run for President. I think I'll run for mayor of Cracow."

The Communists burst into laughter and applause.

Coming as it did only seven weeks before the Democratic National Convention, this barnstorming tour of Poland was no idle pleasure trip. As Joseph Kraft shrewdly observed, Kennedy "seemed to act out the hopes he has never expressed. He demonstrated, once again, the massive pulling power of the Kennedy name. He showed, in his own right, a remarkable way with crowds, and a capacity to dramatize issues. In effect, he put his aspirations and qualities on display." [3]

President Johnson, quite sensibly from his own standpoint, refused to be impressed. He did not choose Kennedy as Vice-President since that would have made his own administration a hybrid affair. In retrospect, it was an astonishing display of arrogance on Kennedy's part ever to have seriously believed that he could bluff or pressure his way on to the ticket. As Theodore H. White has written, the two men shared the knowledge of the bitter, inescapable fact that Johnson could never have become President on his own. No Democratic convention would have nominated him because with his Southern background and ambiguous record on civil rights, he did not look like a winner in the North and West. The Kennedys had opened the White House to him by choosing him for Vice-President.

But Johnson would have had to be a very weak man to reciprocate unless the evidence showed that it was absolutely necessary. In 1960, John Kennedy needed a Protestant partner from the South or Southwest; in short, he needed Johnson. In 1964, with Barry Goldwater as his feckless opponent, Johnson needed no one.

On Wednesday, July 29, 1964, Johnson invited Kennedy to his office to tell him that he would not be chosen. The President so feared Robert Kennedy and the power of the Kennedy name that he could think of no way to rationalize this decision to the public except to announce the next evening that he was excluding from consideration every member of the Cabinet and every official who regularly attended meetings of the Cabinet. He then extracted telegrams from every Democratic state chairman in the country endorsing his decision.

The events of July 29–30 brought the Kennedy era definitively to an end. There was to be no sharing of power in Lyndon Johnson's Washington and no easy right of succession. If Kennedy was to succeed Johnson in the White House, he would have to establish an independent base of power and mount a fight for the succession.

But the Kennedy era had a poignant epilogue. A month later the Democrats held their dull convention at Atlantic City at which Lyndon Johnson and Hubert Humphrey were duly nominated. After four days of heavy-duty oratory, the delegates were shown a brief film on the life of John F. Kennedy. The President had carefully censored its contents and its scheduling: there was to be no mention in it of Robert Kennedy and it was not to be shown until the vice-presidential nomination had been safely made. But since Robert Kennedy could not be barred from the proceedings altogether without producing an unnecessary rift in the party, he was allowed to make a speech of introduction for the film.

When he appeared, the vast crowd in the convention hall gave way to a quarter-hour of intense cheering, applauding, waving. Many were in tears. It was an extraordinary outburst of grief, love, and frustration. As nearly as a large assemblage could, the crowd made a demonstration that was a eulogy to a dead hero. Robert Kennedy stood there, a slight figure in a dark suit and a black tie, with a small, sad smile on his face as wave after wave of sound broke upon him. When he could finally speak, he made a short, moving address highlighted by a quotation from *Romeo and Juliet*.

"When I think of President Kennedy," he said, "I think of these lines from Shakespeare:

> 'When he shall die
> Take him and cut him out in little stars,
> And he will make the face of heaven so fine
> That all the world will be in love with night
> And pay no worship to the garish sun.' "

There is little doubt that at that moment most of the

delegates, if they had been free, would have nominated Robert Kennedy for President. But the applause and tears were impotent. Like the ovations of the galleries for Adlai Stevenson at the 1960 convention in Los Angeles, they were powerless to move events. This convention was locked up for Lyndon Johnson. It could give the Kennedys nothing but sentimental memories. For them, another long march to power was necessary.

Robert Kennedy left Atlantic City for New York to get the march started.

NOTES

[1] Peter Maas, "What Will R.F.K. Do Next?" *Saturday Evening Post*, March 28, 1964.
[2] *Newsweek*, July 6, 1964. The earlier quote on the emptiness of the Vice-Presidency is also from this interview.
[3] Joseph Kraft, "The Ambitions of Bobby Kennedy," *Look*, August 25, 1964, p. 22.

CHAPTER TWO

Enter Kennedy, Triumphant

*"I had few really definite ideas, and the reason for this
was that, instead of obstinately seeking to control circumstances, I obeyed them, and they forced me to change my
mind all the time. Thus it happened that most of the
time, to tell the truth, I had no definite plans but only
projects."*
—NAPOLEON BONAPARTE *in conversation, 1816, quoted in*
J. Christopher Herold, ed., The Mind of Napoleon
(Columbia University Press, New York, 1955), p. 43.

IN that spring of 1964, the fair province of New York
lay ripe for conquest. The local rulers had lost the
loyalty of the populace; the party out of power lacked a
suitable candidate; there was no shortage of mercenaries.
It was a fiefdom waiting for a royal duke to assert his
natural authority and take possession. There was no need
for legitimacy; boldness would win all.

The shrewdest observers recognized that such a conquest would not be an end in itself. It could only be the
first act of a much greater drama. For those seeking to
take Washington and govern the nation, New York is the
traditional recruiting ground. The great moneylenders,
merchant princes, and barons of industry are head-
quartered there; so, too, are many of the poets and trouba-
dours.

Whoever commands the Empire State is inevitably
drawn into further conflicts and rivalries. Only the Presidency can cap a career begun there, only its power can

appease the appetite New York arouses. The awareness
of these traditional truths heightened the excitement of
natives and onlookers alike; a great triumph or perhaps
a great tragedy was about to unfold, and all were eager
for the tale to begin.

Throughout the spring, Robert Kennedy bided his time
and pondered the invasion of New York. Victory was
probable. The seat of Republican Kenneth Keating, the
junior United States Senator, was at stake. He was a
one-term Senator and not an opponent to be feared. It
was not the specter of defeat that concerned Kennedy,
but rather the Senate and New York itself. He had no
desire to go to the Senate; it is a place for old men and
for middle-aged men with the manners of the old. It had
bored his brother John and promised to be no more exciting for him. Moreover, his younger brother Teddy was
already there; a second Kennedy might mean a certain
awkward jostling and unnecessary rivalry. He would
much prefer to be proconsul for this country's interests
in Latin America, or political and military overseer of the
war in Vietnam, or perhaps ambassador to Russia. Robert
Kennedy is no parliamentarian; he is a man of action. He
longed for combat, the stimulus of personal authority,
the zest of the difficult problem and the unexpected crisis.
Let Teddy have the Senate with the courtesy calls on
Richard Brevard Russell and the amendments to the
amendment and all the rest.

New York, too, posed almost as many risks as opportunities. He and his brothers had already mastered the
Irish clan warfare of Massachusetts politics and transformed that state into a safe family possession. But New
York is much larger, more complicated, and less easily
managed; being Irish and Catholic and a Kennedy would
provide much less leverage than in Massachusetts. The
Democratic Party was sorely divided and demoralized. In

working on his brother's campaign there in 1960, Kennedy
had learned that the crosscurrents of selfish intrigues,
obscure feuds, and implacable hatreds were Florentine in
their intricacy. To take possession of it and put its affairs
in order was a formidable political challenge, but it is
not the kind of challenge that interests the Kennedys.
Twenty years after they first became active in Massachusetts politics, the Democratic Party in that state is still
distraught and disorganized. Governing a party, like governing a nation, involves making hard choices and hard
enemies; the Kennedys are too preoccupied with husband-
ing their own popularity for higher, personal objectives
to dissipate it on the wearing tasks of party management.
The very weakness in the New York Democratic Party
that enabled Robert Kennedy to seize it for his own purposes caused him to recoil. If there were a way to stay on
the national scene in a position at once visible and potent,
he would much prefer it to adoption by the unruly constituency of New York.

Robert Kennedy's observation post in New York is a
suite on the thirtieth floor of the Pan-American Building
that sits atop the Grand Central Terminal. The outer doors
to this office bear the uncommunicative title: "Park
Agency, Inc. Licensed Real Estate Brokers." Off the quiet,
thickly carpeted reception rooms run a long corridor and
a series of small offices where sit the accountants and
real estate men who manage the elder Joseph P. Kennedy's
property holdings, the basis of the family fortune. At the
end of this corridor is the pleasant, medium-sized corner
office of Stephen Smith, the husband of Jean Kennedy
Smith, the youngest of the five sisters.

Smith, in 1964, was thirty-six and already well established as the family's "man of all work." He superintends
the management of the family fortune, but his real
passion and focus of concern is politics. He managed

Teddy's campaign in Massachusetts in 1962. He was President Kennedy's confidential agent in New York. He is slim and wiry with a thin, expressive face that can shift in seconds from alert suspicion to a radiant Kennedy-like smile. He has been described as "a hard-boiled Freddie Bartholomew." It is a measure of his qualities that in prep school, he played goalie in two of the roughest sports, lacrosse and hockey. He comes from a wealthy Brooklyn Irish family that made a fortune operating a barge line. After graduating from Georgetown University, he dabbled in oil-and-gas leases in the Southwest before entering the Kennedy family business. In 1961–62, he served briefly in the Development Loan Fund and in the State Department. Smith is exceptionally able and could easily have carved out a successful public career for himself in politics or government, but for reasons of his own, he chose to be the family's inside man. He guards the family exchequer, oversees its public relations, and keeps in touch with its political retainers. His office is unexceptionally furnished except for the innumerable Kennedy family photographs and mementos; its chief feature is the huge window commanding a dazzling view of the skyscrapers of Manhattan.

Smith does most of his work on the telephone (on which his voice sounds uncannily like that of his brother-in-law, Robert Kennedy). His callers in the first half of 1964 almost all gave him the same information: if Kennedy decided to try for the Senate nomination, no other Democrat could stop him.

The arithmetic of power in New York politics at the time was comparatively simple. Both parties chose nominees for statewide offices in conventions. Since the number of delegates was apportioned according to population and since nearly half of the people live in New York City, the candidate who commanded the backing of the city leaders was well ahead from the outset. There are sixty-two counties in the state, but they are far from equal. Brooklyn (Kings County) has approximately three million people and more delegates at a Democratic state convention than twenty thinly populated upstate counties. Smith could assure Kennedy that he had the support of Stanley Steingut, the leader of Brooklyn; of Charles Buckley, the leader of the Bronx; and of John English, the leader of rapidly growing, suburban Nassau County. With the additional support of the O'Connell machine in Albany and of Peter Crotty, the leader in Buffalo, his nomination was assured any time he cared to announce his availability.

Yet so deep was Robert Kennedy's distaste for the whole New York senatorial venture that on June 28, he announced that he had decided against making the race. There followed the trip to West Berlin and Poland and the long weeks of waiting in July until Lyndon Johnson should make known his vice-presidential decision. Only then was Kennedy prepared to move on New York.

Although the nomination was within his grasp, he knew enough about the state's politics to realize how important it was that he be put forward under the right auspices. The Steingut-Buckley-English-O'Connell-and-Crotty quintet had the votes but not the reputation. Except for English, they were stigmatized in public opinion as more or less unsavory bosses. The quality of their sponsorship was further compromised by the gratuitous adherence of Congressman Adam Clayton Powell. The liberal, reform element of the party had rallied in years past to the leadership of Eleanor Roosevelt and former Senator Herbert H. Lehman. In 1960, Robert Kennedy had bent every effort to make sure that the party regulars cooperated with the reformers in his brother's behalf. But Lehman and Mrs. Roosevelt were now dead, and the reform movement had no leaders of comparable prestige. The nearest to a replacement was New York's Mayor Robert F. Wagner, who, with the backing of the Lehman-Roosevelt reformers, had successfully staved off an effort by the regulars to deny him nomination to a third four-year term in 1961. Kennedy now resolved that he could not accept the nomination without Wagner's formal blessing.

Wagner, a man of discreet ambition and much quiet guile, welcomed Kennedy's arrival into New York much as the fifth century Romans welcomed the entry into Italy of Attila. It was an affliction from God which he deemed in no way merited, secretly resented, but could not publicly withstand. He had long coveted a seat in the Senate and had run once unsuccessfully. If he had moved early and decisively, he might have captured the nomination himself; even by mid-summer he could still make difficulties in Kennedy's path. But his wife had died the previous winter after a lingering illness, and the ordeal had so exhausted Wagner as to drain him temporarily of ambition or the will to resist. Although he maneuvered feebly for a time, he did, after many murmurings and mutterings, welcome his "good friend, Bob Kennedy" to New York and the Senate race.

Behind the scenes, Alex Rose, the leader of the small but pivotal Liberal Party, and President Johnson were instrumental in persuading Wagner to accept Kennedy. Rose was eager to clear the final obstacle from Hubert Humphrey's path to the Vice-Presidency. Humphrey had long been the Liberal Party's favorite Senator. Although the President had eliminated Kennedy from consideration for second place on the ticket, his elimination would be confirmed if he were firmly involved in a senatorial race. For this reason, Rose asked the President to talk to Wagner and assure him that even if Kennedy were elected, he (Wagner) would still be regarded as the party leader in New York and consulted on federal patronage. Johnson was happy to comply with this request. He mistakenly assumed that Kennedy would not be troublesome to him as a freshman Senator; and having blocked him for the Vice-Presidency, he did not want to foreclose him from a second political opportunity.

In the week after the national convention in Atlantic City, the New York Democrats gathered in Manhattan for their state meeting. The senatorial nomination was the principal business of the session since no state offices were being contested. Kennedy's only formal opponent was an upstate Congressman, Samuel Stratton. A former radio commentator who had captured a traditionally Republican district in a major upset and then consolidated his position by following a cautiously opportunistic course, swinging now liberal, now conservative, Stratton was well regarded by professionals as a votegetter, but he struck not the slightest spark of enthusiasm in New York City. His studied lack of ideological commitment, his speeches in behalf of government economy, and his occasional votes against housing and other urban programs convinced most city Democrats that he would make a good candidate for governor or Senator—in Ohio or Vermont.

Stratton's name was placed in nomination by Otis Pike, another Democratic Congressman from a normally Republican rural-and-small-town district on the eastern tip of Long Island. Pike bore down heavily on the "carpetbagger" theme in attacking Kennedy.

Before the roll call was half finished, Kennedy had a majority. Former Governor Averell Harriman, who was actively supporting Kennedy, approached Stratton on the convention floor and said, "Sam, how about making it unanimous?"

Stratton replied with a bitter unprintable obscenity. So ended his prospects for a statewide career as long as Robert Kennedy rules the future.

Robert Kennedy was a stranger in New York, but no more so than his brother had been in the Eleventh Congressional District in Massachusetts in 1946. For the

Kennedys of the present generation their only home is Hyannis Port on Cape Cod. Otherwise, theirs is the world of the rootless rich: winter holidays in Palm Beach, vacation trips to the Riviera or Aspen, rented apartments in Manhattan, private planes, unlimited money, unending motion. They could as easily mount a political campaign in Illinois or Pennsylvania or California as in Massachusetts or New York. For a time in 1964, it appeared as if they were, in fact, conducting multiple senatorial campaigns with Teddy running in Massachusetts, Robert in New York, former White House Press Secretary Pierre Salinger in California, and astronaut John Glenn, a Kennedy political protégé, in Ohio. But an accident forced Glenn to withdraw and Salinger was defeated. Only the authentic Kennedys made it.

The ability of the Kennedys to penetrate unfamiliar terrain and reach their political objectives seems to the romantic a triumph of glamorous personal leadership and to the moralist a gross assertion of the power of money. But to the political observer, it is at once more complex and less sinister. It represents the logical culmination of a series of developments, material and intellectual, in the conditions of American politics and society.

First in importance was the impact of radio and then of television. Beginning in the early 1930s, the widespread ownership of radios made it possible for political leaders to simultaneously reach masses of disparate individuals living in widely separated parts of the nation. In "fireside chats," Franklin D. Roosevelt shrank a continent to living-room size. Television completed this annihilation of space and time. Now communication is truly instantaneous, and every spectator, no matter how distant, can become a pseudoparticipant in history as it happens. At the same time, television intensively reinforces the fake intimacy created by the movies. Where once the cameras zoomed in for a close-up of Jean Harlow and Clark Gable, now they enable millions of viewers to be at home with Jack and Jackie or Bobby and Ethel in a "Person to Person" visit.

These technological developments would have had a disintegrative effect on a traditional, deeply structured society. But the United States has throughout its history been exceptionally mobile. In recent decades the tempo of restless migrations has never slowed: Okies and Arkies struggling to California, Negroes fleeing from the rural South and Puerto Ricans from their overcrowded island, West Virginia mountaineers heading for the factories of Detroit, Easterners moving West, and old people following the sun to Florida and Arizona. Between 1940 and 1960, more than seventeen million people left the farms for the towns and cities. At the same time, the children and grandchildren of immigrants are leaving slums and working class neighborhoods for the suburbs. The family may not cross state lines and yet the shift from the Lower East Side to Scarsdale or from South Boston to Natick is a dramatic change. In 1960, only one American in every four lived in the same house or apartment as he had ten years earlier.[1] The junior executive in IBM or Bell Telephone, the welfare recipient, the young man in the Army, and the retired civil servant are all caught up in this relentless flow of people. Increased education and military service have also broken down old parochialisms. Many Americans have ceased to think of themselves as having permanent city or state loyalties. The New Yorker or the Bay Stater has been replaced by the man who knows he is an impermanent resident of Park Forest or Green Acres. The Negro mother from Selma, Alabama, on relief in Chicago is neither an Alabaman nor an Illinoisian. In this peripatetic society, individual voters are not deeply influenced by ties with the past, and social or economic interests that had once seemed enduring are now seen as fluid. Social allegiances and interests are

replaced by appetites; the voter "consumes" political figures as he does athletic heroes and television stars. As in
those fields, his choice is governed by his taste for novelty,
personal attractiveness, and color, and by his need for
wish fulfillment. Voters seek from public affairs the psychic gratifications more proper to entertainment and recreation; politicians respond to this seeking by devoted
attention to their own "image."

As radio and television have made political groupings
far larger and more homogeneous, and as shifts in population have erased old boundaries and undercut old allegiances, more than twenty-five years of prosperity have
drained party loyalties of their intensity and ideological
commitments of their fanaticism. The number of straight
ticket voters steadily diminishes and the ranks of independents grow. Class warfare, which was real in the
1930s, has become an anachronism; the number of blue-
collar workers shrinks and that of clerical, technical, and
service workers rises with the result that the trade unions
fail to grow and middle-class attitudes replace militancy.
Old distinctions such as liberal and conservative are collapsed. In this climate of economic affluence, the public
does not turn to politicians who are disturbers of the
peace. Its approach to issues is not combative but man-
agerial. Intelligence and technique and energy are the
highly prized values, not social idealism or moral commitment to any impersonal cause.

In this new political atmosphere that technology, prosperity, and population change have produced, the two
decisive political forces are publicity and money. These
have never been unimportant. Most of the signers of the
Declaration of Independence and delegates to the Constitutional Convention were, by the standards of their
age, wealthy men, since only men of means could devote
months and years to the conduct of public affairs rather
than their own. And the Federalist papers early demon-

strated the value of skillful publicity. But for long periods in this nation's history men of middle class or even modest means have occupied the Presidency and other places of top political leadership. They were sustained in their rise to power by the support of their local and state party machines. But these party organizations have lost much of their viability and leverage. They cannot deliver the vote because voters move in and out of neighborhoods more frequently, refuse to register under either party label or to vote a straight ticket, and are much more likely to be influenced by what they see of the candidate on television than by anything a block captain or a county committeeman tells them. The decline of the national party conventions as unique institutions is symbolic; because the time-consuming rituals and maneuvers of these conventions are—in terms of show business values— boring, the presence of the television cameras has made the convention itself seem suddenly obsolete and inefficient although, in fact, it is neither.

It takes much greater sums of money from the candidate or the candidate's personal backers to take care of the work once performed by the now-atrophied party organizations. A candidate has to hire his own advance men to make arrangements, schedule his own transportation, and employ his own poll watchers. Since party organizations often do not function in raising campaign funds, he has to raise his own funds or spend his own money.

Intensive publicity and advertising on television are necessary since voters are not reachable by other means. Here there has been a steady retrogression. When radio alone existed, a fifteen-minute or even thirty-minute radio talk by a candidate was not regarded as excessive. But in the age of television, candidates only rarely buy so large a block of time to use for a serious, straightforward presentation of their views. Instead, there are "family shows" as if the attractiveness of the candidate's wife or the number of his children is relevant to his fitness for public office; or there are film clips depicting the candidate racing from one cheering crowd to another. The two-minute, one-minute, and thirty-second "spot" advertisements have crowded out longer programs in the television budgets of most candidates. These spots are a studied insult to the intelligence of voters; since thirty seconds or two minutes is not long enough to provide a clear, responsibly detailed opinion on any major issue, the time is used to make a calculatedly oversimplified and often misleading answer to a single question. The image that the candidate creates of being direct, candid, and sincere is his objective, not the exposition or clarification of any public problem.

The Kennedys are the great success story of contemporary American politics because better than any of their rivals in either party, they have adapted themselves to the requirements of fighting for power under modern circumstances. They have not spent the most money (Nelson Rockefeller has spent more) or been most calculating in their public relations (nobody, not even John Kennedy, spent as much time working on his image as did Richard Nixon) or been most ruthless (again Nixon has outdone them, and Lyndon Johnson has never been far behind). It is rather that the Kennedys have done all of these things more surefootedly, with greater natural ease and singleness of purpose and cool sophistication.

Robert Kennedy managed his own campaign for the Senate with smooth professionalism. He depended upon Steve Smith to oversee the spending of money and to backstop him on details, but he made his own major decisions. At the same time, although it was his first campaign, he made the transition easily from manager to candidate. This can be a high hurdle, and political managers as astute as James Farley and Len Hall have

failed to clear it. The public associates a political manager
with smoke-filled back rooms, with deals for support, and
sometimes with campaign fund-raising among somewhat
dubious people. Robert Kennedy is familiar with the
seamier side of politics, but he escaped these evil associations in the public mind because the Kennedys over the
years have managed their public relations so skillfully as
to avoid the impression that cigar-chewing professional
politicians and back-room deals had anything whatever to
do with John Kennedy's rise to the White House. Moreover, Robert Kennedy's youth, sun-tanned good looks, and
well-known preference, as of that time, for drinking
nothing stronger than milk helped keep him free of the
onus that campaign managers usually bear. Instead, the
only sign that he was a novice candidate was his inferior
performance as a public speaker. He has subsequently
improved considerably, but in 1964, he droned monoto-
nously when he got into the middle portions of a long,
prepared speech and, if he was talking extemporaneously,
he tended to ramble and repeat himself or, what was
worse, fall into short, awkward silences and then resume
abruptly on a different tack.

Kennedy had seemingly four handicaps to overcome in
the campaign. He was from out of state and could not
even qualify to vote for himself. He had been sponsored
in his entry into New York politics by the old-line bosses
in the Democratic Party. There was a widespread belief
that he was not interested in the Senate seat for its own
sake, but only using it as a "stepping-stone" to the Presidency. And, finally, there was his reputation for ruthlessness. All but the last of these handicaps proved more
apparent than real.

The "carpetbagger issue" cut less deeply than many
people had anticipated. It proved to be one of those boring
issues that everyone talks about, but that in the end most
people do not really care about. New York is the nervous,

novelty-hungry pacesetter for a nation of people on the move, and many of the most devoted New Yorkers have come from small towns a thousand miles away. For more than three hundred years, New York has been the cosmopolitan host to immigrants and refugees from all over the world. Why should one more stranger make any difference?* Besides, the years of publicity about Robert Kennedy had made him seem a familiar quantity.

Yet in order to minimize the carpetbagger issue, Kennedy was not averse to molding the truth about his upbringing into a more convenient shape.

"I lived in New York for twenty years. I grew up here. I went to school here. I held my first job here," he told audiences over and over again in the opening weeks of his campaign. In inspired moments, he sometimes added, "I was born here."

Kennedy was, of course, born in Brookline, Massachusetts. His family moved to New York when he was a year old, first to Riverdale, and then two years later to a larger house in Bronxville. He spent ten, not twenty, years of his life in New York. When he was eleven, he went with his family to London, when his father was the U.S. ambassador. In the fall of 1939, when he was not quite fourteen, he was sent back to this country to attend prep school. He spent three years at Portsmouth Priory in Rhode Island and a year at Milton Academy in Massachusetts. After service in the Navy and after graduating from Harvard College and the University of Virginia Law School, he returned to New York in late 1951, where he went to work on his first full-time job as a Justice Depart-

---

* Gerald Gardner has called attention to the fact that three of the principal speakers at the Republican state convention that renominated Kennedy's opponent, Kenneth Keating, were Thomas E. Dewey, who grew up in Michigan; Herbert Brownell, who was reared in Nebraska; and Clare Booth Luce, once a Congresswoman from Connecticut. Gardner, *Robert Kennedy in New York*, (Random House, 1965) p. 11.

ment attorney in the Federal Building in Brooklyn. He stayed several months before resigning to go to Massachusetts to manage his brother's Senate campaign. His family sold their house in Bronxville in 1941.

His sponsorship by party bosses such as Charles Buckley and Stanley Steingut did him even less harm than the carpetbagger issue. Almost all Reform Democrats rallied to his candidacy. Although author Gore Vidal and radio commentator Lisa Howard organized a committee of "Democrats for Keating," its membership was confined to a few other medium-grade celebrities. There was none of the in-fighting by major political figures that had helped wreck the campaign of Frank Hogan, the Democratic candidate against Keating in 1958.

Kennedy was alert to the potential danger of the argument that he was only using the Senatorship as a stepping-stone to something higher. Richard Nixon's gubernatorial campaign in California in 1962 demonstrated that a candidate is severely harmed when there is a widespread belief that he is not interested in state office for its own sake but only as a resting place until the Presidency opens up. Voters never like it when a candidate seems to regard a major office as a consolation prize or a way station to something better because it implies condescension on his part not only toward the office but toward them. Kennedy met this danger head-on by raising this accusation and denying it. His television advertising included a twenty-second spot which simply showed him shaking his head and saying, "Strange as it may seem, I just want to be a good United States Senator."

He was also helped by the ringing endorsements that he received from his two putative rivals for the White House, President Johnson and Hubert Humphrey. Kennedy's posters were changed in the closing weeks of the campaign to accent the picture of him as a good party man. The earlier theme, "Let's put Bob Kennedy to work for New York," gave way to "Get on the Johnson-Humphrey-Kennedy Team."

The reputation for ruthlessness clung to Kennedy to the end and hurt him to some extent. It was linked to two subterranean fears. Since he had worked for Joe McCarthy, was he still a secret McCarthyite? Since his father had been guilty of anti-Semitic remarks in the past, might he not be more like his father than his late brother? No recent evidence argued that he was a McCarthyite, and none at all that he was anti-Semitic. But these were not questions that he could raise himself and directly refute. He had to content himself with making many personal appearances before Jewish audiences. The support of the militantly liberal New York *Post,* which has a sizeable Jewish readership, and the endorsement of the Liberal Party helped diminish these dark worries.

Kennedy, however, could hardly lose. With Republican and independent voters hurrying away from Barry Goldwater's candidacy, the Republican Party was being engulfed by a catastrophe. As it turned out, President Johnson carried every county in the state and won a record-making plurality of 2,666,000 votes. The Republicans lost control of both houses of the state legislature and seven seats in the U.S. House of Representatives. Under these circumstances, the only question was the size of Kennedy's plurality.

His victory might have been in doubt if his opponent had a strong personal hold on New York voters. Jacob K. Javits, for example, might have survived the twin perils of a Johnson sweep and a Kennedy candidacy. But Kenneth Keating was no Javits.

Keating entered the House of Representatives in 1946, leaving a successful law practice, and for a dozen years represented the district which includes his home city of Rochester. He was an energetic, publicity-conscious member, who compiled a middle-of-the-road record. In 1958,

he was elected to the Senate, mostly on Nelson Rockefeller's coattails when the latter won his first term as
governor by an unexpectedly large margin. Once in the
Senate, Keating paid alert attention to the winning ways
of Javits, his Republican colleague, and emulated them.
To build support in New York City, he began to vote on
more liberal lines. He industriously made the rounds of
bar mitzvahs and other Jewish affairs. To please conservative voters, he was sternly anti-Communist; no American
Legion meeting or Communion breakfast was wholly safe
from a Keating speech or telegram inveighing against
"Godless Communism." In the weeks leading up to the
Cuban missile crisis of October 1962, he gained considerable notoriety from his warnings that Russian missiles
were being placed in Cuba. His sources for these warnings
were Cuban refugees whose information was readily available to the Kennedy administration but was not trustworthy until it had been verified by photo-reconnaissance.
Keating also continued his practice from his days in the
House of courting personal publicity. He issued press releases that were worth a paragraph or two in the newspapers because they related some humorous sidelight on
legislation or some oddity from a constituent's letter.

Curiously enough, Keating considerably resembled
Henry Cabot Lodge, whom John Kennedy had ousted from
a Senate seat in Massachusetts twelve years earlier. Keating and Lodge were both moderate conservatives on domestic issues. Both were driven by the voting habits of
their constituencies to adopt decidedly more liberal opinions than they instinctively possessed. They evolved the
same tactics of mystification and maneuver: conservative-
sounding speeches leading up to liberal conclusions, votes
for conservative amendments to liberal measures and vice
versa, and public statements that temporized or looked
both ways or looked no way except upward to God from
whence cometh our help in roll calls and other times of
trouble.[2]

Neither Keating nor Lodge was by any means among the worst of the members of the Senate in their respective periods of service there, but neither did they command the solid respect due to men who stand on their own two feet and speak their minds. When the crunch came, each was rather easily toppled by a Democrat who commanded a natural, as distinguished from an artificial, majority of the constituency.

The respective campaigns of Kennedy and Keating ran on parallel courses until the third and final stage. During the first stage, which extended from Labor Day until late September, each made low-keyed affirmative appeals. Kennedy toured the state making himself personally familiar, stressing his New York background, urging the importance of having at least one Democratic Senator to work with a Democratic administration in Washington, and disarming personal doubts about his character and intentions. Keating was similarly busy visiting around the state and trying to consolidate past support. At the end of the first stage, it was clear that Kennedy was well ahead. Keating was overcoming most of the drag effect of Goldwater's presence at the top of the Republican ticket, but he was not overcoming it entirely. And as a Republican with a weak hold on a constituency with a decided Democratic proclivity, Keating could not afford any losses. He needed strength above and below him on the ticket and all the breaks he could get.

His only hope of avoiding defeat was to gamble and go on the offensive. This marked the opening of the second phase of the campaign. Before audiences of Italian-Americans, he had already been attacking the Senate hearings on the Cosa Nostra, featuring the testimony of gangster Joe Valachi. Kennedy, as Attorney General, had arranged for these hearings to build public support for his wiretapping bill. They were held by the Senate Permanent Investigating Subcommittee of which he had once been counsel. Keating pointed out that the hearings led to no legislation and that the committee had no jurisdiction over the bill that Kennedy was promoting. These were legitimate criticisms but they did not logically sustain Keating's further charge that the hearings "reflected adversely on the good name of the Italian-American community."

Keating's major offensive consisted of a long position paper denouncing Kennedy for his part in the sale of the General Aniline and Film Corporation, which had been seized at the beginning of World War II as enemy property. Interhandel, a Swiss holding company, was the owner on record of most of the stock of General Aniline, but the U.S. government maintained that the real owner was I. G. Farben, the German cartel. When Kennedy took over the Justice Department in 1961, General Aniline was still being operated by management appointed by the U.S. government while suits and countersuits dragged through the courts. Rather than adjudicate the case further, Kennedy eventually decided to make a deal with Interhandel. General Aniline's stock was sold on the open market with the U.S. government and Interhandel dividing the proceeds on a fifty-fifty basis. Kennedy's action could be criticized from the viewpoint that no settlement would be preferable to one that risked the payment of any money to the I. G. Farben interests. But if a settlement was to be made, the one arrived at was reasonable.

Keating had not been opposed in principle to a settlement and prior to the campaign had not criticized the actual terms. But under the guidance of his campaign manager, former Attorney General Herbert Brownell, he now deplored the settlement because it meant money for a "huge Nazi cartel." He was not questioning Kennedy's motives, he added, only his methods.

The General Aniline "issue" was an open bid for the support of New York's Jewish voters. It rested on the cynical conviction that since the case was too difficult for the layman to judge, Keating could get away with anything he cared to say about it. But only a skillful demagogue could have done anything with this intractable material. Keating was no demagogue; he was just a harried, unhappy man afraid of a political defeat. He brought up the charge, fumbled with it just long enough to damage himself with informed voters, and then let it die away.

The New York Times, which supported Keating in its editorial columns, characterized his charge as "a fake issue." *The Times* added: "Attorney General Kennedy did not make 'a deal with Nazis.' He settled an incredibly complicated lawsuit."[3]

Kennedy, who swings hardest when counterattacking, told a press conference, "In all my experience in political campaigning, I have never heard of a charge as low as this one. . . . I lost a brother and a brother-in-law to the Nazis. I'm not making any deals with Nazis."

This was similar to—and may have unconsciously derived from—John Kennedy's argument against religious bigotry in the 1960 campaign when he repeatedly pointed out that no one had asked his or his brothers' religion when they volunteered for military service in World War II. It is an argument laden with explosive emotionalism. Kennedy's dead brother and brother-in-law had nothing to do with the General Aniline case since Keating was explicitly questioning Kennedy's judgment, not his motives, but as argument stoppers those dead heroes are unanswerable.

The Kennedy campaign organization was meanwhile engaged in working up the usual selective sampling and misrepresentation of the opponent's record. A widely distributed leaflet, "The Myth of Keating's Liberalism" and a newspaper advertisement, "By Right-Wing Standards Keating Is an Ultra-Conservative," involved chiefly the use of the incumbent's occasional conservative votes and the careful suppression of his much larger number of progressive votes. There was enough stretching of points and distortion to justify *The Reporter* magazine's observation that the Kennedy forces did not scruple to invent nonexistent bills and amendments for Keating to vote against.[4] Still, this dreary business goes on in many campaigns and most voters are armored against it by their acquired skepticism. It would have provoked little comment if it had not been for the unexpected contretemps over Keating, the Nuclear Test Ban Treaty, and the Fair Campaign Practices Committee. The committee, organized in 1956 on a permanent basis and chaired by Charles P. Taft, is a bipartisan group devoted to research and education. It does not pass judgment on actual unfair tactics by candidates in particular campaigns. However, Bruce L. Felknor, the executive director, was sufficiently incensed by what he regarded as Kennedy's misrepresentation of Keating's position on the Nuclear Test Ban Treaty that he sent him a stiff personal letter. "I say with deep regret that I read your statement with dismay. . . . Your description of his position on the Test Ban Treaty is not only false and distorted, but also appears to be either a deliberate and cynical misrepresentation or the result of incredible carelessness, touched with luck."[5]

Although intended to be confidential, this letter found its way into print in the ardently pro-Keating, New York *Herald Tribune*.

This adverse judgment by a respected bipartisan committee could have been seriously damaging to Kennedy unless reversed. Kennedy set out to reverse it. Ralph McGill, columnist and publisher of the Atlanta *Constitution*, resigned from the committee the next day on the grounds that Felknor was using the committee's name without consulting its members. Other influential members, after telephone calls from Kennedy, protested to Felknor. At the same time, Kennedy sent a platoon of aides to the committee headquarters bearing what was supposed to be new evidence on Keating's position.

Under all this pressure, the committee caved in. It not only disavowed Felknor's letter, which was the right thing to do since it had been sent on a confidential basis, but it went much further and withdrew all criticism altogether. As Felknor later wrote, "The tactical results of the Kennedy counter-foray were impressive. Shaken by the unfair position in which the publication of my letter had put Kennedy, the Committee was for all practical purposes taken out of play so far as the remainder of the Keating complaints were concerned."[6]

Kennedy's original charge had been that Keating, instead of supporting the Test Ban Treaty, had only been "an interested observer" asking questions and making comments and that until the vote was taken, he had "ridiculed" the treaty before finally giving it his "grudging and cautious approval." A rereading of Keating's speech of September 20, 1963, suggests that although it was too much to say that he had ridiculed the treaty, Felknor was also excessive in his indignant reaction. The speech was a fairly typical Keating performance. He made it clear at the beginning and end of his remarks that he intended to vote for the treaty, but the main body of his speech was devoted not to an argument in behalf of its merits but rather to a markedly defensive explanation of why he thought it would not be too harmful for the United States to ratify it. The tone of the speech was apologetic, as if its intended audience was a mailing list of DAR members and Goldwater Republicans.*[7]

---

* The speech contained no ridicule but there was a characteristic bit of Keating's humorous byplay. "Out of all the thousands of letters I received, however, there is one that really puzzles me. It is from a civil defense official who warns: 'The microscopic amount of fallout from an airburst bomb would cause several orders of magnitude less possible birth defects than the custom of men wearing underwear and trousers which keep the temper-

Kennedy's counter-offensive not only immobilized the committee for the rest of the campaign but also cast such doubt on its procedures that it was a year before the committee recovered. Indirectly, the episode led to Felknor's later withdrawal from the post of executive director. He wrote a book, *Dirty Politics,* in which, despite a manful effort to be fair, his bitterness toward Kennedy's pressure tactics shows through.[8]

Kennedy's ability to turn this controversy to his own purposes nullified any chance Keating might have had to overtake him. To prevent overconfidence, the Kennedy headquarters had spread the word in early October that their own polls showed him falling behind. In order to bolster the morale of *their* workers, the Keating headquarters had announced in the same period that their man had overcome Kennedy's lead and now looked like a winner. In fact, Kennedy was always ahead. Ten days after these misleading statements from the rival headquarters, the reliable *Daily News* poll made its first report: Kennedy ahead by twenty percentage points.

The third stage of the campaign encompassed the final two weeks. Kennedy was steadily widening his margin; Keating was sinking out of sight. Kennedy relaxed the pace of his personal campaigning; but his television commercials kept up the pressure. He spent approximately one million dollars for television, most of it for spot announcements and most of it in the last four weeks. One twenty-second spot epitomized the confident spirit of those closing days. It consisted simply of a voice that said:

"Think about it for a minute . . . [pause] which of the candidates running for United States Senator has the better chance of becoming a great United States Senator?

---

ature of the body higher than nature intended.' That makes it sound as if the most constructive thing any of us could do is take off our clothes and stay on the beach," Keating added.

. . . A *great* United States Senator? . . . On November third, vote for Robert Kennedy."[9]

On November third, they did. Kennedy polled 3,823,749 votes to Keating's 3,104,056. His margin of 719,693 votes was barely one-fourth as big as Johnson's astonishing 2,669,597, but Keating was a considerably tougher opponent in New York than Goldwater.

In his victory statement, Kennedy said, "We started something in 1960, and the vote today is an overwhelming mandate to continue."

He made no mention of Lyndon Johnson.

NOTES

[1] Ben J. Wattenberg with Richard M. Scammon, *This U.S.A.* (Doubleday, New York, 1965), pp. 63–117.

[2] It is interesting in this connection to note the conservative tone of Keating's judicial opinions since he became a judge of the New York Court of Appeals in 1965.

[3] Editorial, "Nonsense for New Yorkers," *The New York Times,* September 25, 1964.

[4] *The Reporter,* November 5, 1964, p. 12.

[5] Text of this letter printed in Bruce Felknor, *Dirty Politics* (W. W. Norton, New York, 1966), pp. 279–280.

[6] *Ibid.,* p. 197.

[7] *Congressional Record,* pp. 17619–17621.

[8] The Fair Campaign Practices Committee appointed a three-member panel to study the Keating-Kennedy-Felknor controversy. Its members were Palmer Hoyt, editor and publisher of the Denver *Post,* a Republican; Stephen A. Mitchell, former chairman of the Democratic National Committee, and former Senator Guy Gillette of Iowa, also a Democrat. In its report on April 12, 1965, the special panel concluded that Kennedy's statements were "such as to lead to a substantial distortion in the public's mind as to Keating's position" on the Nuclear Test Ban Treaty. This evoked

a final round of statements by Senator Kennedy and by attorney Louis Nizer. Nizer denounced the panel's conclusion as "unjustifiable" and said that Ralph McGill and Richard Cardinal Cushing of Boston subscribed to his statement. Cardinal Cushing had previously joined McGill in resigning from the committee.

[9] Terry Smith, "Bobby's Image," *Esquire*, April 1965, p. 62, is an excellent analysis of his use of television in his senatorial campaign.

CHAPTER THREE

The Heir Apparent

*"Who sketches Robert F. Kennedy does so at his peril. . . .
The Attorney General is a bundle of many dominant
traits; and these are sometimes in tension, and at all
times finding new forms of expression. Inside as well as
out, he is a man in motion."*
     —JOSEPH KRAFT, *"Riot Squad for the New Frontier,"*
                    Harper's, *August 1963.*

*"He has been called a simple man; it would be more
accurate to say he is many simple men."*
     —PAT ANDERSON, *"Robert's Character,"*
                    Esquire, *April 1965.*

ROBERT KENNEDY stands alone now. No longer the
manager, the trusted deputy, the agent-at-large. He
is head of the family, a major principal in the politics of
his time, the undisputed heir apparent. It is up to him to
achieve fresh greatness for the Kennedy name and fulfill
his brother's destiny. His election to the Senate confirmed
all that. It also brought intense public curiosity and scru-
tiny.

Kennedy flees introspection, but he cannot escape what
he calls "those couch questions." The public wants to know
and understand the quality of mind, temper, and personal
background of a man who seeks the Presidency.[1]

There is a mysterious, provocative, exciting element in
Kennedy's personality. It inspires many and alarms others.

He is "a swinger" who brings to public affairs a hint of danger and unpredictability; he is not a man whose line of development can easily be forecast; what he does or what positions on public issues he adopts may be considerably different ten years from now. In his compulsive athleticism, his reckless risk-taking, his aggressiveness, he seems to be driven by something not accounted for by the realities which engage him and not compatible with the high seriousness of his public ambitions.

When he was his brother's vizier, he did not bother to hide what amounted to habitual rudeness. When politicians complained in the 1960 campaign, he said:

"I'm not running a popularity contest. It doesn't matter if they like me or not. Jack can be nice to them. I don't try to antagonize people but somebody has to be able to say no. If people are not getting off their behinds and working enough, how do you say that nicely? Every time you make a decision in this business you make somebody mad."[2]

This sounds plausible enough until one remembers that other effective politicians do not find rudeness essential in attaining their objectives. It is also unnatural for a person to insist that he does not care whether other people like him or not. A hostile, chip-on-the-shoulder attitude is sometimes encountered in men who are fighting or have fought their way up in the world. But Robert Kennedy was born rich. While still in his early thirties, he achieved the other goals most men strive for—fame and power. What then is he angry about?

One side of a many-sided answer is simple heredity. He inherited his father's choleric temperament. In Joseph Kennedy's case, the explanation was often advanced that he was reacting against the social snobberies of Yankee Boston's ruling class which drew lines delimiting how far an ambitious Irishman could go. But this cultural circumstance is irrelevant for Robert Kennedy; he experienced no discrimination on account of his ancestry or religion. Since there were many other Boston Irishmen of the elder Kennedy's generation who did not react to their city with his overpowering aggressiveness, one suspects that he simply had more fire in his belly than most men, and that his third son inherited his qualities.

"I was the seventh of nine children," Robert Kennedy once said. "And when you come from that far down, you have to struggle to survive."

When he was born on November 20, 1925, his brother Joseph, Jr., was already ten and John was eight. Since his brother Ted did not come along for another seven years, Robert Kennedy spent his formative years as the lone little brother in the middle of five sisters. In some families, that might have meant that he grew up under predominantly feminine influences.

"He was the smallest and thinnest," his mother recalls, "and we feared he might grow up puny and girlish. We soon realized there was no fear of that."

Not only were his sisters extroverts and tomboys but he was also subject to the extraordinary competitive spirit that his father and oldest brother instilled in the family. Joe, Jr., took seriously his duties as a surrogate father.

"Joe taught me to sail, to swim, to play football and baseball," he recalls.

It was Joe who exemplified and insisted upon their father's rigorous code of values. Failure was not to be tolerated; passivity was a disgrace. Unremitting effort was the only door to respect. Exhortations such as "Never take second best" and "When the going gets tough, the tough get going" sound like caricatures of Y.M.C.A. slogans, but they were the rules of life for the Kennedy children.

John Kennedy's keenest memory of his little brother was of the day when Bobby, then four, went sailing with his older brothers and sisters and kept jumping into the water, though it was cold and far over his head, because he was determined to swim or drown in the attempt. He did not drown because Joe, Jr., was swimming nearby and periodically rescued him. John Kennedy, looking back on it, said: "It showed either a lot of guts or no sense at all, depending on how you looked at it."[3]

Bobby grew up to be the runt—not quite five-feet-ten—in a family where all the other men are six feet or taller. But he was the only one of the boys to play in the Harvard-Yale game, which is the prerequisite for winning a Harvard "H." His brother Jack made only the junior varsity. Joe, Jr., played on the varsity for three seasons, but not on the first-string team. When Harvard Coach Richard Harlow failed to play him in the Yale game in his senior year, his father rushed out of the stands in a rage. "He kept up a stream of oaths as he stalked from his seat to the field, where he cornered Harlow and berated him. By one account, the coach had intended to send in the senior for his letter, but misread the time remaining on the field clock. By another account, from no less reliable sources, Harlow resented having received a number of unusual messages from alumni urging him to play young Kennedy against Yale, and so purposely kept him on the bench. In any event, Joe Kennedy reacted as though he and his son had been struck a blow."[4]

The same story had a different ending with Robert Kennedy ten years later. Harlow sent him in for the last play of the Yale game in his senior year, even though Bobby had badly injured a leg in a practice scrimmage, and it was still heavily taped and braced.

Kennedy had no business being on the varsity at all, according to his teammate and close friend, Kenneth O'Donnell, who later served as President Kennedy's appointment secretary. "It was just after the war and all the men were back from the service. We had eight ends who were bigger, faster, and had been high-school stars.

[Bobby] wasn't fast, he wasn't shifty. But he was a quick, tough guy who worked five times as hard as anybody."

He practiced catching passes from O'Donnell for an hour before the rest of the team went on the field and stayed an hour later. He finally made the second-string varsity.

"He'd come in from his end like a wild Indian. If you were blocking Bobby, you'd knock him down, but he'd be up again going after the play. He never let up."[5]

Many undersized men can recount similar exploits in their own lives in which sheer willpower made up for what they lacked in physical endowment, but for them, as for most men, competitive athletics are a peak interest of one's middle teens and fade in importance as one enters manhood. However, the Attorney General of the United States spent a Sunday afternoon in the autumn of 1962 in this fashion: "One icy day . . . with a drizzle coming down, he shamed six reluctant old college football teammates out onto a muddy field to take on brother Teddy and his friends in touch football. They played on, relentlessly, until the Robert Kennedy team pulled ahead."[6]

In March 1965, the spring after his election to the Senate, he climbed Mount Kennedy in Canada, a thirteen-thousand foot peak that was previously the highest unclimbed mountain in North America. He made this climb although he had never before climbed a mountain.

The following November, while touring Latin America, he went on a fishing expedition deep in the Amazon Valley. Andrew J. Glass, a reporter who accompanied him, later wrote:

"It was dark and raining hard by the time we reached the edge of the lake. Just when we were ready to shove off with our guides, the tropical skies burst into torrents of water. Within seconds it became impossible to see six inches. . . . Only by putting our hands on one another's waists were we able to negotiate the 100 yards through the jungle to the nearest light—a native hut.

"The local guides also turned back, but Kennedy could not be persuaded to quit. While Tom Johnston (one of his aides) bailed furiously amidships, Goodwin[7] took the forward seat and Kennedy pulled away—without a light and without a guide in the middle of the jungle. The rain was streaming down too heavily for Kennedy to see either of his two companions; occasionally he would yell to Goodwin to paddle on the other side.

"Forty-five minutes later, without having seen another boat or landmark, the trio returned, triumphantly bearing four fish that had somehow been pulled into their canoe. The native guides solemnly said that they had never expected to see Kennedy or his companions again."

The next day, Kennedy topped that adventure by making a trip with three others to a remote part of the jungle in a single-engine, 1939 plane.

As he kissed his wife good-by, he said: "I must be crazy to get on this thing."[8]

Not crazy perhaps, but certainly imprudent for a father who, at that time, had nine small children at home who need him.

All these aspects of his personality—the obsession with physical courage, the compulsive need to prove himself over and over again although no one doubts his virility, the excessive risk-taking, the rudeness—are interrelated. A first-grader cannot swim as far or throw a pass as well as older brothers who are in the full tide of adolescence, but Bobby Kennedy defined himself as a person through relentless efforts to accomplish these impossibilities. As an adult, he can admire and associate with athletes and astronauts. He can have outsized heroes: Winston Churchill, Herbert Hoover (and J. Edgar Hoover, too—until Kennedy got to know him too well in the Justice Department), Douglas MacArthur, and his father's favorites—

Robert A. Taft, James V. Forrestal, and the mountain-climbing Supreme Court Justice, William O. Douglas. He can act out his belief in the cult of toughness with surprising literalness; thus, when the physical fitness fad swept the Kennedy administration, Pierre Salinger, the roly-poly White House Press Secretary joked about dieting off all that *sauce Béarnaise*, but Robert Kennedy stolidly hiked fifty miles in a day to show that it could be done. And Kennedy can and does articulate the locker-room view of life, telling an appreciative audience of football coaches: "Except for war, there is nothing in American life which trains a boy better for life than football."

Kennedy can do all this and more, from the lonely peaks of the Yukon to the deepest jungles of the Amazon, but since he is competing with his boyhood memories and impressions, he can never win. It is a contest against shadows.

The contest has exacted its price. As a little boy, he was amiable, polite, eager-to-please.

"Bobby was a hell of a nice little boy, one of the nicest I ever met. He always was responsible, friendly, and thoughtful."

That is the recollection of K. LeMoyne Billings, a roommate of John Kennedy at Choate School, who first met Bobby when the latter was nine years old. Others have this same memory of him. It is intriguing to speculate whether his mature personality might have been different if he had grown up in a more relaxed, less competitive atmosphere. As it was, the friendly little boy grew into a moody, inarticulate, intense young man. In his adolescence, he began to acquire the reputation that has clung to him in later years. He is given to quick likes and dislikes; he is suspicious and dour, cannot converse easily with strangers, and welcomes outsiders into his inner circle only after a lengthy waiting period. His temper is furious, instantaneous, biting; only by conscious effort as an adult has he brought it under reasonable control. He is at ease with children since they pose no challenge to him. He admires the West Virginia coal miners or some Southern Negroes or those rank-and-file teamsters who would not be intimidated by Jimmy Hoffa's goons; he is favorably impressed by anyone, that is, who retains his independence in adversity or who will not be beaten down or bluffed out. And there is nothing wrong with his manners. (His mother saw to that.) They can be flawless when he chooses to use them. He is capable of many gallantries and random acts of kindness. When an old Negro messenger retired after decades of service at the Justice Department, Kennedy startled and delighted him with an invitation to the reception for the judiciary at the White House. Encountering an obviously flustered young girl in the corridor of the Justice Department one day, he performed a courtly bow that complimented her and set her at ease at the same time. Meeting him on the opening day of his senatorial campaign in New York, Judy Michaelson of the New York *Post* confessed, "This is my first political campaign."

"It's my first, too," Kennedy replied. "We better stick together."

His fondness for children and his gallantry toward women or the socially disadvantaged are impeccable, but his treatment of many other people is not. Driving one day to the Senate Office Building in a rented limousine, he was taken to the entrance furthest from his office. Discovering his error, the middle-aged chauffeur started the motor again and was about to drive three-quarters of the way around the block to reach the correct entrance when Kennedy vaulted from the back seat to the sidewalk. "No, no," Kennedy exclaimed. "Good God, man, do you think we can't walk three feet?" Casting a glance at the chauffeur's paunch, he added, "You ought to walk more and then you wouldn't be carrying that around with you."[9]

When he travels abroad, he orders about the First Secretaries of American Embassies as if they were flunkies and, when irritable, he has been known to "chew them out" as if he were a Marine top sergeant.

During his brother's administration, he was the terror of the bureaucracy. There was, for instance, a meeting in 1962 of a presidential committee against racial discrimination by government contractors to which he arrived late. Vice-President Johnson was presiding. James Webb, Administrator of the National Aeronautics and Space Agency and a protégé of Johnson, was talking about the difficulties of placing Negroes in jobs in the space program. After listening for a few minutes, Kennedy, without addressing the chair or referring to Johnson at all, cut in and asked, "How many employees are you talking about?"

"Forty thousand," Webb replied.

"How many people do you have working on discrimination problems?"

"One man full-time and another man devotes half his time to it," Webb answered.

Kennedy's face expressed contempt. With scorn in his voice, he said, "You mean you have forty thousand employees and you have only one and one-half men working on this and then you expect to make progress?"

In front of the more than twenty government officials and leading private citizens at the meeting, Kennedy raked Webb for his slack approach to the problem. Unlike his father, who gave "unshirted hell" in earthy language, Kennedy does not normally use profanity but he can be devastatingly cutting. A few minutes later Kennedy abruptly left. Johnson, then in the depths of his vice-presidential depression, sat through this performance slumped in his chair with his eyes half closed. Robert Kennedy has probably forgotten that meeting; it is doubtful that Johnson and Webb have.

Then there was the middle-level State Department official who served on an interdepartmental committee on which Defense, Central Intelligence, and other agencies were also represented by lesser-ranking officers. However, the Attorney General, having been designated by his brother to "bird dog" the committee, usually attended in person. Rarely satisfied with what he heard, he ragged the other members relentlessly, not seeming to realize or to care that they were not in a position to answer him freely because of his higher status and his blood relationship to the President.

After suffering agonies of silent rage at one of those meetings, the State Department member remarked privately to a reporter, "If one of you guys writes one more time about his looking like a choirboy, I'll kill you. A choirboy is sweet, soft, cherubic. Take a look at that bony little face, those hard, opaque eyes, and then listen to him bawl somebody out. Some choirboy!"

Far more exalted officials were targets of Kennedy's brutal candor. At a Cabinet meeting in 1961, he told then Under Secretary of State Chester Bowles that his Cuban policy proposals were worthless and a waste of time. In fact, this was due to the objective situation and not Bowles's fault. Two years later, long after Bowles had departed for New Delhi, the brothers Castro still had the brothers Kennedy hung up.

After Kennedy was elected to the Senate, a reporter for *The New York Times* once sought him out for several days in an unsuccessful effort to get his confidential views as background for a Sunday article on New York politics. He finally caught up with him on a New York-to-Washington flight only to find Kennedy seated next to Republican Senator Jacob K. Javits. At the end of a totally useless ride in which the reporter, because of Javits's presence, had been able to ask almost none of the questions he had in mind, Kennedy turned toward him and asked blandly, "Did you get everything you wanted?"[10]

While campaigning in the West during the 1966 campaign, Kennedy learned of a story that another reporter intended to file that he did not want printed. He went back to the section of the plane where reporters were sitting, excoriated the offender in front of his colleagues, and then had an aide telephone a complaint to the reporter's publisher at the next stop.

Kennedy took note of his own propensities when he spoke to a gathering of federal district attorneys shortly after becoming Attorney General. "It doesn't matter if I hurt your feelings," he said. "It doesn't matter if you hurt my feelings. The important thing is to get the job done."

Rudeness is almost inevitable in a man obsessed with winning and being first. "Nice guys finish last," as Leo Durocher once remarked, and in politics as in sports, it is winning that counts, particularly if one is a Kennedy. In addition to a certain natural savagery inherited from his father, Robert Kennedy also has to relieve the intolerable pressures that he imposes upon himself by being mildly sadistic to others. So much competitiveness is hard on the man who experiences it, and unconscious feelings demand some relief from the inexorable demands of unyielding self-discipline and arduous effort.

The need to win is also a clue to Kennedy's approach to politics. For a long time, he resisted categorizing himself as either a liberal or a conservative, insisting that these distinctions are "merely labels." Since he has emerged as the heir apparent not only of the Kennedy family but of organized political liberalism and as the alternative to Lyndon Johnson, Kennedy has become less gun-shy about his identity as a liberal. But he still prefers to see himself as a pragmatist responding to specific problems and making real choices in the real world. Liberals make him uneasy; he dismisses them as people who would rather talk than act and who are never so happy as when they are all going down to defeat together. But, of course, liberalism is not a mere matter of labels and it has nothing to do with victory or defeat. It has rather to do with the quality of one's means for they ultimately determine the end arrived at, and it has to do with a decent attitude toward power. Adlai Stevenson, the greatest liberal statesman of the post-war period, expressed the liberal attitude when he said in his first acceptance speech in 1952, concerning the power of the American Presidency: "Its potential for good or evil now and in the years of our lives smothers exultation and converts vanity to prayer." In the same speech, he observed, as if it were a truism about which everyone agreed, "Better we lose the election than mislead the people; and better we lose than misgovern the people."

The critic Stanley Kauffmann captured these essentials when he wrote of liberalism: "It is not a political philosophy at all, it is a game: a game of gentlemen, which depends on mutual observance of rules, like tennis. It is a creation of the nineteenth century, of a punctilious and carefully bounded civilization in which one can rely on the etiquette of one's opponents and in which one's allowing a voice to the opposition is at least as important as the achievement of one's own beliefs—perhaps more important. ('It isn't the winning that counts, it's how one plays the game' might be the first tenet of liberalism.)"[11]

It is not a tenet that Robert Kennedy learned in his father's house.

In an interview in 1962, Rose Kennedy remarked, "Bobby has been a great joy and blessing to me and my husband always. He has taken his religion seriously and still does. We never had any worries about him."

As a boy, Robert Kennedy was religious in an enthusiastic, active way. He was a Catholic in the same way that he was a Kennedy, a Democrat, an American; it was part of him, it was his team and he believed in sticking up for it one hundred per cent. When he was sent to St. Paul's School, an Episcopal prep school in Concord, New Hampshire, he wrote to his mother complaining that he had to attend Protestant chapel services daily; he was soon withdrawn and entered in a Catholic school. When his sister Kathleen was married in a civil service to the Marquess of Hartington, a member of the Church of England, Bobby, next to his mother, was the member of the family most upset. In his youth, he served Mass as an altar boy and throughout his life has been faithful in his religious duties. He seems not to have experienced a youthful season of unbelief or an adult crisis of conscience. He and his wife and children say the rosary together, say grace before meals, and attend Mass regularly.

His firmly orthodox attitudes toward religion are typical of Kennedy's basic beliefs in many areas of life. To a significant extent, he has faithfully emulated his parents and adopted the salient convictions of both. Joseph Kennedy once said, "I always felt that if I died, Bobby would be the one to keep the family together. Bobby is a disciple of my theory—if you have your family with you, you have a head start on others who must rely on making friends."[12]

Unlike John Kennedy, who was the Senate's "gay young bachelor" and did not marry until he was thirty-six, and unlike Teddy, who got into an academic scrape that caused his temporary withdrawal from Harvard, Robert has never had any playboyish tendencies. For a long time, his only vices were drinking milk and chewing gum. He was well into his thirties before he began to drink alcohol regularly and only after President Kennedy's death did he take up smoking the small cigars that his brother had favored, later switching to long cigars. In choosing a wife, he stayed close to the pattern of his own family. Ethel Skakel Kennedy comes from a large, wealthy, active, and extroverted family. Like Rose Kennedy, she is a woman of strong Catholic faith. Robert and Ethel Kennedy have not only followed but surpassed the example of the elder Kennedys in producing ten children. In this way, Robert, who until he was seven was the youngest and smallest boy, is enabled now to be the *paterfamilias* at the head of the table overseeing a swarming brood of his own. Then, too, he has his father's dynastic sense; he wants lots of Kennedys for the future.

Out of his religious training and his clan loyalty, Kennedy developed a moralist's view of the world. If life is a matter of "we vs. them," then it is only a matter of substituting new protagonists and new enemies for old as life goes on. Sometimes, the "we" is law and order, or America, or the free world and "them" may be crooked labor leaders, organized crime, or international Communism. "With Bobby, it's always the white hats and the black hats, the good guys versus the bad guys," his wife once observed. This moralism is not to be disdained because it helps account for Kennedy's extraordinary verve and self-confidence in political and intellectual combat. If a man is not in doubt about the rightness of his cause, his strength is many times that of the man who sees all moral issues dissolved in a kind of gray mush. His moralism also enables Kennedy to identify readily with slum youngsters ("I think some of us who were more fortunate might also have been juvenile deliquents if we had been brought up in a different environment," he told a Congressional committee in 1961) and with embattled Southern Negroes. Once he identifies an injustice, Kennedy loathes it with rare intensity and works relentlessly against it. A moralistic, judgmental viewpoint can often though not inevitably lead to arrogance, self-righteousness, and an oversimplification of what is complex. Kennedy has been guilty of these failings at times but less so of late than in the early years of his career. Notwithstanding these offsetting weaknesses, Kennedy's moral force remains one of his major sources of strength. It gives purpose to his other qualities such as courage, loyalty, and intelligence. It is what makes Kennedy a solid man to rely upon in a crisis.

Moralism determined Kennedy's choice of a career in government. His father encouraged all his sons to aspire to the aristocratic ideal of a life of public service since he had, by his financial success, freed them from the abrasive money worries that harass most men. But there are many different careers in the public service. Robert Kennedy could, for example, have become a career diplomat. He chose instead to be a criminal investigator, hunting out evil. His first job after graduating from the University of Virginia Law School in 1951 was in the Criminal Division of the Department of Justice. He was assigned to a district office in Brooklyn where he did research and legwork on graft and tax fraud cases. He quit after several months to devote himself to his brother's senatorial campaign. When that was finished, he went to work as an assistant counsel of the Permanent Investigations Subcommittee chaired by Senator Joseph McCarthy. John Kennedy, a member of the parent Government Operations Committee, advised his brother against it because he could foresee that association with McCarthy would entail a considerable risk for anyone's reputation. Robert Kennedy, however, thought he would have an exciting time exposing corruption and uncovering Communist conspiracies, and his father encouraged him to go ahead.

The subcommittee had earned a favorable reputation under Democratic control in the previous Congress because it helped to expose the "influence peddling" scandals of the Truman administration. McCarthy, when he assumed the chairmanship in 1953, retained Francis Flanagan, an ex-F.B.I. agent who was the respected general counsel, but he set up a second staff headed by a young New York lawyer, Roy Cohn. Kennedy joined Flanagan's group. At first, he did routine investigations of government contracts. He first reached the front pages on May 20 when he presented testimony, drawn from Naval Intelligence data, on the number of British and other allied ships engaged in trade with Communist China at a time when the Korean War was still underway. This was the only major episode of McCarthy's tenure in which Kennedy was involved, and it was not an example of McCarthyism. Rather, it involved the usual divergence in attitude between the State Department diplomats who have to negotiate with foreign countries and Senators who believe that if this country takes a hard line with its allies, it can whip them into agreement. The Democratic Senators on the subcommittee who in a later period would be called "hawks"—John McClellan of Arkansas, Stuart Symington of Missouri, and Henry Jackson of Washington—were in accord with McCarthy and Kennedy on this issue. (Thirteen years later, Kennedy as a member of the Senate opposed amendments to the foreign aid bill that cut off assistance to countries such as India that engage in trade with Cuba and North Vietnam.)

When McCarthy the following month kicked Flanagan upstairs to a job with the full committee and placed the entire investigating subcommittee staff under Cohn, the Democrats withdrew from the committee. Kennedy, who disliked Cohn personally and disapproved of his slapdash methods, resigned a month later. He spent the balance of the year working for the Hoover Commission (his father was a member), which was studying the reorganization of the federal government. The commission provided him with an excellent opportunity to get a panoramic view of the entire government and its internal conflicts and pressure points, but Kennedy found the work too tame. He wanted to be where the action was. When the Democrats rejoined the McCarthy subcommittee in January 1954, he promptly returned as their minority counsel. He was present through those long spring weeks in the Senate Caucus

Room when McCarthy ("Point of order, Mr. Chairman, point of order") and Cohn slowly destroyed themselves in the Army-McCarthy hearings.

Kennedy remained on friendly terms with McCarthy, whom he regarded as more sinned against than sinning. When the Junior Chamber of Commerce chose Kennedy as one of the nation's "ten outstanding young men," he stayed out of the banquet hall during the main address by Edward R. Murrow because the speech was critical of McCarthy. In McCarthy's last months, when he continued to drink despite a serious liver ailment, Kennedy was one of those who visited him and tried to sustain his morale. At McCarthy's death in 1957, Kennedy not only attended the funeral Mass in Washington but also flew to Appleton, Wisconsin, for the interment. Although in this instance Kennedy's loyalty was misplaced, loyalty to friends, particularly those in adversity, remains one of his strongest and most admirable traits.

When the 1954 election restored the Democrats to control of the Senate and McClellan replaced McCarthy as chairman, Kennedy moved up to become chief counsel. He was then twenty-nine. Over the next five years, he became a famous figure in his own right. At first, the Investigations Subcommittee made news by its hearings on the conflict-of-interest cases that plagued the Eisenhower administration; one of these hearings led to the resignation of Secretary of the Air Force Harold Talbott. Then Kennedy became interested in the corrupt affairs of the Teamsters Union, and his long pursuit of its successive presidents, Dave Beck and Jimmy Hoffa, began.

Kennedy told a wry story about his growing fame. While he was riding to LaGuardia Airport in New York, the taxi driver studied him in the mirror a few minutes and then said, "I know who you are. You're Roy Cohn!"

Robert Kennedy, like his brothers, is what teachers call a "late bloomer." His school and college grades are an unreliable clue to the power of his mind, and his intellectual interests are much richer and more diversified at forty than seemed probable at twenty.

He usually dismisses his education—"I think I was in and out of ten or a dozen schools"—but it was not as peripatetic as that sounds. He attended a Bronxville nursery school, a private school for the first and second grades, and then a Bronxville public school for the next three. One of his teachers from those years remembers him as "a nice little freckle-faced kid, his hair some shade of brown, a regular boy. He needed no special handling. It seemed hard for him to finish his work sometimes. But he was only ten after all."[13]

He began the sixth grade at the Riverdale Country School, an expensive private school, but he was withdrawn in the spring of 1938 to go with his family to London when his father became ambassador. There he was enrolled in the Gibbs School, an exclusive preparatory day school where his classmates were the sons of British aristocrats and successful businessmen. After a year and a half in England, he was sent home to the United States at the outbreak of war in September 1939. After his brief stay at Episcopal St. Paul's, he was transferred to Portsmouth Priory, a Catholic prep school in Rhode Island conducted by Benedictine monks. During his three years at the Priory, he drudged along in the lower half of his class, but did well in sports. Since his father was concerned that he might not qualify for college on account of his low grades, he transferred him for his senior year to Milton Academy, a secular school in Massachusetts. His grades were still only middling, but they were good enough to gain him admission to Harvard after the war. (He spent the last two years of the war as a naval officer candidate and then an enlisted man on the destroyer *Joseph P. Kennedy, Jr.*, named for his brother.)

Of Harvard, he later said, "I didn't go to class very much

to tell you the truth. I used to talk and argue a lot, mostly about sports and politics."

It was not until he went to the University of Virginia Law School, where he graduated fifty-sixth in a class of one hundred and twenty-five, that Kennedy showed evidence of having a more than mediocre mind.

Unlike his brother John, who became an inveterate reader in the course of his many illnesses, Robert Kennedy has never found a private world of the imagination. He is a doer who lives by events. He has a quick, curious, open mind. Like his father, who made a fortune as a speculator partly because he did not let preconceptions or sentiment get in the way of learning and judging the facts, he is pragmatic, realistic, able to distinguish "the operational from the purely decorative." He is capable of calculation but not of conceptualization. Large ideas bore him. He makes his decisions from minute to minute as events take shape before him; his responses have a logical consistency that can be read back into them retrospectively but few clues about his future intentions can be garnered from his long-term plans for the reason that he is not a maker of plans.

Like most politicians, he has an aural mind, preferring to learn from briefings than from reading. He has developed a technique of peppering people he meets with innumerable questions. Kennedy undoubtedly learns a good deal this way, and he has a retentive memory. But this technique is mildly suspect on two counts. First, it is an old political ploy. A man asking questions avoids having to answer some himself that might be embarrassing or awkward. It also subtly flatters the visitor by implying that what he has to tell is more important than what Kennedy has to say. Secondly, there is some uncertainty as to how deeply interested Kennedy is in the answers. "When he first arrived in New York, I used to be pleased at how interested he seemed," one important official in city government has said "and I used to fill him in on all the background. But then I noticed that he seemed faintly bored or impatient although he never interrupted or cut me off. So instead of giving him a full explanation, I began giving him abbreviated, two- or three-minute explanations. He seemed just as satisfied with the short, superficial answers as the long, complete ones. So you figure it out. Does he really want to know or does he just like to ask questions?"

Kennedy's developing intellectualism has proceeded, both before and since the assassination, in his brother John's shadow. It was inevitable that he would write a book once his brother won the Pulitzer prize for *Profiles in Courage* in 1957. His book, *The Enemy Within*, was completed two years later. It is an anecdotal, straightforward account of his years investigating the labor rackets. John Siegenthaler, a newspaperman who served for a time on the Rackets Committee staff, assisted him in the writing and editing, but much of it was Kennedy's own, and he labored conscientiously over its revision.

He, too, took a speed-reading course and in recent years has taken to racing his way through works of history and biography. Since his brother prepared himself for the Presidency by meeting informally with Harvard professors, Robert Kennedy organized the "Hickory Hill seminars" in which experts from within the administration give talks at Kennedy's home in Virginia on their specialities. (Begun in the Kennedy years, they have continued with much less publicity under the Johnson administration, the only difference being that experts now are not so eager to have it known at the White House that they are participants.) Increasingly since his brother's death, he has adorned his speeches with quotations from Goethe, Churchill, Robert Frost, Lord Acton, and other greats. It is a little hard to tell whether this is Kennedy emulating his brother or his speech writer emulating Theodore Sorensen.

Robert Kennedy has a rage for excellence. He wants his

historians to be Pulitzer prize winners, his athletes to be All-Americans, and his staff assistants to be brilliant. The reality, of course, does not always match the ideal but the disdain for the ordinary and the second-rate is very much present. Kennedy derived this appetite for the best from his father. A friend traveling with Joseph Kennedy in England in 1933 recalls his complaining bitterly that she was not introducing him to "the very best people." He sent his sons to Harvard, not because he cared much for the college, but simply because he regarded it as the best college. The same craving to travel first-class all the way influenced everything he did from his choice of prep schools for his sons—Choate and Milton—to his selection of a wintering place, Palm Beach.

This striving has its ridiculous side, but it is a necessary obsession for empire builders and founders of dynasties. Robert Kennedy spoke in his father's spirit when he told *Newsweek* following the 1960 election: "We're going to do what we thought Eisenhower was going to do in 1952 and never did—bring a new spirit to the government. Not necessarily young men, but new men, who believe in a cause, who believe their jobs go on forever, not just from 9 to 5; who believe they have a responsibility to the United States, not just to an Administration, and who can really get things done. It really makes a hell of a difference. Our campaign was made up of new faces, to a large extent, and this Administration will be made up of new faces, to a large extent.

"We want the guy in Nashville and South Dakota whom no one ever heard of, people who are never called upon except in a great national emergency. Those are the guys we want. Those are the guys we're going after."[14]

The Kennedys approximated this ideal inasmuch as they chose Dean Rusk, president of the Rockefeller Foundation, as Secretary of State and Robert McNamara, president of the Ford Motor Company, as Secretary of Defense, neither of whom they had ever known before. Later, they fell below this ideal in choosing Anthony Celebrezze as Secretary of Health, Education, and Welfare and John Gronouski as Postmaster General, both of whom were appointed more for their ethnic symbolism than their visible merits.

Robert Kennedy's own appointment as Attorney General violated this ideal because it breached a tradition against presidential nepotism that had existed intact for more than 170 years. The fact that he proved to be a very good Attorney General in no way alters the hard truth that in view of his age and inexperience, he would never have been selected if he had not been the President's brother. A tradition once breached for whatever reason is thereby weakened for the future, and a republic needs as many traditions as it can possibly have against the arbitrary or corrupt exercise of power.[15]

In organizing the top-level administration of the Justice Department, Robert Kennedy demonstrated his good taste in people. No Attorney General in twenty years had assembled so distinguished a team. Not since 1940-41, when Robert Jackson, Francis Biddle, and Thurman Arnold were in the Justice Department were there so many first-line talents. Archibald Cox, the Solicitor General, held an endowed chair at the Harvard Law School. Byron White and Nicholas Katzenbach, who served successively in the post of Deputy Attorney General, were both honor students at the Yale Law School and Rhodes Scholars. The several Assistant Attorneys General were likewise intellectually and professionally outstanding. Burke Marshall, for example, who headed the Civil Rights Division, had been an editor of the *Yale Law Journal*, partner of a leading Washington firm, and, after leaving the Justice Department, became general counsel of IBM.

As Attorney General, Kennedy waged the most personal and intensive drive against organized crime of any Attorney General since the departure in 1940 of that earlier Irish Catholic moralist Frank Murphy. Where political wrongdoing was concerned, he was sternly incorruptible. During his three years in office, the Justice Department prosecuted numerous Democratic politicians including two Congressmen, three State Supreme Court justices, five mayors, two chiefs of police, and three sheriffs. One of those convicted was New York State Supreme Court Justice Vincent Keogh, the brother of Congressman Eugene Keogh, an Administration stalwart on the House Ways and Means Committee and a personal intimate of President Kennedy.

At the same time, the political side of him did not scruple to make a necessary deal. He reached an understanding with Senator James O. Eastland of Mississippi, the chairman of the Senate Judiciary Committee, by appointing Eastland's friend and former law partner, Harold Cox, to the Federal District Court. Judge Cox subsequently referred from the bench to civil rights workers as "a bunch of chimpanzees" and "a bunch of niggers." These remarks were as repulsive to Kennedy as to any other man of conscience and sensibility, but Cox's appointment was necessary if he was to do business successfully with Eastland on legislation and other judicial appointments, most of which were good and many outstanding.

Kennedy relishes combat for its own sake, but during his years as Attorney General, he developed a genuine and special empathy for Negroes. Their battle against high odds kindles his imagination. He freely admits that this is an interest he reached late. "I won't say I stayed awake nights worrying about civil rights before I became Attorney General," he says. This slowness is understandable in a youth who grew up in the sheltered, privileged world of Hyannis Port and Palm Beach. Moreover, Kennedy has the kind of mind that cannot engage a problem theoretically; it becomes real for him only when it assumes practical shape and demands some response or decision from him. The appalling facts of rural poverty only hit him when he campaigned among the unemployed coal miners in the hills and hollows of West Virginia and was moved by their indomitable spirit.

However tardy his start, Kennedy has brought to the civil rights crusade the passion and conviction of an eleventh-hour convert. He has startled bishops of his own church and other solemn dignitaries by asking them bluntly what, if anything, they have done lately to ease the burdens of Negroes. During the first two years of the Kennedy administration, he and the President judged that the Congressional climate would be hostile to any major civil rights legislation. They chose to make maximum use of voting rights laws already on the statute books and to rely on peaceful persuasion. The Justice Department developed more than fifty voting rights cases in the South. Through pressure on the Interstate Commerce Commission, Kennedy and Burke Marshall achieved the desegregation of railroad terminals, airports, and bus depots. They worked behind the scenes to speed the desegregation of the public schools in several Southern cities. When mobs threatened "freedom riders" in Birmingham, Alabama, and tried to prevent the admission of James Meredith as the first Negro student in the University of Mississippi, Kennedy in those crises was patient but firm. He engaged in prolonged haggling with state officials and relied upon the minimum of force—plainclothed federal marshals rather than the Army—to maintain order. He succeeded in Alabama but failed in Mississippi where two lives were lost and the Army had to be used to put down the riot, but no one could contend that he did not make maximum use of all peaceful, moderate methods. When the civil rights demonstrations in the spring of 1963 induced President Kennedy to sponsor civil rights legislation, Robert Kennedy was instrumental in working out the compromises and organizing the bipartisan coalition that brought about its passage the following year.

His record as Attorney General proves that Kennedy learned about civil liberties after his early involvement with Joe McCarthy. In the early 1950s, he saw all issues in black and white and since he knew Communism was black, he had still to learn that all those who oppose it are not necessarily white. As counsel for the Rackets Committee investigating Hoffa and other union malefactors, he stirred controversy among other lawyers by his tactics. He would sit glowering beside Senator John McClellan, the Arkansas Torquemada, and the two of them would take turns excoriating witnesses who frustrated them by hiding behind the Fifth Amendment. But although some legal observers believe Kennedy was abusive and sometimes disingenuous in his examination of witnesses, others point out that he was trying to disassemble a baffling complex of chicanery and lies and that some of the witnesses had lawyers who were exceptionally adept at maneuver and obfuscation. The consensus in the legal community is that Kennedy did not impair the rights of witnesses before the committee.

As Attorney General, Kennedy, like most prosecutors, favored the virtually unrestricted use of wiretapping and electronic devices ("bugs") because these are useful in detecting the activities of underworld syndicates. The Federal Bureau of Investigation had used wiretapping in their investigative work for decades even though evidence gained in this way is not admissible in federal courts. In the winter of 1966–67, when the Justice Department under the pressure of recent Supreme Court decisions adopted a much more strait-laced position on wiretapping, Kennedy tried delicately to disengage himself from the F.B.I.'s record during his tenure. J. Edgar Hoover countered with a sandbagging letter to a member of the House (Representative H. R. Gross of Iowa) in which he virtuously insisted that he never did anything along this line without the full and explicit approval of his superior, the

Attorney General. It is impossible to accept either side of this exchange at face value: Kennedy's zeal to break up the crime syndicates was reminiscent of a sixteenth century Jesuit on the hunt for heresy, and he would scarcely have scrupled at the use of wiretapping or electronic devices; Hoover, for his part, had been operating autonomously for decades and would not have hesitated to follow his own judgment, regardless of what any Attorney General thought. He disliked Robert Kennedy precisely because Kennedy tried to exercise actual, as distinguished from nominal, authority over the F.B.I.

Kennedy's initial impulses are like those of most policemen who believe all that really matters is catching and convicting criminals. He does not come naturally to the notion that "it is better that ninety-nine guilty should go free than that one innocent man be wrongfully convicted." But over the years, without entirely comprehending or accepting the full rationale behind civil liberties, and after many controversies over wiretapping, the Fifth Amendment, and criminal law, he has arrived pragmatically at a basically enlightened position. As Attorney General, he engaged in no witch hunts against dissenters of any kind. He obtained a presidential pardon for Junius Scales, a North Carolina Communist who had been sentenced to prison under the Smith Act. He can now quote Justice Holmes with the best of them, address a Fund for the Republic luncheon with style, and is surely as trustworthy as any other prominent politician with the liberties of the people.

The irony of his career as Attorney General is his undeserved reputation as anti-business. When the steel companies in 1962 raised prices contrary to their implicit pledge to the President not to do so, Robert Kennedy did direct a rapid investigation of the circumstances. But this was part of a bluff to attain the limited objective of a recision of the price increase. Both Kennedys viewed the so-called "steel crisis" as an affront by the steel manufacturers to the prestige of the Presidency, not as a major turning point in government-industry relations. Once the prices were rolled back, nothing was ever heard again of the Justice Department's investigation of the steel industry.

On price-fixing, Kennedy did say on another occasion: "I view the businessman who engages in price-fixing conspiracies in the same light as I regard the racketeer who siphons off money from the public in crooked gambling or the union official who betrays union members."

But again, his bark was worse than his bite. Anti-trust policy is an area of law that bores Kennedy. He provided comparatively little personal leadership on anti-trust issues and the record of that division during his tenure was not markedly better or worse than under his Republican predecessor, William Rogers.

Robert Kennedy's claim to be qualified for the Presidency rests objectively on his record as Attorney General. Politics, sentiment, and glamor aside, he proved in those three and one-half years that he is capable of directing a major department of the government and performing effectively. He showed that he could recruit and hold able subordinates, delegate authority, stay reasonable and unshaken in times of crisis, make clear-cut decisions when decisions were necessary, and has the intelligence and energy to keep a dozen different lines of policy in mind and under control. His residual moralism and his keen political pragmatism were always in unstable equilibrium. "From one day to the next," a friend has said, "you never know which Bobby Kennedy you're going to meet." But this proved to be a creative, not a destructive, tension. He could be rude, restless, impatient, but he was also brilliant, inspiring, forceful. The voters in some future national election will decide whether his style is to their taste or whether the public policies for which he stands meet with their approval, but of his basic competence there is small ground for doubt.

The assassination of his brother put fresh and cruel strains on Robert Kennedy's already complicated personality.

Patrick Anderson, a free-lance writer who worked as a public relations aide for Kennedy in the Justice Department, recalls that after he briefed a reporter on the many youth programs in which Kennedy was interested, the reporter asked why he thought Kennedy spent so much time with children. Anderson suggested that they provided "an antidote" to the Hoffas and the Governor Wallaces he had to deal with so much of the time. When the reporter later asked Kennedy if this was true, he replied with annoyance: "I just like children; that's all."

"Methinks he doth protest too much," Anderson writes, "that such determined simplicity springs necessarily from a basic complexity. Fitzgerald wrote of Dick and Nicole Diver: '. . . the simplicity of behavior also, the nursery-like peace and goodwill, the emphasis on the simpler virtues, was part of a desperate bargain with the gods and had been attained through struggles she could not have guessed at.' "[16]

In Kennedy's case, those silent, internal struggles turned upon his relationships with his demanding, domineering father, his dead hero brother Joe, and his older brother Jack. Love was central in those relationships but resentment and rivalry had also to be accommodated. No one has ever reported hearing him speak a word of criticism of his father or his brothers. Any negative emotions he experienced doubled back upon themselves and found expression in rigid identification with his family and intense, aggressive championship of its values. Crucial to this process was his sublimation of all his energies to his brother Jack's interests. He wanted nothing for himself; everything for his brother. This emotional transfer provided him a moral license for the expression of his natural driving aggressiveness. Any resentment he unconsciously felt at being the little brother or in second place he relieved by directing it outward at the slothful politicians, irreverent columnists, and disobedient bureaucrats who in one way or another obstructed his brother's wishes.

The disaster of November 22, 1963, collapsed the center of his emotional universe. What a friend said is undoubtedly true: "Bob would gladly have taken that bullet for his brother." He felt the anguish of his loss; he felt also the devouring guilt that he had been spared instead of his brother. Fate had made a mistake. How to repair it? He had wanted to compete with his brother at some future time and in his own way. This vagrant wish had peeped through at times. When his brother suggested in December 1960 that he could be appointed to the President-elect's unexpired term in the Senate, Bobby flashed: "Never! The only way I'll go to the Senate is run for it." There was one way he could surpass his brother: Jack was the first Catholic President, but he would be the first brother of a chief executive to be elected President. And he would do it on his own.

Now Jack is dead, and he can never surpass him because the fact of his death has removed him forever as a competitor. He has ceased to be a rival and become a saint. He has joined his father and Joe, Jr., in the gallery of family immortals. Any forward progress on his own will now be in their footsteps, retracing their earlier success; he will not be surpassing Jack; he will be completing his work and fulfilling his destiny. The dark shadow of loss, of what might have been, will always fall across any brilliant triumphs of his own in the future. His older brothers will not be there to share in his success, and he will not have the pleasure of their seeing him in his moments of triumph.

For any man, these would be painful reflections. For Robert Kennedy, who had schooled himself to avoid introspection and to live from moment to moment, the confused feelings of shock, loss, guilt, unacknowledged rivalry, and unremembered anger composed a burden he could barely sustain in the months after the assassination. The very intensity of his emotions embarrassed him. He may well have decided to climb Mount Kennedy in an effort to reassure himself that he was truly a tough Hemingwayesque fellow.

Is it any reason for astonishment that Kennedy, once his victory over Kenneth Keating was won, turned to the memory-ridden Senate chamber with a dragging step? It was to this place that he had fought to elect Jack in 1952. It was here that his brother's national career had been nurtured.

On January 3, 1965, Kennedy received two reporters in his office shortly after he was sworn in. He was asked how he felt now that he was a member of the U.S. Senate. His eyes sorrowful and his face bleak, Kennedy looked like a man who had just lost an election rather than won one.

"I regret the circumstance that led to my being here," he replied.[17]

NOTES

[1] In addition to the sources cited below, I have benefited from reading numerous articles on Kennedy, including James A. Wechsler, "Robert F. Kennedy: A Case of Mistaken Identity,"

Progressive, June–July, 1965; Joseph Wershba, "Bobby Kennedy Today," New York *Post* series, March 23–29, 1964; and Anthony Lewis, "Kennedy's Role as Attorney General," *The New York Times*, September 4, 1964.

2 Quoted in Hugh Sidey, "Brother on the Spot," *The Kennedy Circle* (Lester Tanzer, ed, Robert B. Luce, Inc., Washington, D.C., 1961), p. 209.

3 Robert E. Thompson and Hortense Myers, *Robert F. Kennedy: The Brother Within* (Dell edition, New York, 1962), p. 43.

4 Richard J. Whalen, *The Founding Father* (New York, New American Library, 1964), p. 228.

5 Fletcher Knebel once pointed out how many of Kennedy's Harvard football buddies turned up working in Washington during the New Frontier. In addition to halfback Kenneth O'Donnell at the White House, there was guard Nicholas Rodis, State Department officer; halfback Charles Roche, deputy chairman of the Democratic National Committee; and tackle Dean Markham, executive director of the President's Advisory Commission on Narcotic and Drug Abuse. Fletcher Knebel, "Bobby Kennedy: He Hates to Be Second," *Look*, May 21, 1963, p. 91.

6 Anthony Lewis, "What Drives Bobby Kennedy," *The New York Times Magazine*, April 7, 1963, p. 34.

7 Richard Goodwin was on President Kennedy's White House staff and is an occasional speech writer and adviser to Robert Kennedy.

8 Andrew J. Glass, "The Compulsive Candidate," *Saturday Evening Post*, April 23, 1966, p. 44.

9 Margaret Laing, "Bobby As a Family Man," New York *World Journal Tribune*, November 13, 1966.

10 Penn Kimball, "Kennedy," *Life*, November 18, 1966, p. 34.

11 Stanley Kauffmann, "Mayhem by Muggeridge," *The New Republic*, December 17, 1966, p. 23.

12 Quoted in Nick Thimmesch and William Johnson, *Robert Kennedy At 40* (W. W. Norton, New York, 1965), p. 31.

13 Ann Geracimos, "Bobby Kennedy Was Here," New York *Herald Tribune*, October 11, 1964.

14 *Newsweek*, November 21, 1960, p. 32.

15 The Kennedys, never averse to using a schmaltzy argument when a serious one was deficient, floated the story that Robert accepted the Attorney Generalship because "he had become impressed with the isolation and loneliness of the Presidential office that had begun to afflict his brother. 'I realized . . .' he

confided to intimates, 'what an advantage it would be to him to have someone he could talk to.' " Irwin Ross, "The Kid Brother," New York *Post*, December 25, 1960.

Why the presidency would be lonelier for John F. Kennedy than for any of his predecessors who refrained from appointing their relatives to the Cabinet was left unexplained. One suspects that President Kennedy and the republic would have continued to function if he had declined the appointment.

[16] Patrick Anderson, "Robert's Character," *Esquire*, April, 1965, p. 64.

[17] Personal interview.

CHAPTER FOUR

An Imperial Presence

*"Besides, as far as I am concerned, I have no ambition—
or, if I have any, it is so natural to me, so innate, so
intimately linked with my existence that it is like the
blood that circulates in my veins, like the air I breathe.
It causes me to act neither more precipitately, nor in any
way differently, than do the natural motives that move
me. I never am obliged to fight either for or against my
ambition. Ambition never is in a greater hurry than I; it
merely keeps pace with circumstances and with my general way of thinking."*
—NAPOLEON BONAPARTE *in conversation,* 1804, *quoted in*
Herold, ed., The Mind of Napoleon, *p.* 47.

POWER is the name of the game that politicians play.
Just as a businessman seeks profits, an actor wants
applause and a runner covets speed, a politician naturally
wants power for the personal satisfaction of exercising it.
The scope of his ambition may vary; he may seek influence for his ideas on public policy, or an appropriate
forum for the use of his talents, or the fulfillment of some
objective of personal ambition or family pride; he may use
power for good or evil ends. Inevitably, however, he moves
to find the winning issue, to form alliances, and to put
together majority coalitions; in short, he is in quest of
power. No man enters public life to lose or to diminish his
influence or deliberately to play an insignificant role.

Robert Kennedy, although he approached the Senate
with some inner reluctance, was not in doubt about what

73

he intended to accomplish there. The scope of his ambition was clear: he wanted to be President. The Senate for many men is the summit of their political hopes; for him it would only be a staging ground. The uncertainty was how he would work out his design for power.

He had not been a member of the Senate very long when, the story goes, a colleague approached a committee chairman and complained: "I think you're giving Kennedy preferential treatment."

"Oh no," the committee chairman replied. "I treat him the same way I'd treat any future President."[1]

From the first, the members of the Senate recognized that an imperial presence was in their midst. Despite his lowly seniority ranking, ninety-ninth out of one hundred, he was no ordinary freshman. The Senate has in times past received and quietly absorbed newcomers who arrived with national reputations already made and great expectations for the future prophesied by the press and the public. But it has never had anyone quite like Kennedy. He receives fifty speaking invitations and a thousand letters a day, every day. He seems always to have a television camera crew or a covey of reporters at his heels. Everywhere he walks, a throng of tourists trail after him. His every comment makes news. One Senator remarked with amiable envy: "How can you compete? He has 'future' written all over him."

His arrival in the Senate established another family first. Joseph P. Kennedy thereby became the only man in the country's history to have fathered three Senators. When Edward Kennedy had entered the Senate two years earlier, it had set another precedent. That was the first time a brother of a President served in the Senate. Robert and Edward Kennedy were the second pair of brothers to serve in the Senate at the same time; in 1800, Dwight Foster was elected from Massachusetts and joined his brother Theodore, already a member from Rhode Island. Both served until 1803.

Shortly after winning his seat, Robert Kennedy visited his brother Edward, then in a Boston hospital recuperating from severe back injuries he had suffered in a plane crash the previous June. When both brothers posed for pictures, a photographer asked Robert to "Step back a little, you're casting a shadow on Ted." Edward smiled and said: "It'll be the same in Washington."[2]

The forecast proved accurate. The two brothers cooperate closely; they almost never differ on a roll-call vote. On the one committee on which they both serve—Labor and Public Welfare—they pass notes back and forth during committee sessions and follow the same lines of questioning. On issues such as immigration or the outlawing of the poll tax that Ted has made his own, Robert is careful not to upstage him. But there is no doubt that the older brother is the star.

Robert Kennedy's voting pattern in the Senate is liberal and that was predictable. President Johnson's "Great Society" program of domestic legislation is largely a continuation and an elaboration of the Kennedy "New Frontier" program just as the latter had its origins in the work of the Roosevelt and Truman administrations. Like any sensible politician, Kennedy is responsive to the desires of his constituency, and the state of New York with its progressive traditions, strong trade unions, activist intellectuals, and large communities of impoverished Negroes and Puerto Ricans exerts strong liberal pressures. (New York has not elected a genuine conservative to the Senate from either party in the forty years since Robert F. Wagner, Sr., defeated James Wadsworth, an upstate tory Republican, in 1926.) Kennedy has good reason, therefore, to vote—as he has—for the passage of Medicare, the Voting Rights Act of 1965, the education bills, and the anti-poverty program. There is also the occasional act of sentiment. Kennedy has joined with Joseph S. Clark of Pennsylvania in sponsoring a bill to repeal the loyalty oath provisions of the National Defense Education Act. Clark co-sponsored a similar bill with John Kennedy in 1959.

This liberalism is in accord with Kennedy's own mature convictions as he deepens his understanding of the world. Only thirty-nine when he entered the Senate, Kennedy is still unfolding as a person and enlarging his perceptions. His experience in the Cabinet, the tragedy of his brother's death, and his travels in the United States and abroad have all made him a more sophisticated, thoughtful, and rounded person than the rather two-dimensional, self-righteous young man of a decade earlier.

But it is impossible to determine definitively where honest growth ends and alert opportunism begins in this process of change. He is an astute politician who recognizes that he has no place to go for additional support for the Presidency except to the left. The South cannot be conciliated beyond a certain point and, in any case, the South is Lyndon Johnson's as long as he wants it. The big city machines and the largely Catholic ethnic blocs are already Kennedy's. His efforts have to be directed at the middle-class liberals, the trade unions, the Jewish and Negro organizations, the intellectuals; in other words, at Hubert Humphrey's natural constituency. In the amending and shaping of legislation, therefore, Kennedy usually pushes for the most liberal position, the biggest appropriation, the toughest regulation. What honest conviction prompts, political logic confirms.

The bill to regulate cigarettes affords an example of Kennedy's approach. In the Senate debate on June 16, 1965, Kennedy was militant in opposing the position of the cigarette manufacturers. The bill before the Senate was a weak measure backed by the manufacturers as their best line of defense against what might otherwise have been stringent regulation. The Federal Trade Commission had earlier proposed to require the manufacturers to include in all their advertising a prominent warning that medical research proved smoking is dangerous to health. This requirement would virtually have negated the effect of the advertisements, particularly those on television. To block the FTC, the Senate Commerce Committee reported out a bill that required a warning on cigarette packages, but specifically forbade for three years any Federal, state, or local agency of government from requiring a similar warning in cigarette advertisements. In this form, the bill was a drastically altered version of a bill that Senator Maurine Neuberger of Oregon had been urging for several years. She supported the compromise bill in committee as better than nothing, but on the floor she co-sponsored an amendment to reduce the moratorium on control of advertising from three years to one year. Her co-sponsors were Clark of Pennsylvania and Robert Kennedy.

Kennedy expressed doubt that a warning on the package would help very much in cutting down smoking unless it was accompanied by a similar warning in the advertisements. He pointed out that a bill pending in the House would deny the Federal Trade Commission any authority to require a health warning in advertising "not just for three years but for all time. . . . That provision is what the cigarette industry really wants."

Calling attention to the fact that there is no justifiable medical or scientific reason "for any moratorium whatever," Kennedy attacked the cigarette manufacturers for their "blatant interference with the efforts of federal agencies and state and local authorities to protect the health of American consumers."

The Senate rejected the Neuberger-Clark-Kennedy amendment by a vote of 49 to 29. Kennedy then took the floor to urge defeat of the entire bill. He argued that it would be better to allow the FTC to assert its disputed authority and let the industry challenge it in the courts.

The bill, however, passed the Senate 72 to 5, with only Kennedy and four other Democrats in opposition, and eventually became law.[3]

Kennedy was equally vigorous in defending consumer interests in the Senate hearings on auto safety. These hearings were conducted by a subcommittee of the Committee on Government Operations, chaired by Abraham A. Ribicoff of Connecticut. Ribicoff, an "original Kennedy man," who served in the Kennedy Cabinet in 1961–62 as Secretary of Health, Education, and Welfare, is as close to Robert Kennedy as he once was to his late brother. His subcommittee's assignment is government reorganization, which Ribicoff has broadly interpreted as a mandate to inquire into any problem and determine whether the federal government is properly organized to deal with it. In addition to hearings on auto safety and on pesticides, the subcommittee held the widely publicized inquiry into "the crisis of the cities" in 1966 and early 1967. Kennedy is a member of the full committee and the Ribicoff subcommittee. (His brother John was chairman of the same subcommittee and shepherded on the Senate floor the reorganization proposals submitted by the Hoover Commission.) When Ralph Nader, the crusading author of *Unsafe At Any Speed,* was the witness Kennedy aggressively defended him in an exchange with Republican Senator Carl Curtis of Nebraska:

Kennedy: ". . . What I don't understand is why you don't let Mr. Nader read his statement to find out if in fact . . ."

Curtis: "I have no objection to his reading his statement."

Kennedy: "Then maybe we would understand his position. . . . First, you admit you haven't read the book; and, secondly, you haven't heard his testimony. Why don't you listen to his testimony and then criticize?"

Curtis: "I have no objection to hearing his testimony, but when he loses me with . . ."

Kennedy: "With big words?"

When James Roche, the president of General Motors, testified, Kennedy put him on the spot by calling attention to GM's enormous profits and its puny expenditures on safety research.

As American involvement in the war in Vietnam intensified and commanded an even larger portion of the federal budget, Kennedy became one of the spokesmen for the viewpoint that the United States is rich enough to wage a war in Vietnam and a war against poverty at home at the same time.

"Certainly the war in Vietnam will require great sums from the budget, but to postpone action on our pressing domestic needs would be a terrible mistake," he told the students at Long Island University on December 16, 1965.

He recalled that the McCone Commission that investigated the Negro riots in the Watts section of Los Angeles the previous summer had warned that continued neglect of the Negro ghettos could "split our society irretrievably."

Kennedy added: "To refuse to make the further efforts and the further sacrifices that justice and tranquility require at home would be to invite the very internal conflagration of which we have been warned."

In response to this pressure from Kennedy and others, President Johnson in his State of the Union message in January 1966 vigorously reaffirmed his Administration's commitment to social justice, notwithstanding the distractions of the war. It proved, of course, an easier promise to make than to keep. The difficulty in the year that followed was due, however, as much to the increasingly conservative spirit in Congress as to Lyndon Johnson's own ambivalence. There was little that Kennedy could do about either of these circumstances, but he and Ribicoff scheduled the hearings on the crisis of the cities in part as an effort to keep the problems of poverty and racial inequality alive in the mind of the public. Their hearings provided a forum for some seventy witnesses who represented a wide spectrum of opinion, ranging from Secretary of Housing Robert Weaver and Ford Foundation President McGeorge Bundy to Negro novelist Ralph Ellison and Claude Brown, the author of the moving memoir of a Harlem youth, *Manchild in the Promised Land*. Their interesting if somewhat scattered testimony principally showed that cities have many ills and that those ills are severe, complex, and interrelated. The affluence of the cities draws in Negroes, Puerto Ricans, Mexicans, and impoverished whites from backward rural areas, but the overcrowding, noise, dirt, smog, and traffic congestion expel middle-class whites to the suburbs. The consequent problems of rapidly shifting neighborhoods and *de facto* segregation in housing and schools almost defy solution by hard-pressed municipal governments. The cities hearings produced no immediate legislative result, but much of the work of legislating consists of publicizing issues and testing the reaction to possible solutions until the time is opportune to put together a program that can attract majority support. In these terms, Ribicoff and Kennedy accomplished their purpose.

The political high point of these hearings was the clash between Kennedy and Mayor Samuel Yorty of Los Angeles. Yorty was one of eight mayors of the major cities who testified. All the others received a sympathetic reception, but the subcommittee members zeroed in on Yorty for his failure to do anything to prevent the Watts race riot in which thirty-four lives were lost or to ameliorate conditions once the riot ended. Yorty put on a pathetic display of ignorance, inertia, and frivolous irresponsibility. Asked about unemployment rates in his city, he replied, "I don't know."

Asked about school programs, he replied, "That's not in my jurisdiction."

He offered similar answers when asked about transportation, welfare, health, and housing.

Kennedy interjected, "You might not have the responsibility in each one of these fields, but you certainly are mayor of the city and therefore we need some leadership."

Yorty replied, "I do not need a lecture from you on how to run my city."

Los Angeles has the weak mayor system of government, and authority is fragmented and dispersed among numerous county and local jurisdictions. Nevertheless, a mayor who cared about the plight of the Negroes could do a great deal by personal leadership to focus attention on their specific difficulties and organize community backing to relieve them. Watts, for example, is a community of thirty thousand Negroes in Los Angeles; it suffers from high unemployment, has no hospital, a shortage of doctors, no movie theater, only one swimming pool, few other recreation facilities, and virtually no public transportation system. In a metropolis with as much private wealth as Los Angeles, a mayor with conscience and energy could readily enlist private individuals with the money and public spirit to remedy at least some of these shortages. One has only to imagine what Hubert Humphrey, who was mayor of Minneapolis under a similar weak executive form of government, would do if confronted with a challenge such as Watts.

Yorty, however, is a cynical political adventurer. Elected to the California legislature in 1936 as a New Deal Democrat and a supporter of the Townsend old age pension plan, he shifted in four years from a crusading liberal to a professional anti-Communist. He sponsored the resolution that established the state Committee on Un-American Activities. He served in the U.S. House of Representatives in 1950 to 1954 as a conservative Democrat. His long-term ambition has been to get into the U.S. Senate for which he made unsuccessful races in 1940, 1954, and 1956. Bolting the Democratic Party in 1960 to support Richard Nixon, he wrote a pamphlet called *I Cannot Take Kennedy,* which contained a pointed reference to Kennedy's Catholicism. The following year, he made a political comeback by winning election as mayor of Los Angeles. Although still nominally a Democrat, Yorty gave tacit support to the Republican candidates for governor in 1962 (Nixon) and 1966 (Ronald Reagan). As far as Negroes in Watts and elsewhere in his city are concerned, Yorty uses the stock argument of blaming their unrest on "outside agitators" and criticizing state and federal officials for offering programs that arouse false hopes.

At the hearing, which took place on August 23, 1966, Kennedy clashed intermittently with Yorty, and concluded with the suggestion that the mayor stay for the subsequent hearings to educate himself. "And I think [you] could safely do so, because as I understand from your testimony, you have nothing to get back to."

Ribicoff, however, was actually the sharpest critic of Yorty's shortcomings. Ribicoff: "I would say that the city of Los Angeles right now, from your testimony, does not stand for a damn thing." And again: "You are giving short shrift, and you are shortchanging a few generations by doing absolutely nothing for the disadvantaged groups."

But when Yorty returned to California, he singled out Kennedy for attack, and pictured himself as the innocent victim of Kennedy's political schemes.

"Bobby is an upstart who is trying to ride on his brother's fame and his father's fortune to take over the country," he told a press conference. "Obviously I didn't know what kind of trap I'd run into. The ground had been well laid. Kennedy's tactics are to criticize everything, which is very clever."

Kennedy replied with a formal statement: "Public officials should lead; that is what they are elected for. But in

Los Angeles, progress that has been made has been achieved by the leadership of private citizens, the press, and by neighborhood groups acting on their own.

"The federal government—acting alone—cannot solve our great urban problems; we must rely on local initiative, and it saddened me that Mayor Yorty could give the Congress neither the necessary information nor imaginative proposals of any kind."[4]

On the intellectual merits, Kennedy had the better of that argument. But in political terms, it was at best a standoff. There is never much profit in getting into a running argument with the Sam Yortys of politics.

A secondary objective for Kennedy in the Senate but one he did not neglect was to prove his *bona fides* as a New Yorker and create a clearly identifiable alternative to Governor Nelson Rockefeller and the Republican power structure in New York. Rockefeller, during his first six years in office, had become used to working with two Republican senators who confined any disagreements they had with him to private conferences. One of the ways that Kennedy could assert his leadership in his own party in New York was to demonstrate to local Democrats that now they had a spokesman of their own on state issues who could match the governor in making the front pages.

Senator Jacob K. Javits, his Republican colleague, is an exceptionally energetic, industrious, and useful member of the Senate, who has never been taken quite as seriously as his native abilities would warrant. One reason is that Javits takes himself a shade too seriously. Born a poor boy in a Jewish slum on the Lower East Side, he has had to hustle all his life for what he has achieved, and the hustling has left little room for a sense of humor to develop about himself. Although he has a flawless liberal voting record, and is fertile with interesting ideas and suggestions on international economic policy and many domestic problems, Javits has not attained the moral stature among liberals of a Paul Douglas or a Clifford Case. To sustain an expensive style of living, he has kept busy on the side as a private lawyer. In the 1930s, his practice was principally on the ragged edge of corporations; he specialized in bankruptcies and proxy fights. Since he has attained the dignity of a U.S. Senator, Javits has also moved up in the world as a lawyer. He now represents leading Wall Street investment banking and brokerage houses. A man who does not seriously object to being called "the banker's Senator" is obviously a somewhat special kind of liberal. Javits has also had to demonstrate extraordinarily fast footwork over the years to keep moving ahead in politics. In 1946, when he won a seat in the House of Representatives from an ordinarily Democratic district in Manhattan, he ardently wooed the Communist-line American Labor Party for its endorsement. Ten years later, when he was running for the Senate, reactionaries sought to embarrass him by recalling this involvement. Javits hastened to appear before the Senate Internal Security Subcommittee and avow fervently how much he deplored Communism and admired Richard M. Nixon. This attachment did not, of course, prevent him from supporting Rockefeller against Nixon for the presidential nomination four years later, nor did Javits's alliance with Rockefeller preclude his attempting to supplant him as the Republican gubernatorial candidate in 1966. This last maneuver was an effort on Javits's part to project himself as the first Jewish candidate for Vice-President.

Javits is not a serious threat to Kennedy in national politics, but in New York, he remains a formidable rival. Kennedy's initial instinct was to needle Javits and compete with him for publicity. He began by scoring a small coup: the opening of an office upstate as well as in New York City to handle constituent problems. Javits had been in the Senate for eight years and never had an upstate office. As

soon as Kennedy announced he was opening one in Syracuse, Javits opened one in Buffalo. After some sharp
elbowing in the early months, however, Kennedy arrived
at the more prudent judgment that it would be to his
interest and their mutual convenience to maintain a
facade of bipartisan cooperation. They have co-sponsored
several bills, including one for a federal program of
medical treatment and rehabilitation of narcotics addicts,
and they usually make joint announcements of new federal
projects and contracts in New York.

No such détente has ever been reached between Kennedy and Rockefeller. The two first disagreed publicly on
the question of New York's inclusion in the Appalachia
program. This program, which came before the Senate in
late January 1965, was the culmination of many proposals
dating back four years to the beginning of the Kennedy
administration. The purpose was to assist West Virginia—
to whose voters the Kennedys understandably felt a debt—
and the impoverished mountainous areas in adjoining
states. The premise of the Appalachia plan is that the
region's economic future lies principally in becoming a
tourist and recreation area for the densely populated Atlantic seaboard. To open up this remote back country, the
bill authorized $1,100,000,000, most of it to be used to
build roads but with smaller amounts allocated to sub-
sidiary programs for reforestation, reversing soil erosion,
and cleaning up polluted streams.

Thirteen of New York's sixty-two counties are geographically part of the Appalachian Mountain region. These
are the counties of the so-called "southern tier" that run
westward toward Lake Erie along the Pennsylvania border.
But although geographically in Appalachia, Governor
Rockefeller had opposed their inclusion in the program
because he feared that their inclusion in a "depressed area"
would hurt the image he was trying to create of New York
as a booming industrial state moving ahead on all fronts.

Javits and Keating had deferred to Rockefeller's position, but Kennedy attacked it. He cited statistics showing that twenty-three thousand persons, about 12 per cent of the population of those counties, had incomes of less than two thousand dollars a year. Javits tactfully compromised the dispute by agreeing to support the Kennedy amendment if it were rephrased to make New York's participation contingent upon the governor's approval. In this form, the Senate adopted it. A *New York Times* survey subsequently showed that there was quite enough spotty unemployment, rural poverty, and economic dislocation in the "southern tier" to justify its inclusion in the program.

"City and town officials from one side of the tier to the other, Democrats and Republicans, are unanimous in agreeing that federal help is welcome. Some bristle at the word 'Appalachia,' but none would reject government assistance," *The Times* reported.

Several months later, Governor Rockefeller on May 7 quietly abandoned his opposition and wrote the Federal Appalachian Regional Commission asking it to study New York's eligibility. The state soon afterward began receiving $29 million in federal aid.

Observers of Senate form duly recorded that whereas John Kennedy had waited five months to deliver his maiden speech and brother Teddy had waited sixteen, Robert Kennedy spoke on the floor on behalf of his Appalachia amendment three weeks after taking office. It is also worth noting that his success with the amendment would not have been possible if the Senate did not have a top-heavy, 68-to-32 Democratic majority in which the liberal viewpoint of the Northern Democrats prevailed.

Kennedy also spoke up early on another topic of interest to many New Yorkers: the fate of the commuter railroads. In one of his first public statements as a Senator, he was sharply critical of what he regarded as the evasive attitude of the Rockefeller administration toward the financial crisis of the New Haven Railroad. He contended that it was up to the governors of the four states in which the New Haven operates (New York, Connecticut, Rhode Island, and Massachusetts) to come up with sufficient cash to keep the line running for eighteen months to two years until a long-term federal-state plan could be worked out. Kennedy observed pointedly: "I trust that the Governor of New York will take the lead in arranging it, since New York has a major involvement in the problem."[5]

Kennedy differed with Rockefeller again on the protection of the Hudson River. Rockefeller has an understandable proprietary attitude toward the river. His father helped save the Palisades along the Hudson from exploitation. His brother Laurance is a noted conservationist whom the governor appointed chairman of the Council of State Parks. Since the Hudson River along 95 per cent of its length flows through New York State, Rockefeller believes the state would be falling down in its responsibilities if it turned the river over to the federal government to guard its scenic protection and plan its future use. Kennedy, however, takes the equally justifiable opposing position that the Hudson River, like other scenic treasures such as the Grand Canyon or the California redwoods, belongs to all the American people and not just to the states through which it flows. He introduced a bill to designate the lower portion of the Hudson as a National Scenic Riverway.

In espousing this position, Kennedy was aligning himself with Representative Richard Ottinger, a freshman Democrat from Westchester County, who got himself elected in 1964 in large part on his campaign to save the Hudson.

More startling was Kennedy's surprise attack on the administration of the state schools for the mentally retarded. Testifying before the State Joint Legislative Committee for Mental Retardation on September 9, 1965, Kennedy disclosed that he had recently visited the Willow-

brook School on Staten Island and the Rome State School.
At both, Kennedy said he had discovered serious overcrowding, a shortage of attendants, and many children
who seemed to be receiving no therapy and participating
in no recreation programs. He graphically described children who "just rock back and forth. They grunt and gibber
and soil themselves. They struggle and quarrel—though
great doses of tranquilizers usually keep them quiet and
passive. But for the most part they sit, too often in dim-
ness and gloom and idleness and stench, staring at the
wall or an attendant or an occasional strange visitor."

There followed an inconclusive controversy in which
Kennedy accused Rockefeller of failing to take advantage
of several federal programs to aid the retarded. The governor replied that the state was well aware of these programs and, it developed, was actually participating in
some, in the process of joining others, and chose not to
enter still another for administrative and budgetary reasons. As is true in almost every institutional program—
whether for the retarded, the insane, the delinquent, or
the narcotics addicts—much more could be done if only
more money and more doctors, nurses, and attendants
were readily available.

The controversy over mental retardation not only proves
Kennedy's special interest in that subject but also shows
that the Senate bores him. Many of the failings he criticized could only be corrected by a governor who took a
special personal interest in these institutions and perhaps
infused a new spirit into their administration. Kennedy
is a man of executive energies and imperious will; he
wants to run something. A Senator is an orator, gadfly,
issue maker, and issue popularizer. Kennedy performs all
those functions but he chafes in the essentially spectator
role of a Senator.

When asked in June 1966 about his life in the leisurely

world of the Senate, he grumbled, "They only take about one vote a week here, and they never can tell you in advance when it is going to be so you can schedule other things. If I am not going to be working here, I want to go somewhere I can do something."

The following month, he passed a tedious afternoon at a closed meeting of the Senate Labor and Public Welfare Committee, which was considering a resolution on the national airline strike. Javits and Wayne Morse of Oregon debated at length over the exact words to use in a critical sentence. Unable to stand it any longer, Kennedy suddenly stood up and said, "Oh, hell, why don't you just flip a coin?"

On another occasion, he sat in the Senate chamber waiting to be recognized for a moment to obtain unanimous consent to insert some material in the *Congressional Record*. He had a plane to catch. He kept looking at his watch while two other Senators droned back and forth in an interminable exchange. Kennedy abruptly tossed the papers in the air and strode out of the chamber. They were retrieved by an aide, and Kennedy inserted them the next day.

Kennedy finds an outlet for his executive energies by recruiting dozens of young professors, lawyers, businessmen, and professional men. With the help of this informal corps of volunteers, he has started numerous small projects. Several of these "associates," as these unpaid aides are called, have helped him establish two vest-pocket parks in the Bronx slums. Another tours Indian reservations in the state keeping Kennedy informed on conditions. Others work on hot-breakfast programs and tutorial programs for slum schools and schools for emotionally disturbed children. In effect, Kennedy runs in New York his own private version of an adult "domestic peace corps." Except for special concerns such as the Indians or retarded children, Kennedy and his associates focus on the interrelated problems of the impoverished Negroes and the blighted urban ghettoes.

He outlined his thinking on these problems in three major speeches delivered on successive days, January 20 through 22, 1966. Like most of his speeches, these—particularly the first—were speckled with statistics. He pointed out, for example, that two out of every three Negroes live in towns and cities, most of them in big cities, and fewer than 5 per cent live in suburbs. In 1964, the median family income of Negroes was approximately $3800 and of whites $6800. About 40 per cent of Negro families have incomes below the poverty level of $3000 and live in substandard houses, whereas only 15 per cent of whites do. With segregation rapidly becoming the pattern in the cities of the North, Kennedy called for a renewed effort to break down this pattern.

"Wiping out the ghetto is essential to the future of the Negro and of the city itself. . . . Action must be two-fold—on the one hand giving the Negro complete freedom of choice of neighborhood and, on the other hand, improving existing conditions in the present Negro neighborhoods," Kennedy said.

To achieve these objectives, he proposed a radical strategy for breaking up the concentrated Negro slums and dispersing Negroes to the suburbs. He envisaged "new towns" in which at least 15 per cent of the residents would be Negro. Through federal rent subsidies, Negroes could afford to live there. He urged government money for the more than eleven hundred local public and private agencies around the country which are engaged in promoting racially mixed housing. He recommended that the U.S. Employment Service be drastically overhauled. Using computers and cooperating with local and regional job-and-housing advisory centers, the U.S.E.S. could help migrants—such as a Negro family of ex-sharecroppers leaving Alabama for New York or Chicago—to get matched up with jobs and an apartment in their place of destination before they ever left the South. This plan draws upon the experience of Israel, which has successfully resettled hundreds of thousands of Jews from all over the world; the basis of Israeli success is great care with initial interviews and detailed planning of the flow of migration. This approach is directly opposite to the completely free individualism that European immigrants to this country, as well as Negroes and other internal migrants, have traditionally followed. But since the upheaval of the past half-century that has sent rural Southern Negroes into Northern cities is without precedent, it may require unprecedented programs to reach a successful ending.

For Negro children now trapped in city slums, Kennedy suggested special federal aid to suburban and small-town schools that agree to accept a number of these children either as day pupils who are bussed in or, if distance is too great, as boarders.

In the second of these three talks, Kennedy stressed the need to create jobs in slum areas such as Harlem which the unemployed who live there would get. The construction industry, which uses a comparatively high proportion of unskilled and semiskilled labor, is the obvious target industry. Put Negroes to work building new houses and clinics in their own neighborhoods, Kennedy argued. But he touched not at all on the towering obstacles to this familiar proposal such as the obdurate resistance of the largely white unions in the building trades.

The theme of his third address, which he delivered to a regional conference of the United Automobile Workers in New York, was the desirability of adult education for everyone, but especially for manual workers who have only a high school education or less. If they were enabled to return to high school or go to college, they would be upgraded in the kinds of jobs they would be able to fill in the future, thus making room at the bottom for the young unskilled, particularly the Negro boys and young men whose unemployment runs in the alarming range of 20 to 40 per cent. In effect, Kennedy was making a shrewd appeal to white workers to improve themselves and their own opportunities rather than trying to hold down the Negroes whom they fear as competition. At the same time, he was facing up to a hard fact learned in numerous government and private job-training programs. That is, the employment openings are in professional, technical, and highly skilled occupations, but the unemployed are the least skilled and least educated. No matter how good the remedial reading courses or how long the job-training program, it is impossible to bring very many of these unemployed up to a level where they can qualify for the good jobs that are available.

"It would seem to make better sense," Kennedy said, "to upgrade all of our workers—to give those now employed a chance to move up on the occupational ladder, opening up jobs at levels of skill which would be more easily reached by the presently unemployed. But government job-training programs are primarily directed, not at those now working, but at the unemployed; we have not yet done more than respond to the crises of the moment."

Pointing out that in 1955, only 29 per cent of high school graduates went to college, 33 per cent did so in 1960, and that 45 per cent will in 1970, Kennedy called attention to "an element of unfairness" for millions of young workers. "The graduating high school senior of ten years ago . . . is still only 27 or 28, a young man in the prime of his life, with over thirty years of productive life and work ahead. If that young man, for financial reasons, went to work instead of to college at the age of 18, there is little chance that he will ever get a college education. Yet giving him a college education now would add as much to our national wealth, and to his individual and family welfare, as would aiding many present high school seniors.

"Our society changes rapidly, but we have not provided enough opportunity for people to change with it. . . . Most of our people have, between the ages of 15 and 20, been forced to make a choice—of life and education and career —and that one choice has sharply limited later opportunities."

Eleven months after these speeches came the follow-through. Kennedy announced on December 9, 1966, the formation of two public corporations to try to revitalize Bedford-Stuyvesant, a Negro slum in Brooklyn that has come to rival Harlem in its congestion and the seriousness of its social problems. One corporation is made up of people from the local community, and it is to act as sponsor of programs for housing and rehabilitation and renewal, for job training, and for the creation of cultural and recreational facilities. The other corporation is made up of big names from the business world, such as former Secretary of the Treasury Douglas Dillon, former T.V.A. Chairman David Lilienthal, William Paley of the Columbia Broadcasting System, and Thomas J. Watson, Jr., of the International Business Machines Corporation. This corporation is supposed to work on the economic planning and redevelopment of Bedford-Stuyvesant with the purpose of attracting industry and helping to arrange for the financing of companies that want to locate in the neighborhood.

There is wisdom, social idealism and—in view of how unpopular "open housing" legislation is—political courage in Kennedy's January 1966 speeches. But there are also some unverified assumptions and some intriguing but undeveloped ideas. His Bedford-Stuyvesant experiment will test some of these assumptions and explore the practicality of some of these ideas. Is it really possible to train Negro youths who have no disciplined work habits and Negro

men who have been unemployed for long periods and convert them into skilled building trades craftsmen? And if
this can be accomplished, will there be steady work for
them in the future or after working on a construction
project for a year or two in their own neighborhood, will
many of them be unemployed once again? Why do people
who are moved into a clean, new public housing project
transform it in time into another slum? If slumism has
something to do with fatherless families and attitudes of
dependency, will it reappear in old apartments and houses
that have been renovated and rehabilitated? Can a corporation of local community people make a financial success of renovating and managing slum properties even
with heavy outside financial help? Will the big names who
have lent their names to the second corporation really
have much time to devote to the affairs of Bedford-Stuyvesant? Or have they allowed their names to be used because most of them are personal friends of Senator
Kennedy? David Lilienthal, for example, is not only advising Kennedy on the economic development of Bedford-
Stuyvesant; he is also advising Lyndon Johnson on the
economic development of South Vietnam. Do companies
really want to locate in slum neighborhoods and from the
economic standpoint of their stockholders is it sound
business practice for them to do so?

These are some of the questions that these speeches and
this project evoke. The answers may all be in the affirmative, and it will be encouraging for the United States if
they are. But it will take five years or more before the
corporations in Bedford-Stuyvesant can provide any definitive answers.

Kennedy is admirable for involving himself in what are
the central urban issues of the time; since these are not
directly his responsibilities as a Senator, he could easily
have sidestepped them. Instead, he has shown an initiative and a venturesomeness that are uncommon. But to

sponsor a project like that in Bedford-Stuyvesant is also to assume a commitment to stay with it and provide sustained leadership and personal attention over the months and years to come as the difficult questions are worked out. The quality of Kennedy's commitment is in doubt. He is overextended and overscheduled; he is advising on Bedford-Stuyvesant, advising on the New York State constitutional convention, jousting with the Rockefeller administration on state affairs, flying to Paris to confer with French officials, flying to Chicago to speak to a conference on China policy, issuing statements disagreeing with President Johnson on Vietnam, and by means of all these activities but also in addition to them, he is running for the Presidency. It is an astonishing performance. Under these circumstances, it is only to be expected that Kennedy sometimes raises questions, initiates controversies or proposes projects—and then lets them die. What is extraordinary is that he finds time to remember Bedford-Stuyvesant at all.

The diversity and range of his activities make voracious demands upon Kennedy and his staff. His own tendency is to be somewhat helter-skelter in his work habits and to rely on his random interventions and challenges to keep his associates moving and charged up. This tendency is not new in his Senate years; it has merely become more visible since he left the Justice Department. There he stood at the apex of a large smoothly running bureaucracy, had ample personal staff, and a group of able Assistant Attorneys General. By contrast, his Senate office in Washington resembles nothing so much as a campaign headquarters along about the third week in October. More than thirty persons are shoehorned into five small rooms, not counting the Senator's private office. There is not enough filing space or desk space or people to do all the work that keeps crowding in; the phones almost never stop ringing, and three visitors at one time are enough to create a traffic jam.

Contrary to a popular misconception, Kennedy's staff is not unusually large. Since funds are allotted for staff in the Senate roughly in proportion to the size of a state's population, New York Senators usually have the most employes. As many wealthy Senators do, Kennedy pays for several additional assistants out of his own pocket. He also supplements them with student internes and summer volunteers. Kennedy has roughly thirty people in Washington and another dozen working in New York City and Syracuse; Herbert H. Lehman, who served in the Senate from New York from 1949 to 1957, had thirty employes, half of whom he paid himself.[6]

The core of the staff are six men.[7] Joseph Dolan, forty-five, is a New York lawyer who moved after law school to Colorado, entered politics, was an organizer for the Kennedys in the Rocky Mountain States in 1960, and resigned the following year from the Colorado legislature to join the Justice Department. As an Assistant Deputy Attorney General, he screened candidates for judgeships and performed administrative odd jobs. He and the then Deputy Attorney General Nicholas Katzenbach were the two Justice Department representatives who led Negro students into the University of Alabama in 1963, notwithstanding Governor George Wallace's threat to "stand in the schoolhouse door." As Kennedy's administrative assistant, Dolan supervises the secretaries and clerks and coordinates the internal operations of the Washington office. He is also a discreet, soft-spoken, rather self-effacing confidant; Kennedy values his devotion and his disinterested judgment.

Kennedy's press secretary is Frank Mankiewicz, the nephew of movie producer Joseph Mankiewicz. A former newspaperman in California, he joined the Peace Corps when it was formed and rose to become the Corps' Latin America director. He first met Kennedy in 1965 when he briefed him before his trip to Latin America. He joined the staff six months later.

Dolan at forty-five and Mankiewicz at forty-two are the only men on the staff older than their boss; the other top aides—Peter Edelman, Adam Walinsky, Wendell Pigman, the three legislative assistants, and Thomas Johnston, who runs Kennedy's New York office—have barely turned thirty. (Senator Javits's staff is comparably youthful; staff men on Capitol Hill tend to be young because the work in busy periods demands long hours and reserves of energy. There is also a considerable turnover because there is little opportunity to move up—unless one's Senator becomes President.) Kennedy's bright young men have the outstanding academic records and evident high intelligence that he likes in his aides; thus, Walinsky was Order of the Coif at Yale Law School and Edelman graduated *magna cum laude* from Harvard Law School. But otherwise, they do not differ from dozens of other ambitious young men on Capitol Hill.

Kennedy's aides are generalists; any one of them could write a speech, draft a bill or a press release, research a legal point (even Mankiewicz, the press secretary, is a lawyer), or carry out a political errand. The only complaints ever heard about them is that they are spread too thin, and that they are too few to specialize on particular projects. They seem not disorganized but underorganized.

"I take up a problem with Kennedy and later I never know which of his guys to follow it up with," a New York politician has remarked. "They're all over the lot just the way he is."

But this sense of being in on everything and being on call like firemen to work on a dozen different projects undoubtedly contributes to the élan of the men around Kennedy.

Kennedy is unusual not in the size or quality of his staff but rather in the depth and strength of his unofficial advisers. They spread outward from him in ever widening concentric circles. Closest to the center is his brother-in-law and political manager, Stephen Smith. In the furthermost circles are the young professional men who serve as Kennedy's "associates" in New York and the academic specialists scattered on campuses around the country who are occasionally tapped for advice or information. They get no money, but they have the psychic satisfaction of seeing their ideas at work in the world of high politics and in some instances, the pleasure of saying at the next faculty lunch, "Well, as I told Senator Kennedy the other day . . ."

For advice, speech drafts, and special missions, Kennedy turns most often to three former members of his brother's administration. Theodore C. Sorensen will never be as close to Robert Kennedy—or to any other man—as he was to President Kennedy. But since he finished his book *Kennedy* and left the seclusion of Cape Cod to practice law with a large Manhattan firm, he has gradually begun to move in Robert Kennedy's orbit. Although Sorensen had a rare intellectual compatibility with the late President, he and Robert Kennedy actually have more affinity as political animals. Both are more daring and more prone to move on instinctive reactions to a situation than was the more cautious JFK. As chairman of an advisory committee on the rebuilding of the Democratic Party in New York, Sorensen has become another pair of eyes-and-ears for Kennedy in the state; having participated in the long buildup to the 1960 nomination, he is a knowledgeable source of ideas and advice on national politics; and as one of the great speech writers of the age, he finds time to send along a useful suggestion or a timely witticism that Kennedy's own writers can incorporate. If there is another Kennedy administration, it would be no surprise to see Sorensen in the Cabinet.

Arthur Schlesinger, Jr., is closer to Robert Kennedy and

a more important adviser of his than was the case with President Kennedy. Schlesinger was only casually acquainted with John F. Kennedy before the latter became President. During the White House years, when Schlesinger served as a kind of intellectual-in-residence bringing to the President's attention interesting people and ideas, the two developed a personal rapport. The President enjoyed the quick play of Schlesinger's sharp, witty mind, but the latter was not in the top rank of his assistants. Robert Kennedy, however, consults Schlesinger on most major issues and also enjoys his company in moments of relaxation.

Richard N. Goodwin is the third New Frontier alumnus who is influential in Kennedy's circle. Having graduated first in his class at the Harvard Law School and clerked for Supreme Court Justice Felix Frankfurter, Goodwin looked for a way to stay on the Washington scene in 1958. (He had boasted to Tufts College friends that he would be "working in the White House before I'm thirty.") Too liberal to serve the Eisenhower administration, he joined the staff of the House committee that was investigating fixed television quiz shows. From this inquiry, he went to work as Sorensen's assistant the following year. He took on some of the legislative research and speech-writing chores, freeing Sorensen to travel on political tours with the then Senator Kennedy. Goodwin, who turned out to be a fluent, witty writer, became a compatible collaborator of Sorensen in working on Kennedy's speeches. He naturally was brought along to the White House in 1961, making good his own prophecy with two years to spare. Kennedy asked him to concentrate on Latin America. In this assignment, Goodwin wrote most of the "Alliance for Progress" speech in 1961. Later that year, Kennedy moved him to the State Department as Deputy Assistant Secretary for Latin America. Goodwin began learning Spanish and imparting some Kennedy-style dash to the conduct of hemispheric relations, but the career men in the State Department fought this brash young newcomer at every turn. After a year, he was effectively frozen out. He quit State and switched to the Peace Corps. In late 1963 with the next presidential campaign approaching, Kennedy and Sorensen decided to bring him back to the White House for speech-writing duty. His appointment as Special Assistant for the Arts was made known—on November 22, 1963.

Goodwin did not get the art-and-culture assignment from President Johnson (who chose Broadway producer Roger Stevens instead), but he stayed at the White House as a writer throughout 1964. It was he who wrote the "Great Society" speech that provided Mr. Johnson with his campaign theme. Since leaving the White House and becoming a Research Fellow at Wesleyan University, Goodwin has become increasingly close to Robert Kennedy. He expects to have a third tour of duty at the White House in the not-so-distant future.

NOTES

[1] Richard Reeves, "Kennedy," *The New York Times*, November 14, 1966.

[2] "Topics," *The New York Times*, January 4, 1965.

[3] *Congressional Record*, pp. 13404–13444.

[4] *The New York Times*, August 25, 1966.

[5] "Letters to the Editor," *The New York Times*, February 13, 1965.

[6] Allan Nevins, *Herbert H. Lehman and His Era* (Scribner's, New York 1963), p. 315n.

[7] The best article on Kennedy's staff is Richard Reeves, "The People Around Bobby," *The New York Times Magazine*, February 12, 1967, p. 25.

CHAPTER FIVE

Vietnam and
Counter-insurgency

> *"The guerrilla campaigns being waged in China today are a page in history that has no precedent. Their influence will be confined not solely to China in her present anti-Japanese struggle, but will be world-wide."*
> —MAO TSE-TUNG, *1937*

> *"This kind of warfare can be long-drawn-out and costly, but if Communism is to be stopped, it is necessary. And we mean to see this job through to the finish."*
> —ROBERT F. KENNEDY, *1964*

> *"A negotiated settlement means that each side must concede matters that are important in order to preserve positions that are essential."* —ROBERT F. KENNEDY, *1966*

IMPORTANT as the nation's domestic problems are, the decisive political arena for the contemporary politician is foreign affairs. Potential Presidents are not judged on how they would manage the farm problem or even the civil rights problem but how they would cope with the Russians and the Chinese in this infinitely dangerous period of uncontrolled nuclear armaments.

Since entering the Senate in January 1965, Robert Kennedy has spoken often and pointedly on foreign affairs. His range has been wide. He has deplored the United States intervention in the Dominican Republic, called for a reexamination of policies toward Communist China, and stressed the importance of building bridges to Russia and to Eastern Europe. He has condemned military aid for Latin American countries and urged increased support for the Alliance for Progress. He has devoted considerable attention to the nearly intractable problems of nuclear disarmament.

Vietnam, however, has been the public question with the highest political dynamism during his time in the Senate. It is also a question in which Kennedy was intimately involved during his brother's administration. He had been in the Senate more than a year before he spoke out on the Vietnam War. His move, when it came, had the greatest significance for his future as a possible Presidential candidate.

In February 1965, less than a month after his inauguration for a full, four-year term in his own right, Lyndon Johnson made the critical decision—it may prove the key decision of his tenure in the White House—to introduce American ground forces in Vietnam on a major scale rather than permit an imminent victory by the Communist Viet Cong.

One year later, American troops had reversed the tide of Communist victories and begun to stabilize the military situation in South Vietnam. But in Washington, Johnson's policy was under sharp attack. Senator J. William Fulbright, Chairman of the Senate Foreign Relations Committee, had finally brought his smoldering opposition fully into the open by calling a series of public hearings at which the merits of American involvement were debated. Secretary of State Dean Rusk opened and closed the hearings on behalf of the Administration; he was supported by General Maxwell D. Taylor. The case against the Administration was made by Lieutenant General James M. Gavin and former Ambassador George F. Kennan.

On February 19, 1966, the day after the hearings concluded, Robert Kennedy publicly joined the opposition camp. It was his boldest move in cutting himself apart from the Johnson administration. Kennedy did not make the break lightly, and he did his best to limit its significance. He served in the Cabinet with Rusk and is a close personal friend and keen admirer of General Taylor: the previous year he named his newborn son, Matthew Maxwell Taylor Kennedy. Moreover, Kennedy, having once helped to shape Vietnam policy, knows its tangled history. Many of his colleagues in that effort—Robert McNamara in Defense, McGeorge Bundy at the White House, Averell Harriman in State—were still in office and advising President Johnson. Kennedy conferred at length with General Taylor and other friends and former colleagues while preparing his speech; he sent them advance copies the day before he delivered it. But his break with existing policy was still fundamental and clear-cut.

He defined three alternatives for the United States in Vietnam: military victory, a peaceful settlement, or withdrawal. He dismissed withdrawal as "impossible."

"Unilateral withdrawal would only reward aggression and could offer China no inducement to reach accommodation in a peaceful world," he declared.

He rejected military conquest because it would involve an increasingly heavy American commitment, would heighten the risk of a war with China, and mean increased destruction in Vietnam, all in pursuit of "a goal which is at best uncertain, and at worst unattainable."

He called for a negotiated peace based upon granting the Viet Cong a share in governing South Vietnam. "I believe there is a middle way, that an end to the fighting and a peaceful settlement can be achieved," he declared. "A negotiated settlement means that each side must concede matters that are important in order to preserve positions that are essential."

In the next several days, there were several rounds of statements and counter-statements from Kennedy and Administration spokesmen as the press tried to define the extent of his disagreement with existing policy. He clearly favored the admission of the Viet Cong as a separate party to the peace talks; the Administration position was that Viet Cong views could be "represented" by the government of North Vietnam. But, more important, did Kennedy mean that the Viet Cong was to be guaranteed some share in the government of South Vietnam during the interim period between the truce talks and the holding of a general election in that country? If so, did he really expect the anti-Communist government to work with the Communists?

Kennedy was understandably vague and tentative in outlining the nature of the political settlement he envisaged. "To admit them (the Communist Viet Cong) to a share of power and responsibility is at the heart of the hope for a negotiated setlement. It is not the easy way or the sure way; nor can the manner of the degree of participation now be described with any precision. . . . It will require enormous skill and political wisdom to find the point at which participation does not bring domination or internal conquest."

Between Saturday, February 19, and Tuesday, the 22nd, Kennedy strove to clarify his position. Appearing on the "Today" show on the morning of the twenty-second, he answered the query about how he expected the antagonists to collaborate in an interim government: "Well, it has happened before. . . . I think it's a very, very difficult situation . . . but that has to be our objective and we have to move toward that objective. . . . My point is that the alternatives are so much more unsatisfactory."

During the course of that day in telephone interviews with reporters and in conversations with White House Press Secretary Bill Moyers, he offered additional interpretations. He suggested a Laos-type settlement in which Communist, anti-Communist, and neutral factions shared power by agreement without elections. He also suggested a United Nations or Southeast Asian regional group to administer South Vietnam until elections were held. Such an arrangement would be similar to the interim supervision of the Dominican Republic by the Organization of American States. Late that day, he called a press conference in which he said he was not insisting on any of these alternatives. His view, he said, was not that the Viet Cong should "automatically" have a share of power in the interim government but rather that they should not be "automatically excluded" from having it. The issue, he suggested, could be settled at the peace conference.

In this way, Kennedy arrived at a position sufficiently flexible to permit a temporary cease-fire between himself and the Administration. Undersecretary of State George Ball, Bundy and Moyers, all of whom had criticized what they interpreted as Kennedy's call for a pre-election coalition government, lapsed into silence. For some months thereafter, there was no further clash.

But the meeting of minds was more apparent than real. The Johnson administration has not committed upwards of four hundred thousand troops to South Vietnam to achieve a coalition government in Saigon, either before or after an election. Despite the professed willingness of the Administration to abide by the outcome of an election, its true purpose is to cripple the power of the Viet Cong and thus see to it that the Communists play a small part —or none at all—in the future political life of South Vietnam. The objective is to win the same kind of settlement as has developed in Germany and Korea: a country divided between Communist and non-Communist sectors. Nothing less would justify the huge investment of American men and money in South Vietnam.

In West Germany and South Korea, this pattern of settlement has included the stationing of American troops to underwrite the protection of the non-Communist segment. Kennedy clearly—and accurately—asserted that the Communists would accept this kind of division only as the result of a shattering military defeat. He defined North Vietnam's "one irreducible demand" for entering upon a diplomatic negotiation: "They will not accept a settlement which leaves in the south a hostile government, dedicated to the final physical destruction of all Communist elements, refusing any economic cooperation with the north, dependent upon the continued presence of American military power."

Kennedy's February 19 speech represented his face-saving formula for disengaging from what he regards as an unendurable stalemate which cannot be broken militarily except at the unacceptable risk of war with China. In proposing a coalition government for Saigon, he offered a solution that is distinctly unpromising. It has failed in countries as different as the Czechoslovakia of Eduard Beneš and the China of Chiang Kai-shek. McGeorge Bundy, appearing on a television program on February 20, had no difficulty producing a quotation from President Kennedy that rebutted the pro-coalition view. Speaking in Berlin in June 1963, President Kennedy said: "I am not impressed by the opportunities open to popular fronts throughout the world. I do not believe that any democrat can successfully ride that tiger."

In South Vietnam, which has known very little stability or democratic self-government, there is not much of that "enormous skill and political wisdom" Kennedy suggested as the necessary prerequisites for successful coalition. Vice-President Humphrey was correct when he said that Kennedy's coalition plan would "set the fox to guard the hen house."

Yet for all its visible defects, Kennedy's formula appears

to be the only one that would extricate the United States from its Vietnam commitment in a short time. The disagreement between Kennedy and the Johnson administration then and later has not been over the objective; both want to end the war. The disagreement has been whether the U.S. could get a more permanently viable settlement in South Vietnam if it fought longer and whether that settlement would be worth the military effort and risk. Kennedy's protestations—in February 1966 and subsequently—that unilateral withdrawal and the eventual abandonment of South Vietnam were the farthest thoughts from his mind must be seen as necessary movements in a diplomatic minuet. Charles de Gaulle made comparable protestations about the inviolability of Algeria's relationship with France all the while that he was making up his mind to disown the French *colons* and give Algeria its complete independence. Candor is not only the first casualty in war; it is also useless in making a less than victorious peace. In seeking a formula for disengagement, Kennedy was facing up to the fact that the American public might eventually tire of a limited war that dragged on with mounting losses and no discernible end. In February 1966, General Taylor reminded the Foreign Relations Committee that in 1954 the Communists won more in Paris than in Dienbienphu and that they hoped to repeat this political success in Washington by wearing down America's public opinion and political leadership. Taylor concluded his testimony by quoting President Johnson's brave words: "We will not be defeated. We will not grow tired. We will not withdraw either openly or under the cloak of a meaningless agreement."

But what if Americans do not have the patience and stoicism to wage a long, low-level, grinding war? Who will lead the way for the Democrats if the political pressures mount for an early peace? These were the questions

Robert Kennedy began to answer for himself in his February 19 speech.

There was a political gain and an intellectual loss for Kennedy in taking his stand on Vietnam. The political dividend was immediately evident. One day after the speech, David Broder, then the national political correspondent of *The New York Times,* reported from Bakersfield, California, where the strongly liberal California Democratic Council was in convention: "Mr. Kennedy's public break from Administration policy on Vietnam was the chief topic of conversation."

Gerald Hill, newly elected president of the CDC, prophesied to the delegates—inaccurately, as events developed—that now that Kennedy "has enlisted in this fight" against the Vietnam War, it would hasten a change in Administration policy.

"The new found enthusiasm for the New York Senator," *The Times* correspondent continued, "among the disciples of the late Adlai E. Stevenson is echoed among members of the Democratic left in states around the country and in the capital itself.

"Talks with Democrats in a half-dozen major states during the last three weeks disclosed a shift in their attitude toward Mr. Kennedy. Some self-described liberals who formerly regarded him as a ruthless, cold-blooded and even unprincipled political operator now look to him increasingly as the symbol and exponent of their dissatisfaction with the Johnson administration."[1]

Although Kennedy's shift on Vietnam brought him substantial political gains within the liberal community, he was not motivated solely or perhaps even primarily by considerations of political advantage. Like most men in most situations, he acted upon multiple motives which not even he could clearly disentangle. As a man of feeling, he shared the deepening anguish of people everywhere as they observed the growing number of American casualties and the ordeal of the Vietnamese people, both northerners and southerners. As a former adviser on foreign policy in his brother's administration, he believed that President Johnson had unwisely made an open-end commitment in Vietnam that would probably not end in an American military victory and that it was in the national interest to try to persuade both the President and the American people to cut their losses. As a politician, he astutely perceived that the Vietnam War would eventually mean political disaster for the Democrats and that the prudent course for a political leader who cared about his future was to get on record early in favor of a negotiated peace. There are risks as well as gains in taking the "dove" position, since anti-communism is popular and any war arouses patriotic feeling. The downturn in Kennedy popularity as charted in the public opinion polls in the winter and spring of 1967 was probably due in part to his opposition to the war as well as to the adverse effects of the Manchester book controversy. But the risks are less for Kennedy than for any other politician on the "dove" side of the Vietnam issue because, for entirely separate reasons, he has a strong hold on the emotions of many "hawkish" voters, particularly in the Catholic ethnic groups.

His cold shrewdness and his passion enabled Kennedy to abandon his previous commitment to the Vietnam War. Like his father, he has a speculator's ability to size up a proposition and decide whether it looks like a winner. No emotion, no ideological fixation, no wishful romanticism clouds or confuses this analytic process. Self-interest is the controlling criterion. If General Motors' shares are dropping on the market, what does sentiment have to do with the decision to sell? And why waste more sentiment on Vietnam than on GM? The speculator's approach to foreign policy does not always work: Joseph P. Kennedy wrote off England in 1940 as a losing proposition. But, right or wrong, this kind of cold shrewdness enabled Robert Kennedy in the winter of 1965–66 to reach the conclusion that South Vietnam is not worth a major investment of American men and money—or of Kennedy prestige. Passion, too, played its part. Robert Kennedy's dislike of Lyndon Johnson, bordering upon hatred, made it easier for him to change his mind about Vietnam the more he thought of it as Mr. Johnson's war. Lyndon Johnson in his mind is like the stepfather in classic fiction, a usurper who can never fill the place that rightfully belonged to another. Actions in Vietnam that Robert Kennedy would have stoutly defended if JFK had ordered them became suspect in his eyes since their author was LBJ.

His change of mind with regard to Vietnam represented a major though unacknowledged intellectual defeat for Kennedy. The Vietnam War was the ugly child, grown monstrous and outsized but still recognizable, of the Kennedy administration's belief in the efficacy of counter-insurgency techniques against guerrilla warfare. And no one had been a more devoted proponent of those techniques from 1961 to 1963 than Robert Kennedy.

Kennedy developed his deep personal interest in guerrilla warfare and counter-insurgency in the aftermath of the unsuccessful landing in Cuba at the Bay of Pigs. Along with General Taylor, Admiral Arleigh Burke, and Allen Dulles, he reviewed what went wrong at the Bay of Pigs and its implications for the future. His shrewdness and self-confidence made him an effective participant in that inquiry. He was as willing to ask hard questions of the leading figures in the Central Intelligence Agency or the Joint Chiefs of Staff as he had been of witnesses before the Rackets Committee—and just as scornful privately if the answers were feeble. General Lyman L. Lemnitzer, Chairman of the Joint Chiefs, was one of those who fell steadily from favor in the course of those closed talks.

"Bob thinks Lemnitzer is a very nice man," one of the

Attorney General's aides remarked, "but he thinks he ought to be a grocer in some small town."

Lemnitzer was eventually shifted to Paris as NATO commander and replaced by Taylor as chairman of the Joint Chiefs.

Robert Kennedy was equally influential in choosing John McCone to replace Dulles, who retired as C.I.A. chief. There was sharp disagreement among President Kennedy's advisers over McCone. Liberals recalled him unfavorably for his criticism, as a regent of the University of California, of those professors who backed Adlai Stevenson's position on the nuclear test ban during the 1956 campaign. They also resisted him as a hard-line "cold warrior." But Robert Kennedy had talked with McCone and been favorably impressed; he helped confirm President Kennedy's judgment in McCone's favor.

Kennedy's role in the Bay of Pigs Committee from April to July 1961 and in the personnel shake-ups that followed is well known. What is less well known is that these discussions also engaged the passionate, believing, activist side of his mind. Kennedy became a zealous convert to the doctrines of guerrilla warfare. He became convinced that it is essential for the success of United States foreign policy to develop effective techniques to combat Communist use of terrorism, low-level violence, and brush-fire wars.

He read Mao Tse-tung and Ché Guevara. He sometimes quoted Mao's prophecy of 1937: "The guerrilla campaigns being waged in China today are a page of history that has no precedent. Their influence will be confined not solely to China in her present anti-Japanese struggle, but will be world-wide."

Except for the Korean War, Kennedy observed that the military conflicts with Communism had been neither conventional nor nuclear. In Malaya, the Communist guerrilla war lasted from 1946 to 1957; it involved four hundred thousand armed men and caused nearly sixteen thousand casualties. In Greece, the struggle against Communist guerrillas lasted from 1945 to 1950, engaged three hundred thousand men, and nearly half that number were killed or wounded. There have been similar guerrilla outbreaks in Cuba and Venezuela, in the Philippines and Vietnam.

Here, as in most matters, Robert Kennedy was functioning as the *alter ego* of his brother. The President, too, was engrossed in the guerrilla warfare problem. He personally ordered a six-fold enlargement of the Army's Special Forces, helped select their equipment, and—"over the opposition of top generals"—directed them to wear green berets as a mark of distinction.[2] When the Bay of Pigs Committee completed its work, he appointed a small group of high officials to supervise counter-insurgency efforts. Robert Kennedy was the driving force in this committee. Among its members were representatives of State, Defense, the C.I.A., and the foreign aid agency. The aid agency was involved because it is the conduit for the money to pay for the training of police and special army units in underdeveloped countries. Those from Latin America attend either the Inter-American Police Academy or the Jungle Warfare Training Center in Panama; those from Asian countries attend comparable schools in Okinawa. In numerous countries, the United States subsidizes not only the initial training but the maintenance of these special forces.

Of all the task forces on which he served and all the special missions he performed for his brother, none aroused Robert Kennedy's interest more than this. Other senior officials often sent deputies to represent them at meetings of the counter-insurgency committee, but he invariably attended in person. Within the government, he was regarded as "Mr. Counter-insurgency."

Vietnam seemed a promising place in which to prove

America's ability to counteract Communist tactics. It was on General Taylor's advice that President Kennedy stepped up the number of American instructors attached to the South Vietnamese forces and sent in the Green Berets. Robert Kennedy subscribed wholeheartedly to this decision.

While making his tour of the Far East in early 1962, he was asked in Hong Kong about the war in South Vietnam. He replied: "The solution there lies in our winning it. This is what the President intends to do."[3]

At a news conference during a brief stopover in Saigon a week later, Kennedy expounded on his view of the war: "This is a new kind of war, but war it is in a very real sense of the word. It is a war fought not by massive divisions but secretly by terror, assassination, ambush and infiltration.

"Hanoi may deny its responsibility but the guilt is clear. In a flagrant violation of its signed pledge at Geneva in 1954, the North Vietnamese regime has launched on a course to destroy the Republic of Vietnam."

A British correspondent said, "American boys are dying out here. Do the American people understand and approve of what is going on?"

"I think the American people understand and fully support this struggle," Kennedy replied. "Americans have great affection for the people of Vietnam. I think the United States will do what is necessary to help a country that is trying to repel aggression with its own blood, tears, and sweat."[4]

During the rest of his tenure in the Cabinet, he did not waver from these opinions. In his office, he proudly kept on display a carbine, its stock hand-whittled, its barrel a length of pipe, which had been taken from a captured Viet Cong guerrilla and sent to him by a friend. When he left the Justice Department in 1964, he could look back upon three years of intensive effort in this field, but he was not satisfied.

"We have made a beginning," he said. "We have achieved some notable successes, but we have not mastered the art of counter-insurgency. More importantly, perhaps, in a practical sense, we have not perfected the technique of training foreign nationals to defend themselves against Communist terrorism and guerrilla penetration. This kind of warfare can be long-drawn-out and costly, but if Communism is to be stopped, it is necessary. And we mean to see this job through to the finish."[5]

The experience in Vietnam suggests that Kennedy's confidence in counter-insurgency efforts was misplaced. When the South Vietnamese army and its Green Beret advisers could not defeat Communist penetration, the U.S. in early 1965 had to intervene with regular ground forces to prevent the collapse of the South Vietnamese government and a total defeat. The ensuing struggle has proved "long-drawn-out and costly," and the evidence is at best ambiguous as to whether Americans really want to "see this job through to the finish." If American counter-insurgency techniques fail in Vietnam, they are not likely to succeed elsewhere in Asia. This leaves only the continent of Latin America where they might feasibly be employed. On the basis of the melancholy experience of the Johnson administration in Vietnam, will any future administration try to combat a major Communist military operation in, say, Bolivia or Colombia? The answer will probably be negative.

It is true that counter-insurgency works best if the local government has strong popular support, but neither the Communist guerrillas in Asia nor the Castroite guerrillas in Latin America normally pick countries with strong, popular governments. It is also true that President Kennedy and his brother did not expect the Green Berets or any other U.S. guerrilla force to win brush-fire wars in foreign countries. They both were well acquainted with Mao's axiom: "Guerrillas are like fish, and the people are the water in which the fish swim. If the temperature of the water is right, the fish will thrive and multiply." But until the effort is actually made in a particular country, it is impossible to say for certain whether American guns, training, and advice will produce a corps of local guerrillas to combat hostile infiltration. The effort was made and failed in Vietnam. It has been successful thus far in Venezuela, but an exacting test in the other Latin American countries has not yet been made.

Popular leaders with appealing reform programs cannot be summoned into existence on demand, and without this political dimension, military measures in most instances will not suffice. Despite the good intentions and energetic efforts of the Kennedy brothers, counter-insurgency has not proved the effective American answer to Communist terrorism and subversion.

Robert Kennedy has not yet faced up to the implications of the failure of counter-insurgency in Vietnam. It is one of history's fascinating "if's" to contemplate what might have happened if President Johnson had accepted his offer in 1964 to become U.S. Ambassador to South Vietnam when Henry Cabot Lodge resigned after his first tour of duty. As ambassador, Kennedy in early 1965 would have had the responsibility of giving President Johnson his judgment on what the United States should do to prevent the imminent fall of South Vietnam to the Communists.

On March 2, 1967, one year after his original speech breaking with the Administration over Vietnam, Kennedy returned to this theme in another address to the Senate. He began with an expression of humility. It was not his intention, he said, "to curse the past or to praise it. . . .

"Three Presidents have taken action in Vietnam. As one who was involved in many of those decisions, I can testify that if fault is to be found or responsibility assessed, there is enough to go around for all—including myself."

He placed the blame for the failure to obtain a peaceful settlement on North Vietnam and the Communist Viet Cong.

"The fault rests largely with our adversary. He has pursued relentless and unyielding conquest with obdurate unconcern for mounting desolation. Now his victory has eluded him, replaced by a conflict where violence breeds only endless violence. If our enemy will not accept peace, it cannot come."

Having made those two preliminary observations, Kennedy then turned to the heart of his speech in which he proposed a three-point peace program for the United States to adopt. He proposed a unilateral suspension of American bombing of North Vietnam and an announcement that "we are ready to negotiate within the week." Secondly, once negotiations began, both sides would agree that during the peace talks, neither side would "substantially increase the size of the war in South Vietnam—by infiltration or reinforcement." This agreement could be supervised by an international inspection team patrolling borders, ports, and roads. Third, he envisaged the gradual withdrawal of American and North Vietnamese forces from the South and their replacement by an international peacekeeping force and a final political settlement based on free elections in which all South Vietnamese, including the Viet Cong, would take part.

"If we can follow this course, we cannot be certain that negotiations will take place or that they will be productive. No one can give such a binding guarantee. But measures such as these will enhance the chances of peace while the risks are comparatively slight."

In proposing a halt to the American bombing of North Vietnam, Kennedy stressed the importance of the statement of Russian Premier Kosygin in London two weeks earlier. Kosygin said that the first step toward peace "should be the unconditional cessation of the bombing of, and all other aggressive acts against, North Vietnam. As the Foreign Minister of North Vietnam declared recently, this step is necessary to enable talks between North Vietnam and the United States to take place." Kennedy argued that this statement created a "drastically different" situation than had existed a year earlier when North Vietnam had set much stiffer conditions for beginning peace talks including the withdrawal of American troops from South Vietnam.

Kennedy's second point—international enforcement of an agreement by both sides not to reinforce their troops during peace talks—reflected American experience in the Korean truce talks. From 1951 to 1953, talks dragged on at Panmunjom, and so did the fighting. There were more American casualties during those protracted truce negotiations than there had been in the full-scale fighting of 1950–51.

Kennedy said, "It is unrealistic to think we would sit through prolonged and fruitless negotiations while casualties mount and the war gets bigger. Thus, even if hostilities continue it will be necessary for both sides to refrain from escalating the war on the ground and trying to change the military balance."

If North Vietnam used the negotiations merely as a cover to infiltrate additional men and supplies to its forces in the South, Kennedy argued, we could break off the talks and reexamine our position. If we then resumed bombing or intensified the fighting, we would enjoy "far clearer international understanding [for] our motives and necessities."

This scarcely seems a realistic observation. Public opinion in allied and neutral countries that is hostile to American purposes during the war would scarcely support a resumption of bombing or intensive combat, no matter how repeated or flagrant the provocation from North Vietnam.

Kennedy's third point was a restatement of his main argument a year earlier that South Vietnam could be pacified only if the Viet Cong were brought into the free political life of the country.

After this speech, there was much less effort than there had been a year earlier to paper over the differences between Kennedy and President Johnson. McGeorge Bundy and Bill Moyers, who had served as peacemakers and emissaries the previous year, were now gone from the White House staff. No one had replaced them who could command the confidence of the two antagonists. Although both men avoided an irreparable public break, President Johnson spared no effort to blanket the news of Kennedy's speech. He held a press conference, made a speech on civil rights at Howard University, and released the news that the Soviet Union had agreed to negotiate about the arms race in anti-missile missiles. On the same day, General William C. Westmoreland, the American commander in South Vietnam, issued a rare personal statement urging a continuation of the bombing as necessary to save the lives of American soldiers. Secretary of State Rusk put out a statement insisting that "proposals substantially similar to those put forward by Senator Kennedy" had already been explored with the Communists without result.

"We have had bombing pauses of five days in 1965; thirty-seven days in December–January, 1965–66; and six days just two weeks ago—and we encountered only hostile actions in response. There is, therefore, no reason to believe at this time that Hanoi is interested in proposals for mutual de-escalation such as those put forward by Senator Kennedy," Rusk declared.

On the Senate floor, Senator Henry M. Jackson of Washington, a vigorous supporter of Administration policy, was ready with a letter from the President which he read in defense of the bombing.

All these speeches, statements, and letters were an impressive measure of Mr. Johnson's respect for Kennedy's political pulling power. Not since the days of the late John Foster Dulles had there been such a display of verbal instant massive retaliation. At least a dozen other Senators had made more or less the same suggestions as Kennedy; among the most ardent members of the peace movement, he was regarded as a laggard. But none of the other Senators is looked upon as a potential President. None has a name that captures the attention of the great mass of voters who do not follow foreign affairs closely and who are, according to the public opinion polls, predominantly in favor of bombing and military pressure to win the war.

As there had been a year earlier, an inconclusive flurry of statements, explanations, and clarifications followed Kennedy's speech. Thus, Kennedy had quoted British Prime Minister Wilson who had remarked the week before, "One single, simple act of trust could have achieved (peace)."

"We can—and should—perform that act," Kennedy said.

But columnist James Reston reported that British and American officials agreed that Wilson was referring not to a simple act of trust by the United States, but by North Vietnam. The simple act "was that Hanoi should agree to some military concession to match the U.S. offer to end the bombing, and this proposal—which was apparently supported by Premier Kosygin of the Soviet Union—was rejected by the Hanoi Government."[6]

Kennedy was on stronger ground in arguing that his proposal for a unilateral halt in bombing was exactly what the Administration had been offering Hanoi a year earlier in exchange for talks; now that Hanoi seemed willing to accept such a deal, the Administration had hardened the American terms and was insisting on some military *quid pro quo* such as a halt to infiltration in exchange for a halt in bombing. This was confirmed when North Vietnam released on March 21, 1967, an exchange of letters between

President Johnson and Ho Chi Minh. But if North Vietnam really wanted peace, the President's terms were not onerous. The Viet Cong guerrillas could live off the countryside, without supplies and reinforcement from the North, if there was to be a genuine lull in the fighting. President Johnson was impelled to add this requirement because American military successes encouraged him to believe that sooner or later, he would be able to get Ho Chi Minh to agree to it. Without a halt in infiltration from the North, President Johnson feared that the Viet Cong would steadily strengthen their grip over the South Vietnamese countryside and the United States would, in effect, lose the war while it sat at the peace table.

Kennedy's Vietnam speech had no immediate effect on the course of the war or the prospects for peace in Vietnam, but it had large domestic political implications. It further established Kennedy as the "shadow leader" of the Democratic Party, and an alternative to President Johnson if the party and the nation wanted an alternative. As part of the publicity buildup for his speech, Kennedy made a hurried tour of Western European capitals in late January and early February. In Paris, his interview with a French Foreign Ministry official was the basis of a three-day sensation. Etienne Manac'h, the director of the Far Eastern section of the Foreign Ministry, explained to Kennedy his own impressions, based on talks with North Vietnamese diplomats, of what might be done to get peace talks started. John Dean, a member of the American Embassy staff in Paris who accompanied Kennedy to the interview, cabled the State Department a summary of what Manac'h said. Some pro-Kennedy source in the State Department leaked to the press the report that Kennedy had received a "peace signal" from Hanoi via Paris.

Kennedy, of course, had heard nothing that the Department itself had not already heard since it is in regular contact with North Vietnamese diplomats in various capitals. But so enormous is his political reputation, wishful admirers leaped to the mistaken conclusion that Hanoi had selected him as the chosen instrument for transmitting its peace offer.

Upon his return, Kennedy visited President Johnson at the White House on February 6. It was a tense, angry forty-five minutes. Whether Kennedy called the President "you S.O.B.," as *Time* magazine asserted, will probably never be established definitively. But their exchange was bitter and acrimonious. President Johnson said that Kennedy's comments abroad about peace prospects had been damaging to the secret negotiations in progress with Hanoi. He berated him for stirring up the meaningless furor over the "peace signal." Kennedy countered that this misunderstanding had originated in the State Department, not with him. (Mr. Johnson in subsequent days came around to the belief that this was true.)

But then they moved to the more explosive subject of the domestic political meaning of their disagreement over the war. "We are going to win this war," the President said, "and in six months, all you doves will be politically dead."

The attacks of Kennedy and other critics emboldened North Vietnam to hold out in hopes that American policy would change, Mr. Johnson said, and if the critics persisted, "the blood of American boys will be on your hands." The President threatened to attack Kennedy publicly in those terms.

"If I do, you will be finished," the President declared.

"I don't have to sit here and listen to this kind of talk," Kennedy replied.

This disagreeable conversation, followed soon afterward by Kennedy's March 2 speech and the Administration's hostile response to it, deepened the schism between these two rivals. In effect, the two most powerful men in the Democratic Party have laid opposing bets on the political outcome of the war. Mr. Johnson believes that American military success in Vietnam will vindicate him with the voters. Even if success has not completely materialized by November 1968, he calculates that the electorate in time of war will sustain the commander-in-chief.

Kennedy estimates that a clear-cut military success is improbable in Vietnam. As the war persists, it will become less popular. If the draft is revised to reduce student deferments and take young men into the service by lottery, the human cost of the war will be brought home to many more middle and upper class families than in the past. Opposition to the war may then become more vocal and better organized. If casualties should mount to one thousand deaths a week, if American forces should lose a major engagement, an American Dienbienphu perhaps, then the peace sentiment that is in the minority in 1966 and early 1967 might rapidly become a politically potent majority. If those circumstances should develop, Kennedy would stand ready as the logical peace candidate. What Eisenhower did with regard to Korea in 1952, Kennedy could do with regard to Vietnam in 1968.

NOTES

1 *The New York Times*, February 21, 1966.
2 Theodore Sorensen, *Kennedy* (Harper and Row, New York, 1965), pp. 632–633.
3 *The New York Times*, February 11, 1962.
4 *Ibid.*, February 19, 1962.
5 Robert F. Kennedy, *The Pursuit of Justice*, Theodore J. Lowi, ed. (Harper and Row, New York, 1964), p. 132.
6 *The New York Times*, March 3, 1967.

CHAPTER SIX

The World Image

"The responsibility of our times is nothing less than a revolution. This revolution will be peaceful if we are wise enough; humane if we care enough; successful if we are fortunate enough. But a revolution will come whether we will it or not. We can affect its character; we cannot alter its inevitability."
—ROBERT KENNEDY *in Lima, Peru, November 13, 1965*

FOREIGN TRAVEL has become a familiar form of campaigning for the aspiring politician. Dwight Eisenhower said, "I shall go to Korea." Richard Nixon waggled his finger under Khrushchev's nose in a Moscow kitchen. George Romney tours the jungles of Vietnam. Robert Kennedy is part of this flourishing tradition, and he also transcends it. He arrives in strange countries already a famous figure. In squalid slums and dusty towns, the crowds turn out to see him, the bearer of a famous name and the brother of a slain hero. Whether he is touring Communist Poland or opening a rodeo in Calgary or inspecting a mine in Chile, he arouses fervent enthusiasm. He has a President-sized reputation before ever entering the White House.

Originally, this interest and sentiment belonged to his late brother. But as the years have passed, Robert Kennedy has himself come to embody the legend and to possess the aura. His tousled hair, his shy smile, his well-crafted speeches mingling dry wit, social idealism, and youthful passion make it easy for audiences to think of him not only as the heir and executor of his brother's political legacy but as the man inevitably destined to fulfill it. In many foreign countries, he is greeted as "the future President." In American politics, his world image has no historical precedent.

On November 10, 1965, Robert Kennedy began a three-week tour of five Latin American countries—Peru, Chile, Argentina, Brazil, and Venezuela. "I want to assure the people there that the Alliance for Progress is still as alive and important as it was under President Kennedy," Kennedy declared.

The Alliance for Progress ranks with the Nuclear Test Ban Treaty as one of John Kennedy's two most important initiatives in foreign affairs. The Alliance is crucial because it is this country's effort to lead the way toward a liberal solution for the problems of economically under-developed societies. These societies are not likely to have the time, even if they had the patience and the necessary ethic, to accumulate capital in the slow, scrimping manner of eighteenth and nineteenth century entrepreneurs in the United States and Western Europe. If some swifter yet essentially liberal line of development cannot be worked out for Latin America, there is always the grim totalitarian alternative posed by the Soviet Union and Communist China. The latter have demonstrated that backward societies can be modernized and industrialized if people are willing to accept an anthill existence. It was John Kennedy's immensely optimistic belief that Latin America could achieve both more bread *and* more liberty.

He defined the Alliance in 1961 as "a vast cooperative effort, unparalleled in magnitude and nobility of purpose, to satisfy the basic needs of the American people for homes, work and land, health and schools." He proposed that the Latin American nations work out a ten-year plan for political, economic, and social change that would transform the 1960s into "a historic decade for democratic progress."

The plan drawn up at Punta del Este in Uruguay in August 1961, set a target of at least 2.5 per cent per year growth in income *per person*. (Many countries grow faster than 2.5 per cent annually but their economic gains are eaten up by the even faster growth in population.) The plan also called for a more equitable distribution of national income in each country as between the few who are rich and the many who are poor; diversification to reduce reliance on a single cash crop such as coffee or bananas; rapid industrialization; comprehensive land reform; a sixth-grade education for all children and the elimination of illiteracy; new water supply and sewage systems to reduce endemic disease; and expanded housing and other social services.

This was a program for revolutionary change. In many Latin countries, the ruling oligarchies regard the illiterate peasants as mere beasts of burden. To redress the social balance in favor of those same peasants requires a major change in outlook by those in power. For the United States, change is also required if only in priorities and sense of urgency. In the fifteen years after World War II, the U.S. provided $30 billion in aid to Europe; $15 billion to Asia, and only $2.5 billion to Latin America. The prevailing tendency was to take this hemisphere for granted. Scholars and journalists wrote of the signs of incipient revolution, but the Truman and Eisenhower administrations took little notice of this ferment. It was not until 1958 that the U.S. finally agreed to the creation of the Inter-American Development Bank. Two years later, after Fidel Castro had taken power in Cuba and Vice-President Nixon had been stoned by a Communist mob in Venezuela, Congress authorized $500 million for a Social Progress Fund to be administered by the new bank.

The U.S. financial commitment to the Alliance for Progress has not been equal to its rhetoric. Although President Kennedy spoke of the Alliance as an effort "unparalleled in magnitude," the United States at Punta del Este pledged only $1 billion a year. By contrast, this country contributed over $14 billion in four years to Western Europe through the Marshall Plan. But if the performance of most Latin governments had approximated the bright hopes of 1961, the American commitment could have been increased.

Robert Kennedy began his fact-finding trip in Peru. It has reached the target economic growth rate of 2.5 per cent per person, but in no country is there a sharper cleavage between the Spanish ruling class and the exploited, impoverished mass of Indian peasants. Kennedy's first stop was Lima, where he met with President Fernando Belaúnde Terry and officials of his mildly reformist government. Then he flew to Cuzco, high in the Andes, once the capital of the Inca Empire but now a poor, provincial center. The Indians, normally apathetic because of undernourishment and the thinness of oxygen at high altitudes, turned out by the thousands to greet him and shout "Viva Kennedy!" So great was the crush that he was, at one point, inadvertently pushed against a barbed-wire fence, his pants torn and his face scratched. Kennedy visited Indian villages, schools, a slum neighborhood, and a model agricultural cooperative. Speaking at a boys' military academy, he gave the kind of advice he offers to boys in Harlem:

"Each one of you can make a difference, can make a contribution. Stay in school. Do not drop out. Go to the university. You can make a difference in your country and in Cuzco."[1]

In the most remote villages, he was asked if, or rather, when he would run for President. In one village, the mayor introduced him as President of the United States.

Returning to Lima, he toured the Pama de Comas, a huge slum sprawling across a hillside of red clay where more than one hundred thousand people live. A newspaper correspondent described the scene:

"The people are crowded into small brick shacks with wooden slat roofs. Some shacks have crudely painted hammer-and-sickle emblems on the doors or outside walls. There is no electric power in the *barriada* [the district] and water is trucked in several times a week and sold to residents."[2]

Yet for the Indians who crowd into this slum from their desolate mountain villages, the life and the opportunities of the city hold more promise than the backward rural existence from which they have fled. They had all heard the name "Kennedy," and they, too, gave him a warm greeting.

Kennedy spent most of a day visiting with them in their seemingly endless networks of shacks, reeking with strong odors and teeming with people. After his fourth stop, an indignant Peruvian official exclaimed, "Why does he want to see all this? I've lived here all my life and I've never been in one of these places."

Dan Cordtz, writing in *The Wall Street Journal,* reported that some of the radical, Yankee-baiting university students were equally embarrassed by Kennedy's interest in the worst problems of their countries and his focusing of attention on the arduous, unglamorous work of young Americans in the Peace Corps. He told a group of young Peruvians in Lima, "I've been visiting many of the young students from my country who are out working with the needy of your country. I'd like to have seen more of you out working with them."

"It was perhaps his least popular suggestion," Cordtz observed.[3]

Kennedy also told student audiences that "the responsibility of our times is nothing less than a revolution."

This revolution, he continued, "will be peaceful if we are wise enough; humane if we care enough; successful if we are fortunate enough. But a revolution will come whether we will it or not. We can affect its character; we cannot alter its inevitability."

In these words, he defined the choice for Latin America as either a bloodless, humane, essentially liberal revolution underwritten by the money of the Alliance for Progress or a violent, inhumane, totalitarian revolution along Castroite-Communist lines. If the ruling elites in most Latin countries do not see the future in those terms, neither are many of the officials of the State Department and the AID program administering the Alliance for Progress within that political context. Kennedy's remarks in Peru and elsewhere in his South American tour were unpopular with both sets of listeners.

Chile, his next stop, was an exception. There the Christian Democratic government of President Eduardo Frei Montalva is keenly aware that it represents a non-violent middle course between the reactionaries and the Communists. Kennedy endorsed Frei's social reforms.

"Of all the heads of government I've met around the world and all their administrations," he declared after a two-hour conference with President Frei, "I am as much impressed with this group here as any I've seen. . . .

"If this administration does not succeed," he added, "there is a good chance the country will go Communist, because the people will have lost faith in a democratic government."[4]

In Chile, he encountered the only hostile demonstration of his tour. When he attempted to speak at Concepción University, left-wing students spat on him and threw eggs, rocks, and coins. The eggs and stones missed, but the spittle dribbled on his forehead and clothes. He had been warned by student leaders not to visit the university, but he pressed for an invitation and was finally permitted to risk it. Hundreds of students jammed the university gymnasium, most of them eager to hear him speak, but he could not make himself heard as the Communist students screamed, "Assassin!" and "Yankee go home!" and sang the national anthems of Cuba and Chile.

"I challenge you to a fresh exchange of ideas," Kennedy shouted. "I challenge you to let the rest of the students decide who is right. I challenge you to let me speak."

But after twenty minutes of bedlam, he gave up and withdrew.

The street crowds in Concepción, however, were wildly enthusiastic; an editorial in the next morning's newspaper referred to him as "the future President." In Lota, where he visited miners in an undersea coal mine, and in Linares, a farm town, he was acclaimed. "Practically all the 8,000 people of Linares turned out to see him, and children ran alongside the open car trying to grasp Mr. Kennedy's hands," one correspondent reported. "Women tossed flowers at the Senator and Mrs. Kennedy until the seats and fenders of their car were covered. . . . Crowds have been large, despite very little advance publicity, and their enthusiasm has been astonishing."[5]

The crowds and the enthusiasm persisted throughout the rest of the trip and it did not matter much whether he was in cosmopolitan Buenos Aires or the hungry, poverty-stricken villages of northeast Brazil. In each country, he was interested in seeing the problems rather than the successes, and his favorite platforms were in the universities. "The students usually ask the best questions, and when there's opposition in the audience, it's basically more stimulating," Kennedy once explained.[6] He never hesitated to challenge the prejudices, convictions, or unexamined assumptions of his listeners. He told the four thousand students at the Catholic University in Rio de Janeiro that they would do better to complain less about political abstractions and worry more about their needy fellow countrymen.

"How many of you have ever been in a *favela* [slum]?" he asked. A sprinkling of hands went up.

"How many of you have ever worked in a *favela?*" Even fewer raised their hands.

"If all we do is complain about the universities, criticize the government, carry signs, make speeches to one another, and then leave to take a job with United Fruit or a Brazilian company and then not pay any attention to those who need our help," he declared, "then we have not met our responsibility."[7]

The three-week journey was a personal triumph for Kennedy. Analyzing "the great demonstrations of Mr. Kennedy's popularity," *The New York Times* correspondent wrote:

"There is a reverence in South America for the memory of President Kennedy. It is reflected in the large crowds that greet the Senator. In a sophisticated city like Buenos Aires, the chanting of 'Kennedy!' in the streets was so frenzied that one member of the Senator's party said: 'They don't want him for President. They want him for dictator.' "[8]

Kennedy ended his trip in Caracas, Venezuela, on November 30, where he made his only major policy speech. He told an audience of several hundred members of a national labor federation that Latin American countries should concert their strength by creating additional hemispheric institutions such as a parliamentary assembly, an Inter-American university, a nuclear-free zone, and an institute for conducting joint projects in tropical agriculture. He also urged them to take a more active role in helping the underdeveloped nations of Africa and Asia.

"Latin America can speak to the nations of Asia and Africa from the platform of common problems and understanding which we in the United States do not completely share," he said.[9] (Latin America is, in some respects, only a geographical expression. The author once heard the chancellor of a Mexican university observe that he never met his counterparts from other Latin countries except when they all attended a conference in the United States organized by Americans.)

It was nearly six months later before Kennedy reported to the American people on his Latin American trip. His staff did extensive research on the Alliance for Progress before Kennedy set forth his views. When he rose to address the Senate on May 9, 1966, Kennedy presented an essentially adverse, though not pessimistic, judgement on the record of the Alliance in its first five years.[10] He was encouraged because positive changes were underway but the challenge laid down to the hemisphere by his brother had not been met.

"Economically, the Alliance is moving—" Kennedy said, "but it is not moving fast enough. Governments are working—but they are not working hard enough. The United States is making a contribution—but in many ways, not enough. . . . The ideals of the Alliance stirred men's hearts and minds throughout the continent; now, five years after it began, not enough has been done to fulfill these hopes and keep the passion, imagination, and commitment alive and growing."

He sadly observed, in the words of Francis Bacon: "Hope is a good breakfast but a lean supper."

Even the wealthier countries remain critically dependent upon a single crop or product: Brazil on coffee, Ecuador on bananas, Venezuela on oil.

Kennedy could still recite the same appalling statistics —"which have become almost a litany"—of poverty and degradation and want:

"Income per person is often less than $100 yearly. . . .

"Fifty percent of all Latin Americans are illiterate . . .

"Half of all the people buried in Latin America never reached their fourth year."

Kennedy began his review by sketching in the background that makes change imperative. He described the still unconquered geographic obstacles such as the unexplored jungle of the Amazon, the dividing line of the Andes, and the huge deserts. He recalled the legacy of the past and the tradition of feudal exploitation, and then depicted the poverty he had witnessed.

"To travel in Latin America, to see the terrible reality of human misery, is to feel these statistics with stunning force. In Recife [Brazil], there are people who live in shacks by the water in which they dump their refuse and garbage; the crabs which feed on that garbage are the staple of their diet."

Kennedy developed as his four major themes the importance of land reform, education, economic development, and population control, and he concluded with a discussion of the problems of political leadership.

On each of these themes, he had much to say that was pertinent, liberal, and sensible. Observing that at current growth rates, Latin America's population in just fifteen years will shoot up from 230 million in 1965 to 363 million by 1980, Kennedy had the courage to recommend population control.

"I believe that we should provide assistance to any nation which decides that family planning and population control are in its national interest. To make such assistance more helpful, we should now accelerate our own research into population control devices and techniques.

"We cannot attempt to compel Latin Americans to practice birth control," he added, "but we should stand ready to help."

He also urged a major increase in the foreign aid program to finance faster economic development.

Like most legislators making a major speech, Kennedy

took tacit advantage of the fact that he has no operating responsibility to transform wishes, hopes, and speculations into specific policies and decisions. He made many worthwhile comments about capturing the sympathetic attention of Latin American students, inculcating the ideals of civilian control in Latin American military officers receiving training in this country, and dealing discreetly with military dictatorships. In practice, however, there is often not much that any American official can do. Discussing the Army regime in Brazil, Kennedy observed that "we should confine our identification to those acts of the Government which are in accord with the ideals of the Alliance—projects of social reform in the impoverished northeast, improved education, land and tax reform . . . but we should make clear that we do not wish to be associated with acts of political dictatorship, and not identify ourselves with a government which engages in such acts."

When the United States is cooperating in various economic development projects with the Brazilian government—the same government that censors the newspapers and persecutes student leaders—is it possible for the U.S. to make clear to the ordinary Brazilian that it is for some of the Brazilian government's policies and against others? In the real world, this neat compartmentalization is not always possible.

Speaking broadly about the Alliance for Progress, Kennedy said: "The Alliance is their revolution. . . . If they [the Latin Americans] are willing to work and sacrifice to yield up old privileges and shape new institutions, our help can be of decisive importance. If they are not willing to do these things, then all our effort and money will be as sand cast into the sea."

This is not entirely true. The Alliance was an invention of John F. Kennedy and although it was a response to the pleas of the more enlightened Latin American leaders, its leadership and resources have been American. Only in a partial sense, therefore, is it "their revolution." Moreover, many Latin Americans who are willing to work and sacrifice and shape new institutions are not the same people who enjoy the privileges and control the existing institutions. How much pressure does the U.S. apply to force the pace of change? And at what pressure points? These are the kinds of hard questions that the managers of any policy have to answer from day to day and on which Kennedy was silent.

Nevertheless, for a man prone to think only in facts rather than concepts, this was a wide-ranging and incisive speech. He grappled with most of the right problems even if he did not wrest an intellectual victory in each contest.

The Republic of South Africa is one of the extraordinary political anachronisms of the contemporary world. Although racist customs and attitudes are a familiar, if hideous, feature of many societies, only in South Africa is the doctrine of racial supremacy embedded in the laws of the nation and enforced by the full authority of the government. The system of *apartheid*—compulsory segregation by race—has historical parallels in the Southern United States, in the caste system of India, and in Nazi Germany, but in the present decade South Africa is the outstanding example of a society marching steadfastly away from the liberal ideal of racial equality.

The outside world has registered repeated moral protests against South Africa's racial system. In 1960, Harold Macmillan, the British Prime Minister, frankly told the South African parliament that most Britons disagreed with *apartheid*. He warned that it would eventually have to recognize that "winds of change" are blowing on the African continent. That same year, the Nobel peace prize was conferred on Chief Albert Luthuli, the former head of the outlawed African National Congress and a symbol of native resistance. The newly independent African countries have frequently arraigned South Africa in the United Nations. Robert Kennedy's whirlwind tour of South Africa from June 4 to June 9, 1966, was in this tradition of moral protest.

When it was announced on October 23, 1965, that Kennedy had accepted the invitation of the National Union of South African Students to address their annual "Day of Affirmation" meeting, there was immediate and intense speculation as to whether he would be granted a visa. After some delay, the Johannesburg government decided to admit him but otherwise, like the Communist government of Poland, it hoped to ignore his visit. Visas were refused for forty American newsmen who wanted to accompany him, and a government spokesman huffily observed that the whole trip was probably "a publicity stunt . . . a buildup for a future presidential election."[11] Kennedy's subsequent overtures for meetings with South African government officials were rejected. Throughout his visit, the official South African Broadcasting Corporation reported few of his remarks.

No amount of government discouragement could prevent the journey from becoming an underground sensation and a liberating experience in the closed, repressed life of South Africa. The government had apparently expected that a handful of English-speaking students would welcome Kennedy and that if the press and radio ignored him, the affair would pass off almost unnoticed. The size and intensity of Kennedy's reception was a jolting surprise. The moment his plane set down at Jan Smuts Airport in Johannesburg, more than four thousand students, who had waited several hours, surged toward him, swept him on to their shoulders, and marched triumphantly into the airport terminal. Similar displays of enthusiasm greeted him wherever he went. Whites as well as blacks, Afrikaans as well as English, strove to see him, to touch him, to shake his hand. When he arrived in Durban, a crowd of fifteen hundred students greeted him with cheers, singing in unison, "We love you, Bobby." Peter Mansfield, the acting president of the student union, had explained (when the invitation first became known) that Kennedy was asked because of "his work for human freedom, especially during the time he served as Attorney General," and because "we thought he represented the younger generation of political leaders and the new ideas of youth."

The student union, with 19,500 members, is the largest multiracial organization in South Africa except for the churches. Balthazar J. Vorster, then the Minister of Justice and now Prime Minister, has characterized it as "a damnable and detestable organization," whose leaders are "the offspring of snakes." Although the government has accused some of its members of instigating acts of sabotage, the union has managed to stay within the bounds of legality. The union acts mostly to promote literacy among black Africans and to do welfare work, but more important than its actual accomplishments is the mere fact that it continues to exist in the increasingly totalitarian society around it.*

Three weeks before Kennedy arrived, the government barred Ian Robertson, the twenty-one-year-old president of the student union, from attending any "meeting," defined as three or more persons including himself. Under the

---

* On the annual Day of Affirmation, the students pledge: "We believe that it is the responsibility of a university to insure that no unjust discrimination is practiced in academic life on grounds of race, religion or politics. We pledge ourselves to work for the attainment of this ideal within the realms of all freedoms—of association, of speech, and of movement—for we realize that true academic freedom can exist only in a democratic South Africa whose society is based on the Universal Declaration of Human Rights, and on the highest regard for the integrity of educational and human freedom."

Suppression of Communism Act, Robertson was restricted to the Cape Town vicinity, forbidden to participate in student union activities, and barred from the university except to attend lectures for his law degree. On his arrival in Cape Town, Kennedy visited him in his tiny room and talked with him for twenty minutes. He presented Robertson with a copy of President Kennedy's book *Profiles in Courage* inscribed "With admiration" by Jacqueline Kennedy.

Before entering Robertson's apartment, Kennedy looked around the room and asked, "Is this place bugged?"

"Yes, I think so," Robertson replied.

Kennedy then jumped into the air and landed heavily on the floorboards. When Robertson asked him to explain, Kennedy told him that the vibration would disturb the bugging mechanism for fifteen minutes.

"How do you know that?" he was asked.

Kennedy paused for a moment. "I used to be Attorney General," he replied quietly.[12]

As he left the apartment, students were taking turns thumping a heavy glue pot on the bare boards at fifteen-minute intervals.

When Kennedy spoke that night at the Day of Affirmation ceremony at Cape Town University, an empty chair was placed next to his to symbolize Robertson's absence. The speech was the high point of his trip. More than fifteen thousand persons, about half of them students, crowded the huge hall. Kennedy stated his theme early: "The enlargement of liberty for individual human beings must be the supreme goal and the abiding practice of any Western society."

He outlined the basic elements of individual liberty and as he did so, he obliquely, gently but unmistakably criticized the government of South Africa. "Government must answer—not just to those of a particular religion, or a particular race; but to all its people."

The speech skillfully placed the struggle for freedom in South Africa in the context of the worldwide effort for two centuries to break down barriers based on nationality, social class, or race. Kennedy recalled that his own father had grown up in Boston when signs still said, "No Irish need apply," but his brother became the first Catholic President of the United States. In recent years, the effort at Negro equality had been renewed in his own country but not without bitter conflict—"the violence of the disinherited, the insulted and injured, looms over the streets of Harlem and Watts and Southside Chicago."

Having called attention to the problems and the setbacks in the United States, he then noted the proofs of progress: the young Negro officer training to be an astronaut, the Negro (Thurgood Marshall) who is Solicitor General, and Dr. Martin Luther King—"the second man of African descent to win the Nobel Peace Prize"*—thus linking him to Chief Luthuli.

"Each nation has different obstacles and different goals, shaped by the vagaries of history and experience," Kennedy declared. "Yet as I talk to young people around the world I am impressed not by diversity but by the closeness of their goals, their desires and concerns and hope for the future.

"There is discrimination in New York, *apartheid* in South Africa and serfdom in the mountains of Peru. People starve in the streets in India; intellectuals go to jail in Russia; thousands are slaughtered in Indonesia; wealth is lavished on armaments everywhere. These are differing evils. But they are the common works of man.

"And therefore they call upon common qualities of conscience and of indignation, a shared determination to wipe away the unnecessary sufferings of our fellow human beings at home and particularly around the world."[13]

* Actually, the third. Kennedy forgot Ralph Bunche, who received it in 1950.

The audience stood and gave Kennedy a thunderous five-minute ovation.

John Daniel, the student who was presiding, said, "You have given us a hope for the future. You have renewed our determination not to relax until liberty is restored, not only to our universities but to our land."

The correspondent for the London *Daily Telegraph* later wrote that many people regarded Kennedy's speech as "the most stirring and memorable address ever to come from a foreigner in South Africa."[14]

Kennedy also spoke at the University of Stellenbosch, which has produced all but one of South Africa's prime ministers and is the intellectual center for the *apartheid* movement; at Natal University in Durban, and at Witwatersrand University. He exchanged quips and answered questions, some of them openly hostile, at each meeting. Despite provocation, he was careful never to condemn South Africa as if it existed in a vacuum; he always linked its difficult problems to those in the United States and elsewhere. At Durban, a white man boomed from the gallery, "Can you tell me what President of the United States said in 1885, 'There is an undeniable difference between the white man and the black man'?"

Kennedy shot back, "The one who was beaten in 1888."

The audience roared with applause.

A crowd of two thousand jammed the hall at Natal University and another eighteen thousand listened over a public address system. After the meeting, Kennedy, standing on top of an automobile, joined the crowd outside the hall in singing the hymn of the civil rights movement, "We Shall Overcome." As usual, Kennedy's monotone was dreadful but the effect was electrifying.

He was subsequently host at a dinner in his hotel to a multiracial group of dissenters. Among the guests were Alan Paton, author of *Cry, the Beloved Country*; Archbishop Dennis Hurley, a Roman Catholic prelate who is a frequent critic of *apartheid* policies; Dr. Arthur Lazarus, a spokesman for Natal's large Indian community; Knowledged Guzana, the leader of the anti-government party, the Opposition Democrats, which represents the black Africans; and also two Zulu chiefs.

"I haven't met with so many people in trouble since I was Attorney General," Kennedy said, jokingly.

These South African liberals did not share the reaction sometimes expressed in the United States that his visit was a bit of political grandstanding that would do no practical good. Mrs. Helen Suzman, a white woman who is the only Progressive Party member of parliament, said, "His visit is like a breath of fresh air. He is so willing to learn. He has done his homework on South Africa, too."

His closest approach to the government was a private meeting with the editors of the country's pro-government Afrikaans-language newspapers. One of the editors presented him with a copy of a new book, *The Principles of Apartheid*. Kennedy, with a smile, countered by giving him a copy of *The American Negro Reference Book*. After this exchange of barbed civilities, Kennedy and the editors settled down for more than two hours of candid discussion. He made no converts, and some participants left the meeting more hostile than ever ("He is quite skillful at putting people on the defensive," one remarked). But other editors were favorably impressed by his ready acknowledgment that he had no pat answers to their nation's race problem.

Kennedy obtained government permission to visit Chief Luthuli on the small, remote farm where he lives under house arrest. The Kennedys helicoptered down the Valley of a Thousand Hills at dawn for the interview. They found the chief "a most impressive man, with a marvelously lined face, strong yet kind. [One's] eyes first went to the white goatee, so familiar in his pictures, but then, quickly, the smile took over, illuminating his whole presence, eyes dancing and sparkling. At mention of *apartheid*, however, his eyes went hurt and hard."

To avoid being overheard, the two men walked together under the trees and through the fields.

"What are they doing to my country, to my countrymen," the chief said sadly. "Can't they see that men of all races can work together—and that the alternative is a terrible disaster for us all?"

Kennedy presented him with a transistor record player, two records, and two books dealing with the life of President Kennedy. Chief Luthuli played President Kennedy's civil rights speech of June 11, 1963, in which for the first time, an American President described the relationship of the two races as a "moral issue." The chief, his daughter, two government agents accompanying the Kennedys, and Bobby and Ethel listened to the recording in silence.

"The government men stared fixedly at the floor."[15]

Kennedy later described Chief Luthuli as one of the most impressive men he had ever met. "He has compassion and tolerance and harbors no bitterness against the whites," he remarked.

Outside Johannesburg, Kennedy visited Soweto, a complex of townships where seven hundred thousand Africans live under tightly controlled conditions. Many of the houses there struck Kennedy as more attractive than those in Negro slums in the United States, but the atmosphere is much worse. These are people who cannot leave and who have to obey a curfew and other strict regulations, if they are not to be deported by the police to some distant village in the bush country. The Africans in Soweto, although many of them are illiterate, knew who Kennedy was, and throngs greeted him everywhere. He made several impromptu speeches from the hood of his automobile and from improvised platforms. What to say to people who are trapped in such circumstances? Kennedy told them that people around the world were aware of their situation and that change was bound to come. So as not to incite useless violence or arouse false hopes, he stressed that the best way to get rid of hatred and bigotry is through peaceful methods.

"Master! Master!" the Negroes shouted surging toward him.

"Please don't use that word," Kennedy said, taken aback. But the Bantu know no other English word to describe a powerful white man and their shouting continued until Kennedy's car disappeared into the distance.

Once Kennedy left the country, the South African press began assessing the effect of his visit. Most newspapers echoed the line of *Die Transvaler,* which often expresses government thinking. *Die Transvaler* hinted that he would not be admitted to the country a second time. "A single American circus display on South African soil was more than enough. We definitely don't want a second. . . . Let us say frankly that one can only have the deepest sympathy for the American people if Senator Kennedy becomes their future President."

But the Rand *Daily Mail,* South African's only liberal anti-government paper, wrote that Kennedy's "confident, unabashed idealism" was just what the youth of the country had been yearning to hear. He had enabled them to feel that they are "part and parcel of the continuing tradition of the Western world and not, as they are so often told, something alien, unwholesome, or worse.

"The effects of Senator Kennedy's visit will be felt for a long time to come," the *Daily Mail* concluded. "He has stirred up ideas long in disuse. He has started new controversies among us and about us."

Asked his own reaction to his four days in South Africa, Kennedy at a news conference summed it up in a word, "Unhappy."

Does South Africa constitute a "threat to world peace"

as the nations of black Africa often assert? Kennedy prudently backed away. "I wouldn't use that expression to describe South Africa now. But unless there are changes—if the situation is allowed to continue—it could certainly be explosive."[16]

The rest of his African journey was an anti-climax. He spent a week visiting Tanzania, Kenya, and Ethiopia. In Tanzania, he renewed his acquaintance with President Julius K. Nyerere, who had developed a friendship with President Kennedy. In Addis Ababa, speaking to an audience of African diplomats and members of the Organization of African Unity, he delicately flattered his listeners by suggesting that they could break the deadlock between the great powers over nuclear disarmament. The great powers, including the United States, he said, "are simply not doing enough; not trying hard enough; not sacrificing enough to arrive at an agreement. You must therefore assume a responsibility that others have been unable to fulfill. You must now take the lead and restore the flagging energies of governments and their negotiators.

"In every world capital . . . you must make it clear that you regard as true world leaders only those nations which are willing to walk the last mile, take the last step, in the search for the control of the atom."[17]

The three days that Kennedy spent in the game parks of Tanzania and Kenya bored him. His receptions from the people in these independent African countries were less intense than in South Africa, but here, too, the Kennedy legend has power. A correspondent for *The National Observer* wrote from Addis Ababa:

"The name Kennedy means something here in East Africa, much more so than any of us in the press corps had imagined. It's a name that seems to have penetrated the farthest reaches of illiteracy—in the country, villages, and bush as well as in the cities.

"Outside Mbeya, a Tanzanian village of 12,000 some

550 miles from Dar es Salaam, Peace Corpsmen report that Africans generally hold President Lyndon B. Johnson in low esteem because, they believe, and can't be convinced otherwise, that the President was somehow responsible for John Kennedy's assassination in an African-style military coup.

"One of the 500 Peace Corps volunteers in Ethiopia, a tall, yellow-haired Syracuse, N. Y., lad, Charles Kerr, explains the magic of the Kennedy name in the village where he teaches, eighty miles from Addis Ababa:

" 'The kids call *ME* John Kennedy. The further you get away from the cities, the more you hear the name when a youngster sees a Peace Corps member. When I told my class I was going into the city to see Robert Kennedy their eyes opened wide, they got all excited, and four or five immediately said, 'the brother of John Kennedy?' And little kids who can't speak a word of English come up to me on the street, stick out their hands for a shake, and say 'John Kennedy?'

"This was the reservoir of good will that Robert Kennedy drew upon last week, and by any consensus it appears he did leave that reservoir richer than he found it."[18]

These journeys to Latin America and to Africa were successful because Kennedy showed forth his best qualities, which happen also to be among America's best national characteristics: energy, curiosity, idealism, a willingness to learn and change, and an intelligent, sympathetic concern for people worse off than oneself.

After he had been back in the United States several months, Kennedy quietly launched a follow-up drive to help the black majority in South Africa. In letters to thirty American business leaders having interests in South Africa, Kennedy invited each of them to confer with him about what business could do to ease the burden of *apartheid* on the native population.[19] Among those receiving the letters were Charles Engelhard of New Jersey, who has large gold mining interests, and the heads of General Motors, Ford, the Chase Manhattan Bank, and the First National City Bank. Kennedy emphasized that he did not take the extreme position that the United States should ban further private American investment in South Africa. In his judgment, that would work the greatest hardship on the black population. But, he suggested, private firms would not be breaking the *apartheid* laws if they recognized labor unions formed by blacks; paid at least a minimum subsistence wage to all workers, regardless of color; promoted Africans to responsible positions, and told the South African government, politely but firmly, that *apartheid* is wasteful and bad for business. As might be expected, the reaction of the business community to his intervention ranged from unenthusiastic to downright hostile.

NOTES

[1] *The New York Times*, November 14, 1965.
[2] *Ibid.*
[3] *The Wall Street Journal*, November 18, 1964.
[4] *The New York Times*, November 15, 1965.
[5] *The Wall Street Journal*, November 18, 1965.
[6] *The New Yorker*, October 24, 1964, p. 50.
[7] *The New York Times*, November 26, 1965.
[8] *Ibid.*, November 22, 1965.
[9] *Ibid.*, December 1, 1965.
[10] Kennedy delivered the speech in two sections on successive days, May 9 and 10. Reprinted under the title "The Alliance for Progress: Symbol and Substance" it runs twenty thousand words.

[11] *The New York Times*, October 24, 1965.

[12] New York *Daily News*, June 18, 1966.

[13] *The New York Times*, June 7, 1966.

[14] *The National Observer*, June 13, 1966.

[15] Robert F. Kennedy, "Suppose God Is Black," *Look*, August 23, 1966, p. 45.

[16] *The New York Times*, June 10, 1966.

[17] *Ibid.*, June 16, 1966.

[18] *The National Observer*, June 20, 1966.

[19] Kennedy tried to keep these letters confidential but one came into the hands of a British newspaperman. See London *Observer*, January 1, 1967.

CHAPTER SEVEN

The Absentee Prince

"Abroad and at home I reign only through the fear I inspire."
—NAPOLEON BONAPARTE, *quoted in Felix Markham, Napoleon (Mentor edition, New York, 1966), p. 137.*

ROBERT KENNEDY'S career as leader of the New York Democrats suggests that fear alone is not enough. Kennedy is the most feared man in New York public life. Not since New York Republicans began a dozen years ago to wipe Thomas E. Dewey's shoe polish from their faces has any political figure in the state inspired such uneasiness among politicians of high and middling rank. And where Dewey merely had skill in organization, iron determination, access to money, and an instinct for power, in short, the gifts of the superb technician, Kennedy has all these and the charisma of a prince. No adolescent girls leaped in the streets for Dewey and no middle-aged matrons screamed as he rode by in the night. The Democratic Party county leaders and other regulars fear Kennedy because he can appeal over their heads to the voters with devastating effect. Although he is a thorough realist about political means, they cannot rely upon him always to make the deals and accommodations that are their way of life. He is the great imponderable in their affairs.

Yet New York politics have proved persistently troublesome and intractable for Kennedy. In three years, he has

achieved potential mastery over his party. But personal
dominance has not been translated into effective control.
He overshadows lesser men but he does not lead them; he
is the great reformer who does not reform; his mastery
remains largely potential. In terms of the party's welfare,
though not of his own, he has to be reckoned a failure.
In part, he has failed because he has not made up his
mind where he wishes to lead the party; in part, because
he is afraid to lead it, and most of all because he has
attempted to govern its affairs in a hurried, inconsequent
manner. He is often physically present in New York but
he is only fitfully concerned with its politics. To his
party, he has been an absentee prince.

On the morrow of his victory for the Senate in 1964,
Kennedy moved promptly but discreetly to exploit his new
opportunities. The voters had not only swept him into
office but had also placed the Democrats in control of
the State Senate for the first time since 1938 and of the
Assembly for the first time since 1935. This feat had
been accomplished despite the long-existing Republican
gerrymander of the state's legislative districts. Since the
state was under federal court order to reapportion those
districts, the Democrats in the new legislature had a rare
opportunity to redraw them to conform with the court's
criteria but also with their own political interests. Should
the legislature, meanwhile, have a productive and well-
publicized session in 1965, it would heighten the party's
prestige and extend its growing influence upstate.

If custom were followed, the two Minority Leaders in
the old legislature would automatically be promoted to
Majority Leader of the Senate and Speaker of the Assembly
respectively. Those incumbents were Senator Joseph
Zaretzki of Manhattan and Assemblyman Anthony Travia
of Brooklyn. To call Zaretzki a hack would be undue
praise; Travia was barely adequate.

Kennedy and brother-in-law Steve Smith intervened to arrange for new candidates. They insisted that they were taking no part in these matters. While on an upstate tour, Kennedy said at Jamestown on December 7 that he would remain neutral. The next day in response to questions asked him by reporters in Utica, he blandly asserted, "It isn't important who the leaders are in the State Senate and Assembly." Notwithstanding these protestations, only Kennedy could have put together the subsequent coalition of old-time party bosses and young reformers. No one else so familiar with the bleak realism of the former could fire up the idealism of the latter. At first, it seemed a brilliant coup. In the Senate, the coalition united behind Jack E. Bronston, a graduate of Harvard College, *magna cum laude*, and Harvard Law School, who during six years representing a middle-class constituency in Queens had been a leader on education problems and well above the ordinary member in alertness and initiative. Charles Buckley, the aged, crusty boss of the Bronx Democrats, refused at first to support Bronston as too liberal and independent, but Kennedy brought him into line. For Speaker of the Assembly, Kennedy backed Stanley Steingut, the son of the last Democratic Speaker who had served in 1935. Steingut, in addition to long service in the Assembly, was the leader of the dominant faction of Brooklyn Democrats.

The choice of Bronston and Steingut represented a major challenge to the power of Mayor Wagner, but Kennedy seems not to have thought through the implications of this challenge or anticipated the possible contingencies. The Democrats in the legislature have no binding tradition of deciding internal quarrels in a party caucus. A minority that fears it will be outvoted can merely refrain from attending the caucus and nominate its own candidates directly in the two legislative chambers. This was the course that the Zaretzki and Travia supporters followed when Mayor Wagner decided to make a concerted fight in their behalf. The balloting for Majority Leader and Speaker became a three-cornered contest with two Democrats vying with a Republican, and none commanding a majority. The Democrats had a majority of 33 to 25 in the Senate. Bronston at times polled as many as 21 votes but against the unbreakable opposition of the Republicans and the Wagner Democrats, he never came any closer to the clear majority of 30 that he needed. Similarly, Steingut in the Assembly needed 76 votes (a majority of the 150 members) but could get no more than 52 to Travia's 35. The stalemate that began in early January dragged on for five weeks without a decision.

The chief victim was the Democratic Party itself, and particularly its newly elected Assemblymen and Senators from the suburbs and upstate. The Democrats had the once-in-a-generation opportunity to demonstrate to the public what they could do. But instead of putting on a sparkling display of procedural reforms, progressive legislation, and modern-minded competence, the Democrats became the objects of editorial criticism and general ridicule by their inability even to choose their own leaders and get the legislature started. The newcomers were on Kennedy's side in supporting a change of leadership. Of the ten new Democratic Senators, a majority voted for Bronston and twenty-one of the twenty-two freshmen Assemblymen supported Steingut. Powerless to determine the outcome, they were reduced to repeating pale witticisms. ("We Democrats would rather fight than switch.")

The power struggle in New York City which long antedated Kennedy's arrival in the state made an easy, amicable resolution of the leadership contest impossible. Wagner, who governed the city during his first two terms with the backing of the Democratic Party organizations, broke with them in 1961 and achieved a third term. In the process, he helped to drive Carmine DeSapio out of office as leader of the Manhattan Democrats, but he was unable to dislodge Buckley in the Bronx and Steingut in Brooklyn. With Buckley, he maintained a frayed but durable personal friendship, but he and Steingut became implacable personal enemies as well as political adversaries. Wagner's animosity has contributed to Steingut's ambiguous reputation. In Albany, he is well regarded as an intelligent, industrious, and thoroughly competent Assemblyman and regularly collects the endorsements of the Citizens Union and other disinterested organizations. But in Brooklyn, where he presides as the hard-shelled boss of the party machine, he is under recurrent attack from reformers.

Wagner could have accepted Bronston as Senate leader, although the latter had attacked him in a letter to *The Times* during the 1961 primary as a "weak and inattentive mayor."[1] But the strong man of the new coalition was Steingut, and for the mayor to accept his election would mean not only a temporary blow to his prestige but also the entrenchment of his most powerful opponent in the pivotal office of Speaker. Since New York City's tax and legislative requests have to gain Assembly approval, a Speaker on bad terms with a mayor can block the city's programs or exact a political price for letting them pass. Every compromise proposed during the leadership impasse foundered on Steingut's resolute ambition to be Speaker and Wagner's equally resolute determination not to let him gain control of the Albany toll gates.

Halfway through the leadership conflict, Kennedy intervened publicly. He lined up several party notables who joined him in proposing that the contests be decided by a secret ballot in a closed caucus. Under such a procedure, Wagner's candidates would almost certainly have been defeated. On Friday evening, January 15, Kennedy telephoned Wagner, told him the statement was about to be released, and urged him to go along. This put Wagner in a tight corner. Since the statement of Kennedy and the other party leaders was going to be released whether he agreed or not, he would appear to the public—if he refused—as an obstructionist holdout who was afraid to take his chances on a democratic secret ballot. Wagner yielded. But he left himself an escape route. The proposal would be void unless the county leaders released the legislators to vote freely—"really freely," a Wagner man said later, "not with a wink and a pat on the back."[2]

When the statement was issued, some hopeful language along these lines had been added but in much vaguer terms than Wagner had requested. How much credence Wagner, as an old political realist, placed on the presence or absence of this language is doubtful, but he seized upon its virtual absence as a pretext. At a press conference on Sunday, January 17, he denounced his opponents in harsh terms. According to the mayor, a group of county leaders and influential legislators had gathered with State Chairman William McKeon in an Albany hotel room to strike a bargain. They had attempted to parcel out committee chairmanships bearing "lulus" and "double lulus." (A "lulu" is the phrase invented by Alfred E. Smith when he was in the legislature fifty years earlier; it stands for "in lieu of expenses." Sums of $5000 and $10,000 were involved.) Wagner's denunciation of this "corrupt" dealing destroyed any prospect of a party caucus and led to inconclusive public hearings by the State Investigation Commission which further embarrassed the Democrats.

On February 3, the long dispute suddenly ended. Wagner had reached an understanding with Governor Nelson Rockefeller. In exchange for Republican votes for Zaretzki and Travia, the Wagner Democrats would put through Rockefeller's unpopular request for a 2 per cent sales tax. On that evening, the twenty-five Senate Republicans joined with fifteen Democrats to elect Zaretzki while eighteen Democrats voted for Bronston to the end. The next day, a similar bipartisan coalition elected Travia in the Assembly. The sales tax followed soon afterward.

Wagner suffered severe political damage in forestalling his enemies. For the first time, he took on some of the bad reputation of his enemies, the party bosses, as he traded charges of corruption and back-room deals. Previously, he had stayed aloof from this kind of squabbling. His future hopes for statewide office were also impaired because his expedient alliance with Rockefeller affronted upstate Democrats.

Although Kennedy's forces had been routed, he was spared the opprobrium of defeat. He had skillfully kept himself out of public view throughout the battle. The newspaper stories told of "pro-Wagner Democrats" and "anti-Wagner Democrats." They did not refer to "pro-Kennedy" or "anti-Kennedy" forces. At this precise moment, when an older, cannier politician might congratulate himself for escaping unharmed from a difficult, unsuccessful operation, Kennedy suddenly drew aside the curtains of secrecy and attacked the victors. In a cold, contemptuous letter to Zaretzki and Travia, he warned them that he wanted the legislative staff appointments—worth $4 million in annual salaries—filled on "the basis of merit."

"It has come to my attention," he wrote, "that telephone calls have been made to various political leaders around the state asking them to fill positions on the basis of patronage. Especially in light of the injury which we must agree has recently been sustained by the Democratic Party as a result of the long leadership impasse, I feel constrained to bring to your attention my opposition to filling jobs without paying careful attention to the ability of the men selected for the jobs."

Kennedy went on to urge them to establish "a talent search like that which President Kennedy established in 1960." This operation, he noted, had brought into the

Administration men like Douglas Dillon and Robert Mc-
Namara. He also suggested that all unnecessary jobs be
eliminated and that when jobs were filled, "full disclosure
be made to the public of . . . the duties and responsibilities
and pay, including expenses, attached to each job."

The letter hit hard at genuine evils. In the state legislature, committees are occasionally established for the
sole purpose of creating staff jobs for political hangers-on.
In other instances, a committee counsel or staff director
and one or two assistants may do legitimate work, but
the rest of the staff appropriation is carved up as political
rewards. Men and women are listed as research assistants,
messengers, and clerks who do no work (except for their
party at election time) and receive their salary checks by
mail while holding down regular jobs in private life. In
Albany jargon, such an employe is called a "no show."

But even clubhouse politicians like Zaretzki and Travia
no longer admit that they make appointments on any
basis except merit or that party considerations could
possibly come ahead of "careful attention to . . . ability."
Travia contented himself with saying as little as possible.
But Zaretski turned to Julius C. C. Edelstein, principal
ghost-writer for Mayor Wagner, to draft a reply. Zaretzki's
letter made some surprisingly knowledgeable and effective
counter-thrusts which were beyond his powers but not
those of Edelstein, who had previously served in Washington as administrative assistant to Senator Herbert H.
Lehman. (In subsequent months whenever Kennedy encountered Edelstein, he greeted him, "Hi, letter writer.")

"I am sure that you already know from your brief
experience in the legislative branch of the Federal Government," Zaretzki wrote, "that there is a difference between legislative staff positions and positions of administrative duties in the executive branch of the Government.
Indeed, I am not aware that the specific procedure you
recommend has ever been used by the Congress of the

United States or even by you in filling the staff positions in your own office in the United States Senate."

Zaretzki assured Kennedy that the public would be kept fully informed about the salaries and expenses of the legislative staff. He added, "Indeed, I would be glad to receive from you a summary report of the practices of the United States Senate in this regard, so that we can learn from its experience and its practices. Of course I would hope to improve on that model, if necessary, so as to let in the greatest amount of public light upon all our operations."

In another passage, Zaretzki declared, "As for eliminating useless jobs, you obviously missed seeing a recent joint statement by Speaker Travia and myself in which we pledged to cut down on the appropriation for the Legislature, a saving of over $1 million. We have also emphatically affirmed that we would not sanction or authorize any 'no show' jobs."[3]

Any illusion that the hapless Zaretzki had composed this fierce document was destroyed when he inadvertently sent copies of it to newspaper offices in envelopes marked, "Office of the Mayor."

But regardless of authorship, the letter was an effective riposte. Kennedy had received as good as he gave, and perhaps a bit better. Politicians and newspapermen speculated intensively as to Kennedy's motives in writing the letter. It was suggested that he was attempting to shore up the position of State Chairman McKeon, a former Wagner protégé who had turned against his patron. Another theory was that Kennedy had to challenge Wagner immediately or else the mayor would become so entrenched as to be unchallengeable. Still a third theory was that Kennedy believed that he had to repair his image since his allies had been defeated in the legislature.

None of these theories made much sense. As it turned out, Kennedy had no hidden motive. He acted on impulse, and his impulse was to obtain by personal fiat—"kind of a papal bull," as one politician termed it—what he had not been able to accomplish by electing his own men to the leadership. There was no doubt that Kennedy's proposals were well conceived: the legislature did need reform and a talent hunt modeled on the 1960 Kennedy operation would have dramatized the Democrats' determination to bring about reform. But when Zaretzki and Travia failed to buckle under upon receipt of Kennedy's imperious letter, there was no follow-through. His aides were soon acknowledging that the letter was a mistake and on a subsequent visit to Albany, Kennedy conspicuously made his peace with the legislative leaders. Two years afterward, Travia was still Speaker and Zaretzki— the Democrats in the interim having lost control—was still soldiering on as Minority Leader of the Senate. The legislature was still in need of reform; it still had no journal to provide a public record of its debates and votes; there was still no way in which members could compel a public hearing, much less a vote, on a bill; and there were still numerous "no show" employes. Zaretzki and Travia had forgotten any pledges of reform, and so had Kennedy. Legislative reform had been a foray, not a campaign.

If Kennedy had not been pursuing any persistent long-term purpose, neither did he suffer any political harm. The legislative leaders were powerless to retaliate. The public, if it remembered the exchange of letters at all, remembered only that Kennedy had spoken up against petty politics and for merit.

On June 10, 1965, Robert F. Wagner announced to everyone's surprise that after nearly twelve years in office, he would not seek a fourth term as mayor. His voluntary withdrawal removed the Democratic Party's only functioning leader in New York. Kennedy had worked subtly to undermine Wagner during the struggle to organize the legislature. When rumors of Wagner's retirement began to circulate and there were erroneous press reports that Kennedy had urged him to run, Kennedy made it clear that he was not supporting a draft, although he would back Wagner if he ran. When Wagner abruptly abdicated, the press and the public assumed that Kennedy, as the only Democrat holding a major office, would replace him as *de facto* party leader. But if nature abhors a vacuum, Kennedy does not. He edged his way partly in and then edged his way out again. Six months later, after twenty years in power, the Democrats yielded up City Hall. Although Kennedy was not primarily responsible for this party debacle, neither can he be said to have done much to prevent it.

Kennedy's ambivalent attitude toward Wagner accounts for much of his own ineffectuality. Wagner has a unique niche in the history of New York City politics. He is the first Democratic mayor to break the boss system and govern independently. Since Greater New York was formed in 1897 through a merger of the five boroughs, there have been reform mayors elected with Republican and "Fusion" support, such as Seth Low in 1901 and Fiorello LaGuardia in 1933. But Democratic mayors, regardless of their personal qualities, have been obliged to deal with members of the City Council and the Board of Estimate (made up of the five Borough Presidents, the City Controller, and the City Council President) who were not free men. Instead of considering city business on its merits, these officeholders were essentially agents for the true principals, the five county bosses of the Democratic Party. Democratic governors had similarly been captives of the party organization until Alfred E. Smith broke their grip and demonstrated that it was the governor who gave orders to the party leaders, not the other way around. What Smith accomplished at the state level in the 1920s, Wagner finally accomplished at the city level in 1961. He had captured the mayor's office in 1953 as the candidate of Carmine DeSapio, the leader of Manhattan, and Charles Buckley, the successor to Ed Flynn as the boss of the Bronx. Wagner at first governed in the tradition of the honest machine man. Like Harry Truman or Al Smith or his own father, United States Senator Robert F. Wagner, he respected the traditional prerogatives of the party leaders in dispensing patronage and favors. Personally honest himself, he was yet cognizant as a realist of the lucrative tie-ups among politically well-connected lawyers, contractors, and politicians, and as long as they were legal, he made no effort to disturb them. In short, he was not a reformer; he was with the machine but not of it.

Since New York Democrats enjoy a three-to-one advantage in party registrations over the Republicans and the population is accustomed to government in which all the power brokers—businessmen, trade union chiefs, ethnic bloc leaders—take part, machine rule is not unpopular. In 1957, Wagner won reelection over a weak Republican candidate by 924,000 votes. During the course of his second term, however, Wagner began to chafe under the political tutelage of DeSapio. He gradually reached the conclusion that he could not be his own master in City Hall unless he allied with the reformers and liberated himself from the party organizations. Wagner, phlegmatic, notoriously cautious, addicted to the leaden platitude, achieved a remarkable transformation by 1961 to become "Battling Bob," the foe of the bosses. Skeptics jeered that he was seeking a third term by running against the record of his first two, but he swept the Democratic primary and won a third term on his own. He drove DeSapio from party office, and started Buckley downhill toward the loss of his seat in Congress in 1964 and the defeat of his candidate for Bronx Borough President in the Democratic primary in 1965.

Wagner achieved a personal hegemony over the party organizations but four years proved not long enough to institutionalize it. He alone was able to dominate his party's warring factions, maintain a personal alliance with the small but pivotal Liberal Party, and keep reformers on speaking terms with those regulars who supported him. He demonstrated an impressive skill at political maneuver, had the old Tammany instinct for dealing with ethnic groups, and could bring to bear the tremendous leverage of the mayor's office. Once he stepped aside voluntarily, his personal system of alliances crumbled.

No effort to reform the Democratic Party or to strengthen it as a force for liberalism can proceed except from the basis of Wagner's accomplishment. Kennedy and other successors may improve upon his performance, but they cannot make progress by allying themselves with his enemies or by failing to resist the forces that he resisted. It is almost impossible to overestimate the number of persons who are seeking to make private fortunes out of city government in ways both legal and illegal. There are coteries and interlocking alliances of politicians, political lawyers, contractors, franchised businessmen, public relations men, and fixers and hangers-on of various kinds. Successive municipal administrations, like a retreating glacier, leave behind layer upon layer of these people. Money is their objective and political influence— or at least the appearance of it—is their means. They are constantly patrolling the corridors of power; they want to be "cut in" on a contract, awarded the insurance or the bonding on a public project, or included in an urban renewal redevelopment scheme. Many of them serve as front men and conduits for the money of underworld syndicates moving into legitimate businesses. These influence merchants and political mercenaries are a group entirely distinct from the lowly wardheelers and clubhouse members; they appear to be important and successful in their own professions and businesses and do not admit that they depend, directly or indirectly, upon politics for their livelihood. They are present in the Republican as well as the Democratic Party, as Nelson Rockefeller learned to his sorrow when liquor scandals embarrassed his administration and the Chairman of the Republican State Committee went to prison. But in New York City, the Democratic kind matter more because the Democrats are normally in the ascendancy. If the Liberal Party and the Reform Democrats have any reason for existence, it is to struggle against these corrupting influences. It is combat in which there can never be a truce.

Robert Kennedy, despite his disdain for crooks, underestimated the significance of Wagner's political accomplishment. He did not fully appreciate that this unimpressive, unexciting man had been a competent steward of the city's affairs and the party's good name. In 1932, the personally delightful James J. Walker had resigned as mayor and fled to Europe to escape from a series of scandals. In 1950, the charming, talented William O'Dwyer had resigned as mayor to become ambassador to Mexico and then stayed in Mexico for several years after his ambassadorship ended in order to avoid unpleasant questioning by grand juries. In 1953, Vincent R. Impellitteri was defeated for renomination because of his record of general ineptitude in office. As this brief recital suggests, Robert Wagner was the first Democratic mayor in a long time to leave office neither disgraced nor defeated.

Kennedy, quite unconsciously, acted as if he were bent upon recapitulating Wagner's experience in his first years in City Hall. He was trying to blend the unblendable, to achieve liberal and reformist goals by working with essentially conservative, status quo machine men. Temperament and political style play their part here. Kennedy's impulses and strategy lead him to seek change and to champion the Negroes, the Puerto Ricans, the impoverished, and the other beneficiaries of change. But as a thoroughgoing political realist interested in putting majorities together, controlling nominations, and winning elections, he has the orthodox politician's respect for the wielders of power. Dealing with liberals and reformers is messy and chaotic; dealing with bosses is tight, structured, realistic. Reformers are gabbling about parliamentary points of order at their meetings when they ought to be getting down to business, and liberals are raising abstruse programmatic issues of civil liberties or foreign policy instead of organizing their own district. Kennedy, who is readily bored by gabble of any kind and who distrusts theorists in the practical side of politics, feels more at home with the regulars even when he recognizes they are narrow-minded or not wholly trustworthy.

Stalemated by these divergent tendencies inside himself, Kennedy made no sustained effort to lead the party in any direction in the 1965 mayoralty campaign. He was intermittently active throughout the primary and election campaigns but never to any considered purpose. Rather than imposing himself as the organizer of victory, he became only a traveling companion, illustrious but ineffectual, on the journey to defeat.

The Democrats divided four ways in the mayoral primary. The Wagner loyalists rallied to Paul Screvane, the City Council President, a former career civil servant whom Wagner had elevated to Sanitation Commissioner and then into elective politics on his 1961 slate. Wagner eventually endorsed him. The organization regulars grouped around the Brooklyn and Bronx organizations settled upon Abraham Beame, the City Controller. Another career civil servant, he had been Wagner's Budget Director before becoming the third member of his 1961 ticket. Beame, however, like many municipal employes, had also been active in clubhouse politics as a precinct captain in the Brooklyn Democratic organization. As the 1965 election drew near, Beame decided his future lay with the regulars, not the Wagner faction. The candidate of the reformers was Congressman William F. Ryan from the West Side of Manhattan. Although of Irish ancestry, Ryan is the antithesis of the old Tammany politician. He is the Irishman as radical. This free-swinging, crusading lawyer represents a heterogeneous district which runs west from Central Park to the Hudson River and meanders up Broadway to Columbia University and beyond and contains a sizable middle-class population, predominantly Jewish, and substantial numbers of Negroes and Puerto Ricans. In both national and local elections, its voting pattern is consistently liberal. The fourth candidate was Councilman Paul O'Dwyer, the brother of former Mayor William O'Dwyer; he ran as if intending to prove that an honest lawyer with a well-known name, an engaging personality, and no money could not be nominated for mayor. He proved it.

The contest was obviously between Screvane and Beame, unless Ryan should pull off an astonishing upset. Each of the two leading candidates attempted to strengthen himself in characteristic ways. Beame reached an agreement with Queens District Attorney Frank D. O'Connor, who had been briefly a fifth contender. O'Connor accepted second place on Beame's ticket—the City Council Presidency—in exchange for at least the tacit understanding that he would have the support of Beame and the Steingut-Buckley organizations for the next year's gubernatorial nomination.

Screvane, a modern-minded man fascinated by public opinion polls and eager to run a stylish campaign keyed to the age of television, looked around for two running mates who would help him project an image of youth and newness and vigor. He settled on two political novices who not only fitted these requirements but also the older criteria of an ethnically balanced ticket. Daniel P. "Pat" Moynihan, his candidate for Council President, was thirty-eight, an Assistant Secretary of Labor, the author of the controversial report on "The Negro Family," and the only Democratic candidate in memory to possess a Ph.D. degree. Orin Lehman, his candidate for Controller, was forty-four, a wealthy philanthropist and nephew of the late Senator Herbert H. Lehman.

Kennedy's approach to this political scramble was shrewd in small ways, timid in the large. After Wagner withdrew, he tentatively approached Manhattan District Attorney Frank Hogan as a possible candidate. Hogan, who succeeded Thomas E. Dewey in the District Attorney's office in 1941 and over the past quarter-century has kept it scandal-free, strictly professional, and non-partisan, regularly receives renomination from all parties. If Hogan had announced immediately after Wagner's withdrawal that he was a candidate, would serve only one term, and give the city the same nonpartisan administration he had provided as District Attorney, he would probably have been unbeatable. The big fear in the city was that Wagner's retirement would mean a relapse to the old, corrupt ways that had destroyed several previous Democratic administrations. At the same time, a Hogan promise to serve only one term—he was then sixty-five— would subtly but effectively play upon the sentiment of many partisan Democrats and Liberals who were tempted to vote for John V. Lindsay, the ambitious Republican-Fusion candidate, but hesitated to build him up as a national Republican figure.

Hogan, however, said privately that he would run only if he could get the nomination unopposed, something no one could assure him. His entry might have impelled others to withdraw; Congressman Ryan, for example, who had served under him as an Assistant District Attorney, could scarcely have denounced Hogan with the fire that he directed at his other primary rivals. But with Hogan reluctant to do battle and labor mediator Theodore Kheel also willing to run only if he could have the nomination without a fight, Kennedy dropped back. He refused to join Wagner in supporting Screvane. He recognized that Beame was clearly not of leadership caliber, but he did not wish to affront the Buckley and Steingut organizations. And he would not enter a candidate of his own.

Kennedy calculated that he could afford to be neutral. If Beame were elected, his allies among the party regulars would be in power. If Screvane were elected, he could work with Pat Moynihan. Kennedy had encouraged Screvane to tap Moynihan, one of his New Frontier protégés, for second place on his ticket.

"Whichever ticket wins, I'll have a man in City Hall to look out for my interests," Kennedy remarked privately.

But as events developed, this hedge proved valueless.

Screvane, the early favorite, lost the nomination because of a combination of bad luck and bad judgment. Overconfident, he conserved his television money for use in the later campaign he expected to wage against Lindsay. When he did appear on television during the primary, he came across as pugnacious, abrasive, and, inaccurately, as humorless.

Screvane was also the most luckless candidate of the year. On the day he announced his candidacy, two credit-rating agencies dropped the city's credit standing by one notch. Midway through his campaign, on August first, the city sales tax rose from 4 per cent to 5 per cent. And finally there was the year-long water shortage. Screvane was in no way responsible but, as the Administration candidate, he received the blame.

"Lots of us could see what was going wrong," a leading Democrat reminisced later, "but he always came back at you with those damned polls. No man since Dewey has believed in polls more and no one was ever more misled by them. Almost to the end, they showed him leading 50 per cent to Beame's 33 per cent, with Ryan and O'Dwyer almost nowhere. So Screvane would say, 'Why should I mess around with my style when I'm ahead?' "

Ryan, however, polled over one hundred thousand votes and Beame unexpectedly emerged as the minority victor. The Democratic Party's cause thus passed into the hands of a bossy, fussy accountant. With a bookkeeper's approach to government, he had no social vision to offer the city, no inspiration to lift its morale. He could only promise to administer the status quo in an economical manner. As with Richard Nixon in 1960, where there is no vision, the people may not perish but the candidate surely does.

Beame was especially feeble in his several television debates with Lindsay. He had no program. Even on fiscal matters, which were presumably his specialty, he went no further than a promise to "roll back" the recently increased sales tax, repeal other unpopular taxes, and "go to Washington, where I have friends and where I am sure I will be welcome as a Democrat." If he had gone to Washington, his Eisenhower-esque prose would have sounded familiar to the local press corps. Thus, Beame was fond of pointing to the "most crucial problem" (there proved to be several), seeking taxes that would be "less onerous and also less burdensome," and meeting needs that might cost "four and one-half billions a year annually."

Kennedy campaigned intensively around the city that October for Beame, but nothing could save such a candidate. His colleagues on the city-wide ticket—O'Connor and Mario Procaccino, a hitherto obscure Bronx organization man—were elected but Beame lost decisively.

When a party holds a three-to-one majority in voter registration, the opposition cannot win an election; the incumbents have to cooperate by losing it. Through a series of errors of commission and omission, the Democrats lost the city they had ruled for twenty years. From the standpoint of the city's welfare, this was a welcome result. A complete upheaval in the executive leadership of the city government would produce necessary innovation and stimulate a lethargic bureaucracy.

From the Democratic Party's selfish standpoint, however, the outcome was a disaster. Although Kennedy professed to believe that the Democratic loss did not damage him personally and many observers in the immediate post-election period described him as in a position to "pick up the pieces," he, too, had suffered a serious setback. The defeat of Moynihan and Lehman in the primary eliminated any prospect of reorienting New York City government under "New Frontier" auspices. With Wagner gone, the young Senator was the dominant figure in the party but the first event of his leadership was the stupid Beame candidacy. His campaigning on Beame's behalf had only served to remind liberal Democrats and independents of Kennedy's ties to Charley Buckley and the other old-line bosses, exactly the memory he had spent a year trying to erase. Kennedy's chagrin was deepened when he learned after the election that Beame and his advisers had several times conferred with his mortal enemy, Roy Cohn. One of these conferences occurred on the afternoon of a day in which Kennedy had met with the same group in the morning.

"What will Bobby say if he hears about this?" one participant asked.

"Let's just see to it that he doesn't," Stanley Steingut replied.

The election of John V. Lindsay was a particular defeat for Kennedy. Despite all the easy talk about City Hall being a graveyard for those with higher political ambitions, the office of mayor of New York is still a command post of enormous power and influence. For the Democrats to lose this command post during the first year that Kennedy became active as one of the party's movers and shakers did not speak well for his political acumen. Because New York City is the nation's communications headquarters, its mayor has opportunities for personal publicity and for shaping public opinion surpassed only by those of the President. Lindsay is exactly the kind of alert, imaginative, telegenic politician to exploit these opportunities to the limit. He is a competing attraction to Kennedy in a way that Governor Rockefeller, battered by fate, and Senator Javits, who will be sixty-four in 1968, are not.

Kennedy departed for Latin America a week after the city election. After a futile autumn on the street corners of New York, the Amazon Valley jungle looked inviting.

The winter of 1965–66 passed quietly in New York Democratic politics. While Kennedy was on his post-election tour of Latin America, the correspondent accompanying him for *The New York Times* filed a dispatch from Buenos Aires suggesting that Kennedy might reopen the legislative leadership struggle. The story was that, according to "friends of Senator Kennedy," he would be pleased if Joseph Zaretzki were moved into a judgeship and replaced with an abler man as Senate leader. Speaker Travia, it was further suggested, would receive Kennedy's support for reelection if he chose a younger, more liberal floor leader as his partner in the Assembly. But these suggestions were more nearly cocktail-hour conversation than considered plans. No one had the stamina for a second round of struggle over the leadership. When Kennedy returned to New York, he took no action.

Political interest focused on the coming gubernatorial election. Would the Democrats capitalize on the opportunity to defeat Nelson Rockefeller whose standing in the public opinion polls was spectacularly low? How large a role would Robert Kennedy play in choosing the Democratic candidate?

In the midst of these speculations, Kennedy unexpectedly interjected himself into an obscure Manhattan judgeship contest and scored a major political coup. In New York City, the judges of most courts are nominated and elected by the political parties. It is the custom of the majority Democrats to work out bipartisan deals with the GOP to avoid the expense and inconvenience of a contest. Of all the judgeships, that of Surrogate is most coveted. The Surrogates (there are two in Manhattan and one in each of the other counties) supervise the probating of estates and protect the interests of families, infants, and incompetents involved in wills by appointing lawyers to serve as guardians or administrators of estates. Since Manhattan is the nation's financial capital, the wills of many out-of-state businessmen are probated there because that is where their assets are. From the judge's viewpoint, the Surrogate's Court is a pleasant quiet place to work free of the emotional conflict of criminal cases or the business complexities of many civil suits. For the political party, the patronage flowing from a Surrogate judge to politically dependable lawyers is a vital source of strength. During the 1930s, when Tammany was out of power at City Hall under the LaGuardia regime and out of favor in Washington with the Roosevelt administration, it managed to survive partly because it still controlled considerable judicial patronage. In the late 1960s, with the Lindsay reform administration in City Hall, Tammany again looked to the courthouses for sustenance. In Manhattan, estates worth nearly one billion dollars are probated each year.

In May 1966, it looked as if the usual comfortable arrangement had been worked out between the parties. In exchange for a joint endorsement of a Democrat for Surrogate, the Democrats promised the Republicans a number

of lesser-ranking judgeships. The only question in doubt
was the identity of the Democrat. The Tammany regulars
decided upon Supreme Court Justice Arthur G. Klein, an
old-timer who had served as a district leader on the Lower
East Side and a Congressman. Most Reform Democrats
would have preferred another candidate but once outvoted
in the party executive committee, they moved to make it
unanimous. It was all routine, and *The Times* on May 7
ran a brief account of it on page thirty-four.

The editorial pages, the traditional guardians of the
integrity of the judiciary, expressed disapproval. "Despite
their numerous defeats in recent years, the old-line leaders
of the Manhattan Democrats have learned nothing and
have forgotten nothing," *The Times* editorialized on May 9.
"A veteran of the Tammany machine, Mr. Klein owes his
public career to his party regularity and his personal affa-
bility. . . . Nothing in his record recommends him for this
significant promotion. . . . It is imperative that the Republican and Liberal parties unite in choosing a truly impressive lawyer."

The *Post* weighed in that afternoon with a similar expression of distaste. The Liberal Party in a bid for an
alliance with the GOP nominated a Republican. But the
alliance between the two major parties held firm. On Friday, the thirteenth, the Republican County Committee
unanimously endorsed Klein. Despite the newspapers and
the Liberals, the way seemed smooth.

The following Thursday, May 19, James A. Wechsler,
who doubles as columnist as well as editorial page editor
of the *Post* wrote a column fiercely attacking the Klein
nomination. He harked back to an earlier judgeship controversy. In 1943, when gangster Frank Costello was a
major influence in Tammany, he had steered a judgeship
nomination to one of his political protégés, Thomas Aurelio. Wechsler printed a portion of the wiretapped conver-

sation Aurelio held on that occasion with Costello. The date was August 29, 1943; the transcript released by District Attorney Hogan read:

"Aurelio: Good morning, Francesco, how are you and thanks for everything.

"Costello: Congratulations. It went over perfect. When I tell you something is in the bag, you can rest assured.

"Aurelio: It was perfect. Arthur Klein did the nominating; first me, then Gavagan, then Peck. It was fine."

Wechsler added: "This excerpt is not offered to suggest that Klein knew he was taking Costello's orders, or to cast asperations on those he named. It is cited only to dramatize the intimacy of his relations with the old Tammany cabal in which Costello's hidden hand loomed so large. I would hardly damn Justice Klein for this solitary episode. But nothing in the ensuing record indicates that he has ever turned his back on his old cronies or that, in the position of Surrogate, he would coldly forget them.

"The larger question is why, of all the jurists and attorneys in this crowded city, he became [Manhattan Democratic leader] Ray Jones' choice for Surrogate and so promptly received the Republican blessing."[4]

Wechsler's column appeared May 19. Robert Kennedy had an appointment to meet Alex Rose of the Liberal Party for drinks that same day in the bar of the Prince George Hotel on Twenty-eighth Street, around the corner from the Fifth Avenue office of the Hatters Union of which Rose is president. The get-together had no specific purpose; it was just another in the endless round of meetings which politicians have to "keep in touch" with one another.

Rose sipped his customary sherry, Kennedy drank his vodka-and-tonic, and conversation languished—as conversations often do when Kennedy is one of the partners.

"He's not the easiest fellow in the world to talk to, you

know," Rose recalled later. "I had this copy of the *Post* with me opened to the page with Jimmy Wechsler's column, and just to make conversation, and not really expecting anything much to come of it, I asked him if he had read it. He said, 'No,' and I handed it to him.

"As he read through it, I could see his face change. You could tell he was interested."

Kennedy hates gangsters with a pure, holy passion. The knowledge that Arthur Klein was involved, however peripherally, in any political operation of Frank Costello gave the Surrogate election a point and an interest that it had not previously had for him. Kennedy also realized that he would strengthen his ties with Rose if he made common cause with the Liberals in this controversy. But these and related political calculations were subordinate to his reflexive moral response.

Kennedy returned to Washington that evening, but he put Steve Smith, William vanden Heuvel, and other members of his entourage to work exploring the possibilities of making a fight in the Democratic primary against Klein. Who was the best judge willing to make the race? Several judges were sounded out until agreement was reached on State Supreme Court Justice Samuel J. Silverman. Was it possible to organize an effective campaign in the five weeks remaining before the June 28 primary? The consensus was that it could be done. The regulars counted upon the normally light turnout in a judicial primary to ratify the choices of the leadership, but there was no certainty that they could withstand a vigorous opposition drive.

On Sunday evening, May 22, Kennedy returned to Manhattan to attend a meeting he had called of all the Democratic district leaders belonging to the reform faction. Discussion dragged for three hours. Some of the leaders were reluctant to wage a primary fight against Klein since they had participated in the selection process and joined in making his nomination unanimous. Others were dubious because they did not think it possible to beat the machine in the short time available. Kennedy finally overrode these scruples and doubts. He peptalked them into making a fight and declared it the sense of the meeting that Judge Silverman was their candidate.

Kennedy's personal participation had to be fitted around his trip to South Africa, but he deputized Smith to manage Silverman's campaign, assigned aides and outriders to specific duties, and helped recruit well-known lawyers for endorsements. Since Silverman had been a member of Paul, Weiss, Wharton and Rifkind, one of the city's best known law firms, before joining the bench, he attracted impressive professional support. Bruce Bromley, a former judge of the Court of Appeals and a well-known Republican attorney, and Irving E. Engel, a long-time leader in the Democratic reform movement, agreed to serve as co-chairmen of a Lawyers Committee for Silverman. Typical of the score or more of lawyers who worked actively in Silverman's behalf was his former partner, Adrian W. DeWind, who had been chief counsel to the House committee that exposed the tax scandals in the Truman administration.

With Kennedy, as with any successful politician, the first rule for winning a campaign is to select a quality candidate who evokes respect and some measure of personal support. The second rule is to have the resources of staff and money and deploy them effectively.

"If we had been trying to run Silverman's campaign on our own," remarked a leader of the Lexington Democrats, the reform club on the Upper East Side, "we would have rounded up some volunteers and had them telephone voters in the evenings. But Steve Smith had the lists of registered Democrats broken down by neighborhoods, picked the neighborhoods that looked promising for Silverman, and just called one of these professional telephone services and placed an order for ten thousand calls.

"Volunteers are all right if you have six months to organize them but money moves faster when you only have three or four weeks to whip up a campaign."

No marginal source of strength was overlooked. Kennedy asked Herman Badillo, the Borough President of the Bronx, to run as a delegate to the state constitutional convention in the Twenty-ninth Senatorial District. This district is two-thirds in the Bronx but one-third in East Harlem, a predominantly Puerto Rican neighborhood. Since Badillo is the only Puerto Rican to hold major office in the city government, his presence on the ballot would help to get out the vote in East Harlem. (The effort was worthwhile; Badillo won and Silverman carried East Harlem, though narrowly.)

Kennedy's final contribution to the campaign was his own name and electrifying legend. The crowds might not know the difference between a surrogate and a magistrate and be unable to recognize Silverman when he was introduced from a platform, but they had all heard of Kennedy. After his return from Africa, he campaigned with Silverman on street corners each night in the last week, drawing sizable crowds.

The regulars supporting Klein played into Kennedy's hands by making him the issue. Former Mayor Impellitteri said, "Kennedy is making a vicious grab for power. . . . He is trying to take over the Democratic party, in the city and the state, that's my opinion."

J. Raymond Jones, the leader of Tammany who had arranged Klein's bipartisan nomination, said Kennedy was engaged in a "vendetta" against him. "He who seeks to conquer aims at me, the office, the Court—all principle is shoved under the rug," Jones solemnly announced.

Since Jones and Impellitteri are implausible as foes of bossism, their criticisms of Kennedy on this score were something less than convincing. In desperation, Jones, known in Harlem as "The Fox" and the only Negro county leader in the nation, raised the cry of racism. Four prominent Negroes joined with attorney Morris Ernst in a statement declaring that the opposition to Klein was really a devious attack on Jones. Negroes, they warned, might see the defeat of Jones's man as "an attempt to constrict the power and prerogatives of any political office attained by the Negro."[5]

Kennedy countered by bringing James Farmer, formerly the head of CORE (Congress for Racial Equality), and James Meredith, the first Negro to graduate from the University of Mississippi, into the campaign to speak in Silverman's behalf.

The outcome was a dramatic triumph for Kennedy. Silverman polled 70,771 votes to Klein's 47,625.

"I'm pleased. I think the results show how sophisticated the voters in New York are," Kennedy said on election night.

His success threw terror into the hearts of every county leader from Brooklyn to Buffalo. What he had done to Ray Jones and the Manhattan regulars he might conceivably do to any one of them. His intervention in the Surrogate race was a bold move, for national politicians can find their strength and reputation nibbled away by defeats in obscure, complicated local elections. It also took moral imagination; no other major politician, not even Mayor Lindsay so recently elected on a reform platform, had perceived that this dull judgeship primary might ignite public indignation. In a swift month-long campaign, Kennedy had wiped away the stigma of his initial sponsorship by the party bosses and established himself as the hero and leader of New York's liberal Democrats. The absentee prince had reasserted his authority.

NOTES

[1] "Letters to the Editor," *The New York Times*, August 15, 1961.
[2] *The New York Times*, January 21, 1965.
[3] *Ibid.*, February 11, 1965, February 12, 1965.
[4] New York *Post*, May 19, 1966.
[5] *The New York Times*, June 13, 1966.

CHAPTER EIGHT

In Search of a Viceroy

"I start out by believing the worst."
—NAPOLEON BONAPARTE, *quoted in*
Herold, ed., The Mind of Napoleon, *p. 6.*

ON THE NIGHT of the Silverman primary victory, all
things seemed possible in New York politics for
Robert Kennedy. With a state election coming in the fall,
he had a promising opportunity to lead his party back to
power and elect an ally as governor. Secure in the knowledge that for the next four years a trustworthy viceroy in
Albany was protecting his local interests, Kennedy could
then turn his full attention to national politics and international issues.

"He [is] now the ruler of the Democratic Party in New
York," wrote Pete Hamill, the young columnist of the New
York *Post,* on primary night.

"Fresh from directing a major political victory, Senator
Robert F. Kennedy is expected to endorse one of the Democratic candidates for Governor before the party's nominating convention in early September," wrote Warren
Weaver, Jr., in *The New York Times.*

John Burns, the Democratic State Chairman, predicted
that Kennedy would make known his choice "after he
analyzes how the candidates appear to be doing as to
popularity within the Democratic party."[1]

Since Manhattan Democrats do not differ much from

those elsewhere in the state, Democrats would follow Kennedy if he backed a candidate for governor and fought for him. His task was to divert the party from the drift and fumble of its practical politicians. "A practical politician," Disraeli once remarked, "is one who practices the errors of his predecessors."

The practical politicians already had their candidate for governor. He was Frank D. O'Connor, the President of the New York City Council. A slight man of medium height with thinning gray hair, large eyes, and a leprechaun's smile, O'Connor, at fifty-seven, looked a dozen years younger.

The *National Observer* wrote of O'Connor, "His is the kind of political biography that went out of print twenty years ago."[2]

He is the son of Irish immigrants, his father having come from County Sligo and his mother from County Limerick. Born on the West Side of Manhattan, he grew up in Queens, where many aspiring Irish began to move around World War I. His father was "a gentle, quiet man" and his mother "one of those terrific women." Like her, he joined his local Democratic club as soon as he was of age and shortly became a district captain. After St. John's College and Niagara University Law School, he opened a local practice in Queens, was elected a county committeeman in a factional fight, and became active in the Elks, eventually becoming their state leader and a friend of past Grand Exalted Ruler James A. Farley.

O'Connor obtained a State Senate nomination in 1948 "because it was the year Truman ran against Dewey and there weren't many candidates." He won in an upset, served two terms, was defeated in the 1952 Eisenhower landslide, and recaptured his seat in 1954.

O'Connor went to Albany as conservative and parochial as his middle and lower-middle class constituency. "He had as much social idealism," another politician pointed out, "as you would expect a man to acquire sitting around the Elks Club." He introduced bills to require loyalty oaths from teachers and jurors, to censor obscene books, to compel all students to recite the pledge of allegiance in the schools, and to deny public welfare assistance to any one not resident in the state for at least one year. Another of his bills would have forbidden candidates to accept endorsements from more than one party, a favorite scheme of organization Democrats trying to kill off the Liberal Party. He also offered resolutions calling for an end of Marshall Plan aid to Great Britain after the British recognized Communist China and for a plebiscite to reunite Ireland.

O'Connor was already thirty-nine when elected to the State Senate but, in a sense, he had never left Queens. Albany is not normally thought of as a center of the higher civilization, but for O'Connor, service there was educational. If he introduced some inane resolutions, he also was more interested and industrious than the run-of-the-mill members. His horizons widened. When he regained his seat in 1954, he had the endorsements of the Liberal Party, the Americans for Democratic Action, and the non-partisan Citizens Union. In 1966, he could look back upon the bills and resolutions of his first term and truthfully say: "That all happened when I was young and foolish. They raise those old bills every time I run. I don't blame them. I'd do just the same."

In 1955, in the middle of his third senatorial term, O'Connor was elected District Attorney of Queens. He was twice reelected by increasingly large pluralities. As he tried to position himself to win higher office, he adopted more discernibly liberal opinions. He was the only District Attorney in the state to oppose capital punishment; he endorsed the Supreme Court decisions restricting police interrogation and the use of confessions; he criticized the

John Birch Society. He urged a revision of the divorce law (previously adultery was the only grounds for divorce in New York), and a liberalization of the laws governing narcotics offenders.

If O'Connor's opinions on public policy were becoming more liberal, his administration of the District Attorney's office remained resolutely old-fashioned. His Assistant District Attorneys were party regulars hired on the recommendation of their district leaders. He permitted these assistants to have private practices on the side. His standards were different from those observed in the best District Attorneys' offices. Frank Hogan, the Manhattan prosecutor, chooses his assistants on a nonpartisan basis, forbids them to be active in their party clubhouses, if they belong at all, and requires them to work full-time. The relaxed, political atmosphere of O'Connor's office bred no major scandal but it perpetuated the long-standing belief that if a lawyer were a well-connected Democrat, his client's chances of obtaining an out-of-court settlement or a reduced sentence were better than average.

Columnist Murray Kempton stated the defense for O'Connor's style as a district attorney in charming terms: "He was District Attorney of Queens for ten years; but he had been a criminal lawyer for much longer. And, if he is sometimes criticized as having been less passionate in the job than the District Attorney of tradition, it is because he is incurably defense-minded and because to him to be a policeman was still a little bit to have taken the king's shilling."[3]

There were others, however, who regarded O'Connor's prosecuting record less tolerantly, among them Robert Kennedy. Having spent nearly ten years lusting after the conviction of James R. Hoffa, he could scarcely comprehend, much less approve, a District Attorney of such amiable spirit.

O'Connor is typical of the Irish in towns and cities

across the nation who, in the ninety years between the Irish potato famine and the New Deal, built both the Catholic Church and the Democratic Party and who kept the faith, political as well as religious, in good times and bad. Like them, he is an organization man in an old-fashioned sense of that term, a man with an understanding of the importance of institutions, a respect for hierarchical authority, an affection for the past, and a fatalistic attitude toward the future. Honest and conventional in his own life, he has a wry, un-Puritanical tolerance for the failings of others, whether their sin be taking a bribe or a drink too many. One hates the sin, not the sinner. Kennedy's grandfathers in Boston would have felt at home with O'Connor; Kennedy did not. In O'Connor's case, a charitable attitude toward human frailty was laced with an engaging sense of humor about himself. Not since Adlai Stevenson had one encountered a politician with such genuine humility and such a propensity for making small private jokes about the madnesses and incongruities of politics.

In short, O'Connor was exactly the kind of Irishman that Robert Kennedy was not: a political regular, a man given to humor about victory and defeat, a fatalist, a loser. They understood one another and they even liked one another, but they could never be close. O'Connor was vaguely uncomfortable around this tigerish young man with his brooding eyes and fierce ambitions; Kennedy could basically not respect an organization man who would rather lose as a gentleman than win—period. The contest for the Democratic Party's nomination for governor of New York in 1966 became a duel between these two men, so united by their common cultural past and so divided by their present ways of viewing the world.

"He is such a nice man," Kennedy said of him. On this assessment, there was unanimous agreement. No one could personally dislike Frank O'Connor. But he was not tough enough, efficient enough, modern-minded enough to serve as Kennedy's viceroy in New York. A Kennedy aide offered a candid assessment: "Frank is the best of the old breed, but we are looking for the best of the new breed."

But O'Connor was still the choice of his peers in the party organizations. A year earlier, he had helped the regulars put together their ticket by withdrawing his own candidacy for mayor and agreeing to run for the honorific but empty office of President of the City Council. He had survived the Beame debacle and in winning the Council Presidency, he polled two hundred thousand more votes than Mayor Lindsay. It was, as the professional politicians like to say, "his turn," and he had earned it. O'Connor had the nomination firmly within his grasp unless Kennedy could shake it loose.

Of O'Connor's active rivals, Franklin D. Roosevelt, Jr., was the most dramatic figure and the saddest. He had hopes for the nomination but they were fragile and totally dependent upon Robert Kennedy's favor. He who had once been the man of destiny in New York politics looked out at a world in which an upstart from Massachusetts enjoyed a primacy that might have been his own.

In the spring of 1949, when Kennedy was twenty-three and a first-year student at the University of Virginia Law School,* Roosevelt was thirty-four and made a perfect political debut. Running as an independent candidate, he defeated a Tammany Democrat for a seat in the House of Representatives from Manhattan in a special election. The future seemed open before him. He had every requisite

---

* Roosevelt, incidentally, is also an alumnus of the University of Virginia Law School. It was at his son's law school commencement on June 10, 1940, that President Roosevelt made his famous speech denouncing Italy for entering the war against France and Britain: "The hand that held the dagger has struck it into the back of its neighbor."

political gift. He was intelligent, tirelessly energetic ("that damn Roosevelt extra gland"), handsome, a fluent and forceful speaker, and possessed of personal magnetism and charm.

"He could really turn an audience around," an old politician later recalled. "Put him before an audience of women in those days, and he was unbeatable."

But impatient ambition undid him. In his eagerness to achieve the governorship and begin moving toward the Presidency, he courted the support of machine politicians and blighted his budding reputation as a man of independence and principle. In 1950, he made his first bid for the governorship. Older, wiser men tried to warn him off, pointing out that with scarcely a year of service in the House, he did not have the experience and stature to qualify. But he plunged ahead and encountered the rejection he could have foreseen. In making his futile bid, he incurred obligations that later plagued him. One was to Joseph Sharkey, a Brooklyn Democratic leader who supported him in that convention. The following year, Sharkey was the Democratic candidate for President of the City Council in a special election. The Liberal candidate was the late Rudolph Halley, counsel to the Kefauver Committee crime investigation. Roosevelt reciprocated Sharkey's support by campaigning for him rather than Halley. The Liberals, believing that they deserved Roosevelt's prior loyalty since they had backed him in his first compaign, were incensed.

In 1952, Roosevelt opportunistically enlisted as Averell Harriman's campaign manager for the presidential nomination in the hope that Harriman, a multimillionaire, would reciprocate by helping to finance a Roosevelt campaign for governor two years later. Harriman, a great public servant but a close man with a dollar, not only never invested any money in Roosevelt but became so enamored of running for President that he decided to annex the governorship of New York as a staging ground. In 1954, he did just that. Roosevelt led in the public opinion polls, had strong support both upstate and in the city, and would have won a primary if there had been one. But at the convention, Harriman, shrewdly advised behind the scenes by Liberal Party leader Alex Rose, was the choice of the well-disciplined delegates.

Roosevelt accepted the nomination for Attorney General as a consolation prize only to lose that, too. While Harriman squeezed through to victory by fewer than 12,000 votes, Roosevelt lost to Representative Jacob K. Javits by 173,000. Javits, although a Republican, had an almost perfect liberal voting profile in the House, a strong hold upon normally Democratic Jewish voters, and a more plausible, if no more substantial, record of accomplishment in the House. As legislators, Javits and Roosevelt were as powerless to affect events as other fledgling members. But Javits contrived a better reputation out of press releases, bills introduced (but not passed), and timely gestures. Striving to hold his tenuous grip on a normally Democratic district, he was unsleeping in his assiduous attention to work. Roosevelt, relaxed, a bit overconfident, and his mind on higher things than the chores of a Congressman from a safe district, evinced a streak of self-indulgence. He sometimes failed to show up at political and civic meetings where he had promised to speak; he missed more than his share of routine roll calls; and he acquired a mildly playboyish reputation. These seemed mere peccadillos but in the hard-fought 1954 campaign, Javits exploited them successfully.

The "anti" votes were more important than Javits's virtues. Roosevelt found that some Liberals were voting against him because of his defection in the Halley campaign and some organization Democrats, particularly Catholics, because of his mother's quarrel with Cardinal Spellman over aid to parochial schools. Conservative Democrats were happy to have the opportunity to vote against "young Franklin" in order to avenge themselves in ancient quarrels with his father. Memories of FDR's feuds with James A. Farley and Alfred E. Smith were still fresh. And, despite Javits's liberalism, upstate Republicans would vote for him or for Satan rather than for the son of "that man."

If there is any moral to the political destruction of "young Franklin" between 1949 and 1954, it would seem to be that sons of famous men are best advised to avoid seeking high elective office too soon. If they wait fifteen or twenty years, old enmities have a chance to fade, their father's contemporaries no longer feel that they are being hurried off stage before their time, and a wave of nostalgia has time to form. Whether or not this is true as a general principle, it certainly was true of the younger Roosevelt. If he had waited until 1962 or 1966 to project himself toward the governorship instead of beginning in 1950, he would have emerged upon the scene as a fresh figure. As it was, he had become by 1966, if not a political dead man, at best one of the walking wounded.

The intervening dozen years had not been kind to Roosevelt, except financially. Raised in privileged circumstances but without a hereditary fortune, he had expensive tastes that he could not afford. He turned first to the practice of his profession, but like his father before him, law was never his first interest. Among his clients for a six-month period was Generalissimo Trujillo, the malodorous, barbarously cruel dictator of the Dominican Republic. Since the liberal community had only begun to withdraw its tolerance from Latin dictators in the post-war years, Roosevelt may be forgiven for failing to realize that times had changed since his father had traded jovial courtesies with Getulio Vargas of Brazil, Fulgencio Batista of Cuba, and this same Trujillo.

From dabbling in the law, Roosevelt turned with greater success to the importation of foreign automobiles. Roosevelt Motor Co., the principal distributor in the southeastern United States of Fiats, is a thriving business and has at last assured its owner of the financial independence he desired. In 1960, in search of a route back to politics, Roosevelt allied himself with the Kennedys against Hubert Humphrey. Roosevelt's name had value because John Kennedy, bidding for liberal acceptance, needed to strengthen his links with the party's New Deal past. Nowhere was the name more valuable than in West Virginia where the coal miners and their mountain neighbors still worshiped President Roosevelt as their friend and savior in depression days.

Franklin Roosevelt, Jr., not only campaigned for Kennedy but also attacked Humphrey's war record. (Humphrey was deferred by Selective Service for various reasons during the war, and finally rejected on medical grounds.) After Kennedy won the primary, Roosevelt apologized publicly to Humphrey and made peace.[4] But this self-inflicted wound permanently and deservedly scarred Roosevelt's reputation. Ironically enough, John Kennedy, who was cognizant of Roosevelt's intended slur on Humphrey and derived political benefit from it, suffered no harm to his reputation. Neither did Robert Kennedy, who persuaded Roosevelt to do it.

"You helped get us into this [the West Virginia primary] and it is up to you to help us win it," Robert Kennedy is said to have admonished Roosevelt.[5]

John Kennedy had a genuine liking for Roosevelt, strengthened by the fact that the latter's wife, Suzanne, was one of the few political wives whom Jacqueline Kennedy found congenial. The Roosevelts were among the guests at the first private dinner party the Kennedys gave in the White House. Kennedy proffered several diplomatic posts, including the ambassadorship to Italy, but Roosevelt turned them down, preferring a job in Washington that would keep him close to the New York political scene.

Eventually, he became Undersecretary of Commerce. If Kennedy had lived, he would probably have elevated him to the Secretaryship in his second administration. From the Cabinet, Roosevelt would have been well-positioned to run for governor, perhaps even as the unofficial "administration candidate." As events actually developed, President Johnson eased him out of the Commerce Department and transferred him to the chairmanship of the Equal Opportunities Commission. It was from this post that he resigned in 1966 to return to New York and try again for the governorship that had twice eluded him.

At fifty-one, he still possessed the physical assets of his heritage: the large head, the strong upthrust jaw, the powerful shoulders. Standing six-foot-four, he had the warm smile, vigorous handshake, and personal presence of a commanding figure. Only a few tired lines around his eyes and the slight pouchiness of his face hinted at the past defeats and disappointments. He could still make a better speech than any of the Kennedys. He had an ease of manner on the platform, a natural political style, and a familiarity with New York and its problems superior to his rivals. To observers who had known him when he was young, he evoked a haunting sense of what-might-have-been. He had made no more mistakes than most major politicians make on the way up, but he had paid more dearly for them because everybody had held him to a higher standard. His family name had provided the instant recognition and visibility that most politicians spend half their careers striving to attain, but he had been careless. If he had been less arrogant, if he had been less insistent on rushing headlong for success, if he had been able to develop his native powers in an elective job that challenged and interested him, if . . .

As he waited in the early summer of 1966 for the word of approval from the new man of power in New York politics, the word that never came, Franklin Roosevelt,

Jr., the son of one President and the grandnephew of another, had reason to ponder the fate of dynasties. Like a royalist *émigré* returned from exile to wait attendance at Bonaparte's court, he was grateful to be back and yet remorseful that he held by sufferance only a portion of what had once seemed his by right. Memory and desire continued their ceaseless warfare in the secret places of his mind.

Of the candidates for Kennedy's favor and the party's nomination, Howard J. Samuels was the least known. A native of Rochester, New York, where he was a high school tennis champion, a graduate of the Massachusetts Institute of Technology, and, at twenty-five, a lieutenant colonel on General George Patton's Third Army staff, Samuels made a fortune in the post-war years in the plastics business. His MIT thesis, "The Manufacturing and Distribution Problems of a Vinyl Coated Sisal Rope as a Clothesline," became the basis for founding the Kordite Corporation in 1946 with his brother Richard in a rented school building in a village near Rochester. It eventually became the nation's largest producer of plastic packaging, including "Baggies," which housewives use to wrap sandwiches and leftovers. After selling the business to the Mobil Chemical Company, Samuels now a millionaire, turned to politics.

He did not run for elective office, but he became involved in a staggeringly long list of civic causes. He chaired dinners and fund-raising drives of everything from the March of Dimes to the American Histadrut Cultural Exchange Institute to the National Association for Prevention of Addiction to Narcotics. As upstate chairman of the President's Club, the Democratic Party's elite group of financial contributors, Samuels became a familiar figure at party gatherings. He also interested himself in various school projects and wrote pamphlets on education. With the ad-

vice of Paul Buiar, a gifted public relations man, Samuels
projected himself as a public-spirited young businessman
—in 1966 he was forty-six—with a fresh, constructive
approach. At each of the party forums at which the gubernatorial hopefuls spoke in the spring and early summer,
he made a point of always offering a positive proposal
such as a new plan for higher education or the appointment of deputy governors for each of the regions of the
state.

A slim, tall, heavy-lidded rather handsome man with
an unruly mop of gray hair and an eager smile, Samuels
is vain, self-confident, smooth. He is at home on television
and with all the modern arts of advertising and promotion; if nominated, he would have run the most sophisticated, television-oriented campaign.

Samuels made no impact in New York City where he
was barely known but he had a sizable bloc of convention
delegates from the small, normally Republican counties.
He also had eight children. One asset he did not have was
Robert Kennedy's good will. Whether it was that Kennedy
disliked his quietly aggressive manner or resented, perhaps
subconsciously, a potential rival with that unruly hair
and a houseful of children, or did not judge him a dependable political ally, the fact remains that the two did
not hit it off. Samuels, therefore, never really had a
chance of obtaining the nomination. But his wealth, his
persistence, and his upstate delegates kept him a factor
in a complex situation.

The fourth candidate was Eugene Nickerson. On paper,
he was the ideal candidate. Scion of a wealthy Republican
family, Nickerson had converted to the Democrats as a
young man. He was educated at Yale and Harvard Law
School, clerked for Judge Learned Hand, practiced law as
a partner of a leading Manhattan firm, Donovan, Lumbard
and Leisure. In 1959, he upset a long-dominant Republican machine when he was elected county executive of

Nassau County, the huge, sprawling middle section of Long Island adjoining New York City. In 1963, he was reelected by a greatly increased majority. As chief administrative officer of one of the nation's major suburban areas and a proven vote-getter in an independent, politically volatile constituency, Nickerson, at forty-six, seemed like the ideal candidate for a party trying to widen its political base outside New York City. He was the most programmatic of the candidates, informed on the issues, seriously concerned about the nuts-and-bolts details of transportation, water pollution, and fiscal planning. No one doubted that Nickerson would make a competent, effective governor.

But he lacked that indefinable quality of electric vitality that "turns on" an audience. He gained the respect of his listeners but rarely stirred them. This need not have been an insurmountable obstacle since he was a more polished speaker than Judge Silverman, whom Kennedy had just succeeded in nominating for Surrogate. But as events developed, it was to prove a fatal handicap.

Faced with the necessity of having to choose among O'Connor, Roosevelt, Samuels, and Nickerson, Kennedy's first private reaction was to reject them all.

Earlier in the year, he had searched briefly for a prestigious candidate from outside of politics. Secretary of Health, Education, and Welfare John W. Gardner was approached, but turned out to be a registered Republican. Dr. James Perkins, the president of Cornell University, was also considered but he had not been resident in the state for the necessary five years. Theodore Kheel, attorney and labor mediator, was again briefly discussed as he had been during the maneuvering for mayor, but nothing came of it.

Kennedy next espoused a proposal to hold a series of open forums in which prospective candidates would speak and answer questions. The theory was that the forums would refute the nasty Republican charge that a few party bosses in New York City usually chose the Democratic candidate. Since the charge was true, this was expecting a lot from the forums. Moreover, they served to constrict Kennedy's area of maneuver. Since O'Connor and Roosevelt were unenthusiastic about a round of joint appearances with their lesser rivals, Kennedy could only keep the forum idea alive by insisting that he would refuse to support a candidate who failed to take part. At least nominally, this declaration limited his field of choice to the four participants.* Nickerson was generally regarded as having made the best impression in the forums, but not clearly enough to make any difference. The decision still lay with the county leaders unless Kennedy organized a personal coalition behind a candidate of his choice.

O'Connor had working for him the same power combination as had nominated Kennedy himself two years earlier. With 1,145 delegates, a majority of 573 was needed to nominate. O'Connor had the 129 votes from his home county of Queens and the backing of the Buckley organization in the Bronx (90 votes) and the Steingut organization in Brooklyn (184 votes). The leadership of Erie County (Buffalo) traditionally worked in concert with the New York City leaders which, if this past custom prevailed, meant another 90 votes. In addition, O'Connor had scattered support upstate which would bring his total comfortably above 600.

O'Connor, however, could take no comfort from these calculations. He remembered his defeat in the 1962 convention; indeed, there are those who believe that his

---

* There was a fifth participant, Lee Dennison, executive of Suffolk County, but he was not a serious candidate.

strongest incentive for winning the 1966 nomination was his determination to wipe out that previous defeat. Four years earlier, he had lined up much the same support. Samuels was a dark horse, then, too, but Nickerson and Roosevelt were not candidates and in the absence of any other big name contender, O'Connor appeared to have the nomination won. But a public opinion poll decided otherwise. Studies by pollster Louis Harris indicated that the "ideal" candidate would be a Jew with a liberal, reformist appeal. Harris was then a confidant and adviser of Mayor Wagner, Alex Rose of the Liberal Party, and the Kennedys. Since each of them was unenthusiastic about O'Connor, they searched for a candidate to fit Harris's specifications. Kennedy proposed Robert Morgenthau, the United States Attorney in New York, and a member of one of New York's most distinguished Jewish families. (His grandfather had been ambassador to Turkey in the Wilson administration; his father was Secretary of the Treasury in the Roosevelt administration; his mother was Herbert H. Lehman's niece.) Wagner, using a mayor's patronage powers as the lever, broke up O'Connor's city support and put across Morgenthau. O'Connor carried the fight to a second ballot, the only time that has ever happened at a Democratic state convention in New York, and Morgenthau was soundly defeated in the election, but neither event provided solace for O'Connor.

Wagner was now out of City Hall but Kennedy had been transformed from a remote presence in Washington into an active and interested force in New York. O'Connor had reason to worry. A politician familiar with the inner workings of the party later explained why: "Kennedy wanted Nickerson. Now, Nickerson had ninety delegates from Nassau. If Bobby had endorsed him publicly, he would have picked up another hundred and fifty to two hundred delegates upstate and also just about finished off Samuels and Roosevelt. Nickerson also had most of the reform clubs in Manhattan and the Bronx. If Bobby had gone to Ray Jones the morning after the primary and said, 'You get behind Nickerson and we'll let bygones be bygones,' Jones would have been glad to make peace and brought most of the Manhattan regulars along with him. The Kennedys have always had an 'in' in Erie, first with Peter Crotty and now with Joe Crangle. If Bobby had really put the arm on Crangle, he could have switched Erie."

If Kennedy were as ruthless and daring as his legend suggests, he might have transformed O'Connor's fears into realities. He tried but he did not try to the maximum of his strength. He never endorsed Nickerson because he would not risk a public defeat. The most he would do was authorize John English, the Democratic leader of Nassau, to tell delegates privately that he (Kennedy) would be pleased if they got behind Nickerson.

Kennedy temporized with Jones after the primary, neither mounting a campaign to drive him from the Manhattan leadership nor coming to an understanding with him. There were persuasive reasons for his caution. He did not want to give credence to Jones's charge, ludicrous though it was, that the Surrogate clash was really a covert racist attack on the nation's only Negro county leader. Moreover, Jones was an ally of Wagner, and Wagner's help might be useful at the convention.*

As for Crangle of Erie County, Kennedy through Steve Smith told him what he told all upstate leaders, which was, simply, to stay uncommitted. Unless and until Nickerson came within striking distance of a majority, there was no point in pressuring the Erie leaders to do what they did not want to do.

Kennedy concentrated his main attack on O'Connor's

---

* Jones retired from the county leadership the following year, blaming his decision partly on Kennedy's refusal to work with him.

strongest point: Brooklyn and the Bronx.* The Steingut-Buckley agreement was the hinge on which O'Connor's strength turned. Buckley, seventy-five, an irascible, outspoken, old-fashioned party boss straight out of the pages of *The Last Hurrah,* was already dying of lung cancer but he had not yet relaxed his grip on power. Like many Irish politicians of the older generation, he saw John Kennedy's election to the Presidency as a kind of justification and fulfillment, and he had a sentimental, almost fatherly affection for Robert Kennedy. The latter now tried to shake the old man from his commitment to O'Connor. Four years before, Buckley had switched to Morgenthau, and he was not averse to switching again, but he had given his word to Steingut and would not move unless they moved together.

Steingut was adamant. His ambition was still fixed upon becoming Speaker of the Assembly. His only prospect of attaining that goal was with the help of a Democratic governor, and he had more reason to hope that Frank O'Connor in the governor's chair would assist him, perhaps by easing Speaker Travia into a judgeship, than would any other candidate. Kennedy's triumph over the Manhattan regulars also had the effect of frightening Steingut. What kind of dangerous ally had he produced for himself by sponsoring Kennedy in New York? Would he be safe if Kennedy's power grew?

When his frontal assault failed to break Buckley or Steingut, Kennedy attacked on their flanks. Having used Roosevelt as a hatchetman in West Virginia in 1960, he now resorted to him again.

---

* A sound Napoleonic tactic. "The principles of war are the same as those of a siege," Napoleon wrote. "Fire must be concentrated on a single point and as soon as the breach is made, the equilibrium is broken and the rest is nothing." Quoted in David G. Chandler, *The Campaigns of Napoleon* (Macmillan, New York, 1966), p. 135.

In the course of canvassing party leaders for their support, Roosevelt had a fascinating conversation with Charlie Buckley at the latter's home in the Bronx. In explaining why he could not support him, Buckley recounted to Roosevelt a meeting that had occurred in the same room exactly one year earlier on July 7, 1965. Present were Buckley, Steingut, Abraham Beame, O'Connor, Lawrence Perez, a lawyer and political adviser to O'Connor, and two businessmen, Martin Tannenbaum of the Yonkers Race Track and Frank Barry of the Circle Line, which operates sightseeing boats around Manhattan Island. According to a memorandum that Roosevelt prepared the next day, this is what occurred as Buckley recalled it:

"Stanley Steingut asked O'Connor to take the second place on a ticket to be headed by Abe Beame for Mayor. Both O'Connor and Perez turned down this suggestion.

"Buckley then told the group about a parallel situation in 1917 when the county leaders of New York City had decided to run Hylan for Mayor and Alfred E. Smith threatened to run against Hylan in the primary. The problem was resolved when the leaders got together with Smith and asked him to run for President of the Board of Aldermen (now the City Council). In return the leaders agreed to back Alfred Smith for Governor the following year. Smith agreed, was elected as President of the Board of Aldermen, and the following year the leaders turned the Governor nomination over to him and he won the election.

"Charlie Buckley then said to Frank O'Connor that he suggested a similar deal with Steingut and himself agreeing to back O'Connor for Governor in 1966 if he would run for President of the Council with Beame in 1965. Buckley then turned to Steingut and asked if he did agree. Steingut gave his agreement. O'Connor and Perez then said this was acceptable to them and O'Connor, therefore, did run for the second spot on the Beame ticket.

"The deal was made and the meeting broke up at 2 A.M. on July 8, 1965.

"Buckley then said to me that he was a man of his word and that he considered himself to be bound by this deal to support O'Connor with the 90 votes he controls in the Bronx delegation—the Reformers have 18. But he then told me to talk to Stanley Steingut and to ask Steingut whether he considered that he was still bound by the deal to support O'Connor. He then said to me that if Steingut was not bound by the deal that he, Charlie Buckley, would consider himself released and in his words, 'I will not be left out on a limb alone.'

". . . I believe that Buckley gave me this information because he does not feel that O'Connor can win and he is looking for a way out of the deal."[6]

Roosevelt showed this memorandum to Kennedy, who encouraged him to circulate it privately among other party leaders. Roosevelt's original hope was that the memorandum would bluff the leaders out of going ahead with the O'Connor nomination. Rather than begin the state campaign by handing the Republicans the issue of "bossism" and "back-room deals," they would turn to another candidate. Kennedy shared this hope although he knew that if there were a shift, Roosevelt would not be the beneficiary.

The contents of the memorandum were "leaked" to the press as was inevitable once it was shown to more than a few people. O'Connor and Beame at first denied that they had attended such a meeting, then said that they had met with Buckley and the others at a later date for the implausible purpose of discussing the direct election of district leaders in the Bronx, and finally agreed that just the two of them had encountered one another at Kennedy Airport and worked out their joint ticket while walking around the parking lot. Kennedy was privately derisive of these scatterbrained cover stories; his view was that the participants should simply have confirmed the fact of the meeting and pointed out that in politics bargaining for future support goes on all the time.

There was little reason to doubt the authenticity of Roosevelt's memorandum. O'Connor would obviously not have agreed to withdraw from the race for mayor without obtaining some *quid pro quo* from Beame's backers. In telling Roosevelt about the arrangement, Buckley was speaking with his characteristic blunt candor and implicitly trusting Roosevelt to abide by the politician's code of protecting confidences. The memorandum's circumstantial details were of a kind that could not be invented since only an old-timer like Buckley would be likely to recall the Smith-Hylan deal of 1917.

The reaction within the Democratic Party to Roosevelt's disclosure was less effective than might have been anticipated. The timing worked against it, since late July when many people are on vacation is not the best time to launch a civic crusade. Roosevelt's enemies naturally discredited his memorandum as the product of a sorehead. Except for the New York *Post*, most of the press was slow to take up the issue, and the *Post* is discounted among many Democrats because of its pronounced editorial sympathy for the Liberal Party. The Liberal Party attacked the "deal," but many Democrats were eager to defy the Liberals and prove that they could win without a Liberal endorsement.

The decisive factor, however, was the unwillingness of any party leader to spell out for the public the significance of Roosevelt's charges and dramatize the underlying issue. That issue was not whether there had been just another deal—scarcely a new event in the long history of politics —but rather whether O'Connor would be a strong, independent governor or only the honest front man for machine politicians and their business allies. The presence at the disputed July 1965 conference of Martin Tannenbaum of Yonkers Raceway symbolized that issue. Tannenbaum is one of three brothers who made a fortune in textiles during World War II and then branched out into other businesses, including harness racing. In 1956, they helped lobby through the New York state legislature a bill establishing a construction fund into which one-half of any future increase in parimutuel receipts at harness tracks would be deposited. The money was used to modernize and expand the tracks. Some legislators asked why these profitable, privately owned businesses could not borrow money from banks for capital improvements or else why the state did not lend the money rather than grant it outright. As one opponent argued, "We might as well take part of the alcoholic beverage tax and start refurbishing all the saloons." But there were enough sympathetic legislators to get the bill enacted into law. It was repealed three years later when the State Investigation Commission disclosed evidence that accounts had been padded and that much of the subcontracting on the construction had been done by firms controlled by gangsters. During those three years, $21 million in public funds from racing receipts had been committed to pay for construction at Yonkers Raceway.

Other good fortune came to the track from a beneficent government in Albany. The New York Thruway, a six-lane super-highway, was routed right by the track's front gate. The state paid $775,000 to the raceway for right-of-way land that had been carried on the track's books as worth only $100,000.[7]

Tannenbaum contributed to both political parties and was equally adroit in lobbying the legislators of both parties, but he was especially active in political campaigns in which Charlie Buckley was interested. He had, for example, raised over $100,000 for Beame's mayoral campaign. His track also provided jobs for Buckley's rank-and-file supporters, thereby serving as an extragovernmental source of patronage. There was nothing illegal in Tannenbaum's activities; indeed, lawfulness was an essential feature of his operation. But should this man and men like him choose the Democratic Party's candidates for mayor and governor?

This was the question that no leading Democrat was willing to raise in the summer of 1966. In past campaigns, Robert Wagner had campaigned against Buckley, Steingut, and their backers. In the Surrogate primary, Kennedy had charged that the bipartisan arrangement worked out by the party bosses was tainted by "suspicion of corruption." But he could scarcely bring himself to raise the same suspicions against Buckley, his father's old friend and his brother's first supporter in New York. Since Roosevelt was obviously too self-interested to be effective by himself and no one else would dramatize his charges, the "deal" sensation was muffled.*

There were ten weeks between the Surrogate primary in late June and the Democratic state convention in early September but after three or four weeks, it was clear that the psychological impact of the Surrogate primary had faded. Then came Roosevelt's disclosure, which was first made known on July 23. When this failed to change sentiment, Kennedy by August 10 was willing to abandon his resistance. John English, Nickerson's manager, pleaded for one more week, and Kennedy let him go ahead with his soliciting of delegate support using his (Kennedy's) name for another several days.

O'Connor counter-attacked. He negotiated with the leaders of Suffolk County, among them Congressman Otis Pike, the same man who had made the nominating speech for Representative Sam Stratton against Kennedy for the senatorial nomination in 1964. Suffolk's delegates caucused and declared for O'Connor. Suffolk is back-door

---

* The chief effect was that O'Connor lost Tannenbaum's money-raising talents. He announced, after he was nominated, that he was barring "racetrack people" from his campaign, and Tannenbaum was seen no more around Democratic headquarters.

neighbor on Long Island to Nickerson's home county of Nassau. Without the support of the other suburban counties, Nickerson clearly had no chance.

So the nomination of O'Connor went forward and under the guidance of its professionals the Democratic Party drifted inexorably to another defeat, its sixth in the past seven statewide elections. It was increasingly clear that the Liberals planned to run Roosevelt as an independent candidate. Kennedy let it be known that he doubted if O'Connor could win without the backing of the Liberal Party and without the editorial support of any major newspapers. He floated a trial balloon for another prestige candidate, Sol Linowitz, the board chairman of the Xerox Corporation. But nothing availed. On August 15, Nickerson withdrew. The next day, after a breakfast conference with O'Connor in Washington, Kennedy issued a declaration of neutrality.

"On the basis of information I have been able to gather over the last several weeks, I am convinced that a number of distinguished Democrats can defeat Governor Rockefeller," Kennedy said.

". . . It is the responsibility of the convention delegates to make the assessment as to which candidate combines the qualities to best serve the state and attract the broadest coalition of support to win in November. I do not plan to support or oppose any individual candidate prior to the convention."[8]

The ticket nominated at the state convention in Buffalo on September 8 provided a final fillip to Kennedy's summer of frustration. He attended the opening day of the convention, conferred with O'Connor on the lesser nominees, and then left for Washington. When the agreed-upon slate was submitted to the convention, the upstate delegates organized a revolt in favor of Samuels for lieutenant governor. At the critical moment, Jones threw the support of the Manhattan delegates behind Samuels.

Rather than risk a defeat on the floor, O'Connor let the delegates have their way. One of his aides then passed the word to newspapermen that O'Connor had been willing to accept Samuels all along, but had ruled him out in deference to Senator Kennedy's well-known antipathy to Samuels. Kennedy, in fact, scarcely cared about the identity of O'Connor's running mates since he did not expect any of them to be elected. But these little games at his expense had to be countered for the sake of his own prestige. Publicly disavowing any animosity toward Samuels, he arranged one of those ritualistic press conferences in which politicians trade compliments. As with his public reconciliation with Travia and Zaretzki after his failure to unseat them as leaders of the legislature, Kennedy had to make the best of an unsatisfactory situation.

In the campaign itself, Kennedy made a limited commitment of his forces. Steve Smith agreed to serve as campaign "coordinator" but not as campaign manager. Kennedy and Smith refused to raise any funds for the campaign. They also declined to ask Papert, Koenig & Lois, their favorite advertising agency, to handle O'Connor's campaign. The agency was reluctant to take the assignment, but no one doubted that it would do so if Kennedy asked.

Yet Kennedy made more than a score of appearances around the state for O'Connor, and Smith gave the limping campaign such direction as it received.

"Frank never really had a manager," one O'Connor staff man recalled. "There was naturally tension between his friends from Queens and the Kennedy people. The two never really meshed, and Smith would not force it. I sat in meetings in which a decision could have been made on the question under discussion if the man at the head of the table wanted to make it, but when there was no consensus, Smith did not give orders. I don't think that's how he ran Bobby's campaign in '64."

Rockefeller defeated O'Connor by nearly 400,000 votes. The results were Rockefeller 2,690,000, O'Connor 2,298,-000, and Roosevelt 507,000.

"Win or lose, changes should be made in the party," Kennedy said in an interview on the weekend before Election Day, 1966. In the aftermath of the election, the inevitable round of newspaper stories asserted that Kennedy was now in a position to "pick up the pieces," take charge of the Democratic Party, and rebuild its organization.

His record as a politician in New York provides little support for these assumptions. The guerrilla warfare for the leadership of the legislature ending in an ambush, the erratic interventions in the mayoralty campaign, the refusal to offer open battle for the governorship—this is a record of defeat, inconsequence, and confused purposes. Aside from his own election to the Senate, his one success was the Surrogate primary, which was a lightning-swift sortie rather than a major, prolonged effort. That success accorded with the nature of his previous political experience. Before coming to New York, Kennedy had gained all his experience managing his brother's campaigns. He was working with an exceptional candidate with whom he had complete rapport; he also had unlimited funds, a corps of volunteers with which he could bypass the regular organization if necessary, and full time to devote to winning the election. On the morning after one of those campaigns, he could walk away and leave Massachusetts as he found it, having no responsibility for its party organization. As his brother's political agent during the presidential years, he had political influence on a national scale and so diverse in its nature that it was not comparable to state party-building.

Kennedy is a superb campaign organizer, the political equivalent of a hundred-yard-dash man, but reorganizing a party is slow, time-consuming work, more like a ten-mile cross-country run. It involves attending scores of meetings, keeping in touch with hundreds of local politicians, and maintaining a vast correspondence. In some states, it would be possible for the chairman of the State Committee to undertake this work. However, in New York, the state chairmanship has historically been a powerless post. James A. Farley carried the title as so much excess baggage for nearly fifteen years, during much of that time serving also as national chairman and Postmaster General. The state chairman is normally the agent of the incumbent governor and in the absence of a governor, he is named by whoever in the party has the most patronage to dispense. In the pre-Kennedy years, it was usually Mayor Wagner. Kennedy has obtained the election of John Burns, a former mayor of Binghamton, at an annual salary of thirty thousand dollars. Since the committee was six hundred thousand dollars in debt at the time of Burns's election in 1965, politicians assume that Kennedy guarantees the payment of this salary. Burns, a tall, likable, soft-spoken man of forty-three, is by temperament a peacemaker. As a mediator among factions and a discreet Kennedy emissary, he performs a useful role but he does not have the personal prestige or authority to make decisions, attract recruits, or draw crowds to party meetings. Only Kennedy can provide that kind of leadership.

Through Burns, Kennedy in early 1967 arranged the appointment of Theodore Sorensen, once his brother's most important assistant and now a practicing New York attorney, as chairman of a top-level advisory committee on plans to strengthen the party for the future. Kennedy himself in a speech to party leaders exhorted them to get the party active in their communities in year-round work on civic problems such as juvenile delinquency, slums, and racial integration. But a study committee and an occasional speech do not add up to party reorganization.

Kennedy is actually remote and inaccessible to most

lesser politicians in New York. Two well-known members of the State Senate, both admirers of his, said privately in January 1967 that in the preceding year, Kennedy had talked to them only once. An upstate county chairman who is an enthusiastic Kennedyite in public confesses that he is not certain that the Senator would know him if they were to meet on the street. These are not the relationships of a master politician intent upon rebuilding his party.

Kennedy let it be known in November 1966 that he intended to spend almost all of his time during the next three months in New York in order to concentrate on the constitutional convention, which began meeting in April to rewrite the state's fundamental law. (This was before Kennedy realized how much of his time he would be devoting in that period to the Manchester book controversy.) The Democrats won control of the convention, and Kennedy appointed teams of lawyers, businessmen, and educators to prepare policy papers.

"The Senator said all along that the election of convention delegates was more important than the gubernatorial election," declared William vanden Heuvel, lawyer and Kennedy confidant, who was elected a delegate. "He wants to leave his mark on the new constitution."[9]

Once again, Kennedy's reach considerably exceeded his grasp. Most of the Democratic delegates were judges, legislators, and district leaders, all of them defenders of this or that part of the status quo. As president of the convention, they chose Anthony Travia, the same party wheelhorse Kennedy had tried to block two years earlier as Speaker of the Assembly.

Unlike John Kennedy, who coolly kept his distance from the misgovernment of Massachusetts and from most of his party's factional fights, Robert Kennedy has a recurrent impulse to dabble and dominate. This is to his credit; he cares more and more passionately about electing an honest judge and an effective governor than his brother did. His involvement is also a reflexive response; he is a combative man with an itch to run things. But he does not persist day in and day out in the struggle to reshape the Democratic Party into a serviceable instrument of reform government and social idealism. At bottom, he lacks the patience and the interest to rebuild a party at the state and local level. And there is good reason to doubt whether it is to his own advantage to devote a major portion of his time and energy to it. His personal horizon extends far beyond the Hudson River. A man who wants to be President can get closer to his goal traveling to South Africa or Berkeley, California, than he can addressing party meetings in Great Neck or Gloversville. To win the presidential nomination, all that Kennedy needs to control is New York's delegation to the national convention, and that control is reasonably assured.

The outlook is for more Democratic defeats and more Kennedy frustration. Defeat only breeds defeat, and disintegration only produces more disintegration. Rather than getting picked up, the pieces only get more fragmented. Unless Kennedy evinces a willingness in the future to break with the party regulars, fight them openly for control, and devote much more time consistently to party affairs, the momentum of mediocrity will run on. The likelihood is that the Democratic candidate for mayor of New York in 1969 may be the same Frank O'Connor and for governor in 1970 the same Anthony Travia. They will presumably go down to defeat before more sophisticated, more attractive, and better financed Republicans of the Rockefeller-Lindsay-Javits variety. The Democrats are not in shape to win back New York's City Hall or the governor's Mansion in Albany. But even without them, Kennedy can carry New York in his own drive to win back the White House. No New York Democrat, be he regular or reformer, can challenge him. The risk he runs is that the successful New York Republicans have leaders whose ambitions also run beyond the Hudson. If Nelson Rockefeller, Jacob Javits, and John Lindsay can defeat Robert Kennedy's party in New York, they may be the men to defeat it in the nation.

NOTES

[1] The Hamill quote is from New York *Post*, June 29, 1966; the second and third quotes from *The New York Times*, July 1, 1966.

[2] *National Observer*, September 5, 1966.

[3] New York *Post*, August 16, 1966.

[4] For Roosevelt's detailed criticism of Humphrey's war record, see *The New York Times*, May 7, 1960; for his apology, *The New York Times*, June 23, 1960.

[5] Confidential source.

[6] The text of Roosevelt's memorandum was printed as an advertisement in *The New York Times* on July 29, 1966.

[7] See excellent series by Michael J. Berlin, Marvin Smilon, and Leonard Katz, "The Tannenbaum Brothers: Horses, Taxis, Money and Politics," New York *Post*, October 31–November 5, 1966.

[8] *The New York Times*, August 17, 1966.

[9] *Ibid.*, November 14, 1966.

CHAPTER NINE

The Rivals

*"It seems to me that Senator Kennedy would easily win
against Romney. And in a second Nixon-Kennedy contest
. . . the prodigious Kennedy myth would operate against
Nixon. I do not hesitate to say that if Robert Kennedy
were the Democratic candidate, the best man to beat him
would be Governor Rockefeller."*
—CLARE BOOTHE LUCE, McCall's, *March 1967*

"Lindsay—The District's Pride, The Nation's Hope"
—John V. Lindsay's campaign slogan, *1964*

THE ROAD to the White House does not run through
Albany.

Nelson Rockefeller resigned as a Special Assistant to
President Eisenhower on December 31, 1955, and spent
the next two and one-half years in a carefully calculated
and successful pursuit of the governorship of New York.
His purpose was not to bring better government to the
Finger Lakes or to restore the blessings of a balanced budget to the commuters of Westchester County. He wanted a
solid base of elective political power from which he could
return as a dominant figure to the scene of his real interests: Washington, D.C., and the great issues of world
affairs.

He made it to Albany, and has been marooned there
ever since. By the fall of 1966, he had no choice except
to seek a third four-year term if he was even to stay alive
as a public figure. He doggedly campaigned in each of

New York's sixty-two counties, and his campaign literature set forth some exciting accomplishments of the previous eight years:

"Legislation to combat bill padding, price gouging, and fraudulent selling techniques by funeral directors.

"New Division of Motor Boats.

"Initiated new program of land treatment which has virtually eradicated golden nematode as a threat to the potato industry.

"Reorganized State Police and expanded force by 1,000 troopers.

"Permanent State Office for the Aging in the Executive Department."

Raising his eyes and gazing at the horizon across a land free of the menace of price-gouging funeral directors, golden nematode (virtually), and unregulated motor boats, Governor Rockefeller occasionally thinks of Washington, where in those same eight years three successive Presidents have grappled with the life-and-death challenges of Vietnam, the Soviet Union, Communist China, General de Gaulle, and Castro's Cuba.

And although he is naturally ebullient, Nelson Rockefeller thinks of these matters and he is sad.

Rockefeller began his political career by destroying the presidential dreams of Governor Averell Harriman, once dubbed "the Albany Adenauer." In the spring of 1958, private polls showed Harriman winning reelection in November with 60 per cent of the vote against any Republican opponent. If he had been successful, Harriman planned a major drive for the Democratic presidential nomination two years later with only his age as a serious obstacle—he was to be sixty-eight in 1960. Rockefeller and Harriman are remarkably similar. Both are handsome, physically tireless, relentlessly ambitious and able. Both inherited great wealth, although Rockefeller is vastly richer. Both entered public life through appointive jobs conferred by Franklin D. Roosevelt. Both have held a wide variety of important posts in the federal government, but their deepest interest is the same: foreign affairs, and particularly the cold war challenge of the Communists.

In the election of 1958, Harriman proved unexpectedly vulnerable. Always an awkward speaker, he did not improve with practice. The most visible trait he brought to politics was determination; it had earlier enabled him to master every challenge from croquet and championship polo to railroading and Kremlinology. Often effective in talking to a small group of people, Harriman could occasionally break through before larger audiences with a burst of spontaneous passion that was convincing and moving. But these moments of eloquence were infrequent and unpredictable; most often, the passion remained clotted at the source, and he wandered ineffectually through fields of cliché and broken syntax, uttering now and then a strident imprecation against the Republican enemy. Against the late Irving Ives, his Republican opponent in 1954, Harriman's failings as a candidate were unimportant. Ives by then was a weary, used-up man who had no keen desire to leave his quiet berth in the U.S. Senate and seek the governorship.

Rockefeller was another story. He pulsed with enthusiasm and the zest to win. Only moderately better than Harriman in reading a prepared text, he communicated a delightful sense of zest and warmth and optimism as a street corner campaigner. He plunged into crowds like a beggar diving for a dollar; "Hi, ya, fella," he exclaimed with a grin, his eyes crinkling into small laugh lines; he ate Nathan's Famous Frankfurters at Coney Island, munched bagels and lox on the Lower East Side, and wolfed pizza like a hungry twelve-year-old. His gusto was his own and largely unforeseen. It also turned out that a

Rockefeller is not, like Harriman, just another rich man. A Rockefeller is part of the American legend and language: there is a New York landmark (Rockefeller Center), an American institution (Rockefeller Foundation), and even an item on the menu (Oysters Rockefeller). From old John D. with the prune-wrinkled face and the famous dimes through John D., Jr., who restored Williamsburg, Virginia, saved the Hudson Palisades, and donated the land on which the UN is built, and on to the five Rockefeller brothers of the present, the family has itself become an American institution. Its incomprehensibly huge fortune (perhaps $10 *billion* or more) makes the members of the family objects of fascination as much as envy. The awe, the curiosity, the admiration, both open and sneaking, redounded to Nelson Rockefeller's benefit as a candidate. In his first campaign, he had the fresh glamor of a new baseball hero or a film star. Just to have shaken hands with him became a conversation piece. Harriman could not compete in this glamor league.*

Rockefeller stirred echoes of the past. He reminded many people of Franklin Roosevelt; it was his style as a patrician democrat, his air of absolute confidence, and perhaps even the similarity in names. Whatever the reason, reporters traveling with him sometimes heard older voters make a slip of the tongue: "God bless you, Mr. Roosevelt!"

Election Day, 1958, was a disaster for Republicans across the nation. The loss of twelve seats in the Senate and forty-seven in the House foreshadowed the end of the Eisenhower era two years later. But in New York, it was as if the Grand Old Party had discovered a new Vermont.

---

* The league now extends to Arkansas where Nelson's brother Winthrop, a Republican, has been elected governor and to West Virginia, where his nephew, John D., IV, a Democrat, has been elected a member of the state legislature and is already talked of for governor.

Rockefeller defeated Harriman by 573,000 votes. He carried Representative Kenneth Keating to the U.S. Senate and maintained the usual Republican majorities in both houses of the legislature. Seeing Rockefeller come from political obscurity to capture the gubernatorial nomination and then blitz Harriman, many observers were impelled to pessimistic speculations about Richard Nixon's future. Would not the story of New York in 1958 become the story of the nation in 1960?

Upon his election in 1958, Rockefeller took command of one of the more powerful Republican parties in the nation. In his subsequent efforts to sell himself as a presidential candidate to the hard-shelled Republican organizations around the country, Rockefeller liked to point out that since the New York GOP controlled the governorship, both U.S. Senate seats, and substantial majorities in both houses of the legislature, New York ranked with Kansas as one of the two most Republican states. Most conservatives never quite bought this argument in 1959–60 or in 1963–64 although it was statistically true. They noted that New York is notoriously unfaithful to the GOP in national elections, and they doubted that New York Republicans are of the same breed as themselves.

The hard core of the New York Republican Party is, in fact, very much the same as its counterpart in Ohio or Iowa. The dairy farmer in Chenango County, the bank manager in New Paltz, and the suburban matron in Scarsdale are as orthodox and conservative in their social viewpoints as successful farmers, small businessmen, and prosperous suburbanites in the Middle West. They believe that taxes are too high, government interferes too much in the conduct of private business, and most social welfare programs are probably excessive because anyone can get along in this country if he just stands up on his hind legs and takes care of himself. Republicans of this viewpoint accepted Nelson Rockefeller in 1958 because of his family name and background; a Rockefeller, by definition, must be a good person and a sound conservative. When, upon taking office, he immediately requested a substantial tax increase, he distressed these voters, and they have been increasingly uneasy about him ever since. By the end of his first term in 1962, the new Conservative Party had been formed for the chief purpose of defeating Rockefeller; it failed in that objective but its candidate, David H. Jacquith, an unknown upstate businessman, polled 141,000 votes. An equally obscure Conservative candidate four years later polled 520,000 votes, many of them anti-Rockefeller protest votes. Most orthodox Republicans voted each time for Rockefeller, of course, because participation in minority parties is not part of their style; they are as "regular" as old-time Tammany Democrats, but they have stayed with their party with diminished enthusiasm and more than a little grumbling.

The significant difference between Republicans in New York and those in the Middle West is not in their economic status or social outlook, but in the strength of their opposition and the sophistication of their own leadership. Rank-and-file New York Republicans, if left to their own devices and prejudices, would rarely win a statewide election because New York City, which used to cast almost half the statewide vote and still contributes forty per cent of it, is heavily Democratic. The party leadership has met this difficulty by refusing to allow the rank-and-file to have its own way; the leaders regularly choose candidates who are somewhat more liberal than their followers and who can appeal to independents and Democrats. This sophisticated strategy has kept the Republicans in power for most of the past twenty-five years in a state where the Democrats have a lead in registration of over eight hundred thousand.

The Republicans were a long time learning this lesson.

They elected a Republican governor in the Harding landslide of 1920 and did not elect another for twenty years. When Governor Nathan Miller conceded defeat to Alfred E. Smith in 1922, he said, accurately enough: "Evidently the voters prefer your brand of government to mine." Mr. Miller became counsel for United States Steel, while Smith, Franklin D. Roosevelt, and Herbert H. Lehman over the next two decades transformed New York from a normally Republican to a normally Democratic state.

The Republican comeback started with Thomas E. Dewey, and the party which Rockefeller inherited is largely Dewey's creation. In his first race for governor in 1938, Dewey, then an exciting young District Attorney of thirty-five, rallied to the polls virtually every potential upstate Republican voter and came down to the New York City line ahead by 619,000 votes. But the city produced a 683,000-vote majority for Lehman. On his next attempt Dewey won easily, but the way was opened by a Democratic division. In 1942, Lehman retired and James A. Farley carried his feud with President Roosevelt into the Democratic state convention to force the nomination of state Attorney General John J. Bennett, a lackluster candidate who could not hold the support of the liberal Democrats.

Once in office, Dewey exploited with masterly skill the opportunities for broadening his base of support. He courted the growing Negro and Puerto Rican vote with a fair employment practices law. He pushed for low-income and middle-income housing and kept rent control on the statute books long after it had been dispensed with in every other state. He neutralized the opposition of trade unions to the Republican Party by improving workmen's compensation, by appointing union officials to public office, and by refusing to sponsor anti-union legislation during the post-war period when resentment against strikes was high. None of these moves changed the Republican Party into the party of the working class; but Dewey did reduce the size of Democratic majorities in the city sufficiently so that upstate Republican strength could prevail. Equally important, his record and his progressive approach convinced the young married voters in the newer suburbs, whose number shot up in the post-war decade, that the Republican Party is modern-minded and responsive to their needs. As a result, although their parents back in Brooklyn and the Bronx were still voting Democratic, many of these "young marrieds" were voting Republican in the new Long Island subdivisions.

Rockefeller has carried forward and considerably expanded this positive approach to government. To rescue the commuter railroads, he sponsored the creation of the Metropolitan Commuter Transportation Authority, which purchased the Long Island Rail Road, the nation's biggest commuter line, for $65 million and undertook a major modernization program.

On civil rights, Rockefeller and the New York Republicans have moved far beyond their party in Congress. New York not only bans racial discrimination in the sale or rental of private housing and commercial space but also specifically forbids discriminatory practices by real estate brokers, banks, and savings-and-loan associations. New York is also the first state in the country to require municipalities to devise a plan for racial integration in order to qualify for state urban renewal assistance.

Water pollution, which during the 1960s has become one of the big, new environmental issues, provided Rockefeller an opportunity to act. Under his leadership, the voters approved in 1965 a bond issue to pay for the state's share of a $1.6 billion pure water program. With regard to another environmental issue—recreation, Rockefeller sponsored a land acquisition program, costing $100 million to protect 360,000 acres of open space and develop new facilities. Education at the college and university level was one area where the Dewey administration and the Republican legislature fell down badly. Rockefeller had been in office for some years before he responded to the plight of the new state university, which was grandiose on paper but an administrative chaos in reality. By the end of his second term, however, there was a $1 billion fund to construct new buildings, enrollment had tripled to more than 100,000 students, the number of scholarships had kept pace with that growth, and the faculties had been enlarged and strengthened in quality. The state's appropriation for higher education rose in less than a decade from $93 million to $535. New York is now well on its way to emulating California in the creation of a complete system of public higher education, even to the extent of choosing Dr. Samuel Gould, formerly president of the University of California at Santa Barbara, to serve as state university chancellor.

Some of Rockefeller's initiatives as governor betrayed a yearning for a larger stage. Does New York really need an Atomic and Space Development Authority? Is the desalting of ocean water primarily a state responsibility? But Rockefeller likes to think big, and so do many "swing voters" in New York. His positive, enthusiastic approach to government leadership kept the Democrats off-stride and put the Republicans, in his favorite phrase, "in the mainstream" of life in the 1960s.

Timing is crucial in any bid for the Presidency. By the cruel nature of the presidential political system, success on the first attempt is essential. Even those few, such as Thomas E. Dewey and Adlai E. Stevenson, who get a second chance never succeed where first they failed. Rockefeller's sense of timing failed him in 1959–60 and again in 1963–64. In each instance, his failure of judgment developed out of the nature of his strength.

One of his strengths is his enormous personal fortune.

It provided him with immediate entrée into the top levels of the Republican Party in New York when he decided to seek the governorship. Much earlier, it gained him access to President Franklin D. Roosevelt and led to his appointment as Coordinator of Inter-American Affairs at thirty-two. Wealth has inevitably conditioned Rockefeller to the conviction that the decisions that matter are made in the executive suite. But politics is one activity where this rule does not always hold true. No man or no small group of men can control or definitively predict the actions of millions of individual voters. Rockefeller overlooked this truism in the fall of 1959 as he made his round of duty calls on the wealthy businessmen and political leaders of his party. Wherever he could speak directly to the voters and to the rank-and-file party workers, he received a warm reception, but the moneymen and the political bosses were cool. They had reached a consensus in favor of Richard Nixon. He was a capable campaigner and a known quantity; he was safe, conservative, and a regular, yet not stodgy or old-fashioned. In short, he was not great but he would do. These men of power warned Rockefeller that if he disturbed this consensus, they would stand firm against him.

Coolness from the elite was a new experience for Rockefeller. Accustomed to making things happen by convincing the people at the levers of power, he quickly concluded that his cause was hopeless. On December 31, 1959, four years after he had left Eisenhower's White House staff to seek national power on his own, he issued his fatal statement of renunciation. "The men who control the Republican Party have made it plain that they do not want a contest for the nomination," he said bluntly.

The statement was an error tactically and strategically. Tactically, it offended loyal Republicans who did not like to see one of their national leaders suggest, in effect, that their party's nomination was rigged. Strategically, it was a miscalculation. If he had fought Nixon in the primaries for the nomination, he stood close to a fifty-fifty chance of winning. It would have been a savage, rending struggle like the Taft-Eisenhower contest of 1952, but its outcome was not certain to be in Nixon's favor. Nixon was popular with the party workers, but Rockefeller was exciting to the ordinary voters. Nixon already had the smell of defeat about him; while Rockefeller then had the air and assurance of a natural winner. Nixon would have the Midwestern party organizations and most of the South, but Rockefeller commanded New York, had allies in other Eastern states, and might have shifted the sentiment of the party with one or two primary victories. Nixon's appeal to the party—as to the nation—was widespread but thin and superficial; it was vulnerable to the counterappeal of a dramatic new figure. Rockefeller might well have been that figure; instead, it turned out to be John Kennedy.

Rockefeller, who virtually personifies the power of positive thinking, spends little time on regrets, but his 1959 withdrawal is one decision which he has come as close to regretting as anything he has ever done. The regrets began almost as soon as the statement was issued. By late spring, it led him to an uncharacteristically impractical, half-hearted flirtation with a draft movement. Drafts can occur in presidential politics, but there has to be a multiplicity of weak candidates with the logic of the situation pointing to one strong, unavowed candidate. The Democrats found themselves in that situation in 1952 when they turned to Adlai Stevenson. But in 1960, the Republicans did not have many candidates; they had only Nixon and the logic of events—his eight-year apprenticeship in the Vice-Presidency, his tacit backing from General Eisenhower, his popularity with the party machines, his relatively good showing in the public opinion polls—pointed toward his nomination, not away from it.

Yet under these circumstances, Rockefeller suddenly decided to make a public fight for a platform more to his liking: stronger for civil rights and social welfare programs and calling for increased defense spending. Such a platform made intellectual sense only if Rockefeller were to be the candidate; it made political sense only if he were attempting to revive his candidacy. Rockefeller, however, saw it as a fight for principle, and that is how it is presented in sympathetic biographies. More probably, the fight over the platform is understandable only in psychiatric terms: Rockefeller was venting the aggression that had not found its natural outlet in a straight-out fight with Nixon in the primaries.

Nixon with his usual opportunism made nonsense of the whole platform controversy. He visited Rockefeller in New York, accepted the essence of the governor's demands except for minor jousting over language, and then proceeded to forget most of these platform pledges during the campaign.

This platform fuss further weakened Rockefeller. He offended Republicans who were otherwise well disposed toward him by what they construed as his deliberate attempt to embarrass the party's new leader on the eve of his nomination. It created an unhelpful impression of amateurism mixed with arrogance. It also soured his personal relationship with General Eisenhower. Rockefeller had never been one of his intimates, but their relationship, though formal, had been reasonably friendly during Rockefeller's service in the Administration. Eisenhower preferred Nixon as the nominee because he was fiscally more conservative, but he was not hostile to Rockefeller. Rockefeller's criticism of the Administration's record on defense spending, disarmament, and conduct of the cold war altered everything. Eisenhower since 1960 has exchanged letters with Rockefeller and received him in audience twice, but he has never been willing to do the slightest thing that would advance the younger man's career. In the days in early June 1964, when even an implicit Eisenhower disavowal of Barry Goldwater would have been important in the California primary and an outright endorsement of Rockefeller would probably have been decisive, the old general made no move.

Rockefeller's second bid for the Presidency was crippled from the outset by adverse public reaction to his marital difficulties. In 1962, he was divorced from his wife of more than thirty years and the mother of his five children. The dissolution of what outsiders had regarded as a happy marriage shattered Rockefeller's image as a solid, middle-aged family man surrounded by attractive children and grandchildren. He then became "the other man" in a divorce case in which his wife-to-be yielded custody of her four small children in order to gain her freedom. In an ideal world, these painful private events would have no political impact since they in no way affect Rockefeller's views on public issues or his capacity to hold high office. But in choosing a President, the public is not only registering a judgment on issues and parties but also casting a vote of confidence in one man's moral character and emotional strength. At least for a time, many of his fellow citizens revised downward their previous estimate of Rockefeller's personal qualities.

Rockefeller, however, refused to heed the storm warnings. His extraordinary self-confidence and buoyant optimism convinced him that he would come out all right if he just sailed through the storm. Only after he had encountered a series of disasters from New Hampshire to California did he acknowledge what ordinary mortals had recognized from the first: 1964 was his year to stay close to port.

An urbane Democratic Senator once suggested in private the only solution that might have solved Rockefeller's public relations problems at that time.

"Rocky should have tried the Duke of Windsor gambit," this Democrat suggested. "When he got married a second time, he should have said, 'I am giving up my chance for the Presidency for the woman I love.' If he had said that, the same public that was ready to tear him apart would have been clamoring for him to run."

Historical reality, as distinguished from tradition, provides little support for the belief that the New York governorship is a good jumping-off place for the Presidency. In the past hundred years, only two men—Grover Cleveland and Franklin D. Roosevelt—have gone directly from Albany to the White House. A third—Theodore Roosevelt —needed the fateful assist of McKinley's assassination. The tradition holds better for winning the nomination since five others—Horatio Seymour, Samuel Tilden, Charles Evans Hughes, Alfred E. Smith, and Thomas E. Dewey —at least got that far.

But if tradition is an uncertain support, hope is a powerful motive force. Rockefeller's decisive victory in winning a third term revived his hope of achieving the Presidency. Six months before the 1966 election, his own polls showed that less than thirty per cent of the voters favored his reelection; State Senator John Hughes of Syracuse, one of the Republican Party's upstate conservative stalwarts, was openly leading an effort to replace him with Senator Javits; and one of the governor's brothers advised him to retire rather than risk probable defeat. Under these circumstances, Rockefeller's reelection had the dramatic quality of a personal comeback. He again proved that he is a formidable campaigner.

Rockefeller remains the Republican Party's most experienced and best qualified man for the Presidency. At thirty-two, he became Coordinator for Inter-American Affairs in 1940; four years later, he became Assistant Secretary of State for Latin America and was an important participant in the San Francisco Conference that organized the United Nations. In 1950, he returned to government as chairman of the committee that set up the "Point Four" technical assistance program. In the Eisenhower administration, he reshaped the old Federal Security Agency into the new Cabinet-level Department of Health, Education, and Welfare, and served in 1953–54 as its Undersecretary. In 1955, as a foreign affairs adviser on President Eisenhower's staff, he was instrumental in pushing the "Open Skies" program at the Geneva summit meeting. In the interim between leaving Washington and his election as governor, he organized the Rockefeller Brothers Fund studies of foreign policy, national defense, foreign trade and aid, economic development, and education. As Walter Lippmann once remarked, these Rockefeller Reports were the intellectual basis for John Kennedy's 1960 campaign. When Kennedy cried, "Let's get this country moving again," he was pointing the country in the directions charted by the teams of experts that Rockefeller had assembled.

Merely to cite Rockefeller's record is to underscore the comparatively shallow experience of competitors like George Romney and Charles Percy. Moreover, Latin America is likely to be of crucial importance in the years just ahead, and that continent and its problems have been Rockefeller's strongest interest for more than thirty years. He is fluent in Spanish, vacations annually at his ranch in Venezuela, and has dealt as a government official and private citizen with two generations of Latin American leaders.

Clare Boothe Luce, who argued for the logic of his candidacy in the March 1967 *McCall's*, is not alone in thinking that Rockefeller would make the strongest Republican nominee against Kennedy. His experience, his liberalism, and his zest as a campaigner would provide keen competition, while his age—sixty in 1968—would actually be a drawing card for voters who distrusted Kennedy's youthful style.

Since Rockefeller in his two past attempts has seemed to have a tin ear for the sensibilities of the Republican Party outside of New York, he is fortunate that his final attempt, if there is one, will depend more upon the cool assessment of the party's power brokers than upon his skill in courting the delegates. The odds are not in his favor, but a man as rich, resolute, and persistent as Rockefeller can sometimes make his own luck. It is just possible that he may yet find the route from Albany to Washington.

If 1972 is Robert Kennedy's year, the New York Republicans have another potential candidate who would be delighted to oppose him.

John V. Lindsay is not embarrassed to be called "The Republican Kennedy"—but he means JFK, not RFK. In his winning campaign for mayor of New York City in 1965, Lindsay shamelessly invited comparison with the late President by paraphrasing some of his famous lines: "Let's get this city moving again" and "As a great American who was killed while serving his government said, 'Ask not what your government can do for you, but what you can do for your government and your city'."

Tall, tousle-haired, and strikingly handsome, articulate, intelligent, and determinedly ambitious, Lindsay has some notable similarities with John Kennedy. He, too, is a deeply tanned, coolly elegant Ivy League Lancelot come to rescue a disordered Camelot. There are some substantial differences as well, as Robert Kennedy is not the last to point out. But in political terms, the similarities are more impressive and significant. If the GOP turns to a Kennedy-type candidate, there is no one else in the party remotely as well cast for the role as Lindsay.

Although sharing some qualities with John Kennedy and emulating certain others, Lindsay has for years been feuding and tilting with brother Robert. When the latter

conferred with the Soviet ambassador in 1961 and report-
edly discussed the Berlin crisis of that summer, Lindsay,
then a second-term Congressman, fired off a note to Secretary of State Dean Rusk asserting that "I am deeply
disturbed" because such a meeting "bypasses your office
and your department, and in so doing runs great risks."

"It appears," Lindsay wrote, "to be part of a growing
pattern—namely, the conduct of foreign relations in a
casual or loose-reined *ad hoc* manner, too often involving
personalities untrained in foreign policy and the art of
diplomacy. . . . I would appreciate your frank opinion as
to whether this is a proper way to conduct foreign policy
in general or to negotiate on the explosive question of
Berlin."

When Robert Kennedy made his trip to Indonesia in
1962 and other excursions into foreign affairs, Lindsay
jabbed each time with a letter to Rusk or a speech in the
House. Occasionally, he made a generalized attack: "Time
spent on . . . the [Justice] department's legislative program—civil rights, for example—would be time better
spent than meddling in the area of foreign policy, ham-
burger fries in the great halls of the U.S. Department of
Justice and other superficial publicity gimmicks."

Lindsay had a proprietary attitude toward the Justice
Department, having served for more than a year as executive assistant to one of Kennedy's predecessors, former
Attorney General Herbert Brownell. He also had sound
political logic behind his needling. Lindsay was often
under attack within his own party, even being censured
by the New York Young Republicans of which he had once
been president, for his votes in behalf of Kennedy administration bills. By leading partisan raids against Robert
Kennedy, he helped retain his *bona fides* as a Republican.

Lindsay also had principled differences with Robert
Kennedy's decision to "litigate, not legislate" on civil

rights issues in 1961–62 and with certain of his positions on civil liberties.

Their most memorable clash occurred when Kennedy appeared as the first witness before the House Judiciary Committee in behalf of his brother's civil rights proposals. (They formed the basis of the historic Civil Rights Act of 1964.)

"Let's be frank about this," Lindsay said. "There are rumors in the cloakrooms all over Capitol Hill that the Administration and the leaders have made a deal to scuttle public accommodations [as a section in the bill]."

Kennedy replied angrily, "I am surprised that you would come out in open hearings and say you've heard rumors in the cloakroom without any further substantiation. Neither the President nor I have to defend our good faith to you or anyone else."

Despite this jousting, Lindsay and Kennedy worked responsibly together in the many compromises and redraftings that finally produced the civil rights bill. But their personal animosity has lingered. On the Kennedy side, Lindsay is regarded as an intellectual lightweight; an official who worked with Kennedy on the civil rights bill said of Lindsay, "He ain't very bright but he sure is pretty." On Lindsay's side, Kennedy is seen as a publicity hound and a "sharpshooter" always on the alert for political advantage. A head-to-head struggle between these two for the Presidency—or for a lesser office such as governor of New York in 1970—could prove to be a bruising, ungentlemanly encounter.

When New York City, a fantastic ethnic complex composed of Russian Jews, Italians, Puerto Ricans, Negroes, Irish, Germans, and more than sixty other nationalities, elected John Vliet Lindsay as mayor, it chose a member of one of its tiniest minorities—he is English-Dutch, Episcopalian, Ivy League, Republican. A native New Yorker born

on Thanksgiving Day, 1921, as one of twin sons of a well-
to-do investment banker and his wife, Lindsay was educated at a good private school in Manhattan (Buckley), a
fashionable prep school (St. Paul's) and Yale College and
Yale Law School. He was a page at the Republican National Convention of 1940 that nominated Wendell Will-
kie. Between college and law school came three years in
the Navy during World War II as executive officer of a
destroyer.

Just as Robert Kennedy, fresh out of the Navy in 1946,
took off a few months to work in his brother's successful
House primary race, Lindsay, upon leaving the Navy that
spring, also worked in a Congressional primary contest
but with a different outcome. The Republican machine in
Manhattan was out to purge Representative Joseph Clark
Baldwin because he too often voted with the Democrats
in the House. Lindsay and other liberal Republicans rallied
to Baldwin's support in the primary, but he lost to the
organization choice, Frederic R. Coudert, a starchy corporation lawyer.

After graduating from Yale Law School in 1948, Lindsay joined a prominent New York law firm and became
active in the Republican Party. He organized a "Youth for
Eisenhower" club and was one of the many young lawyers
who worked for Brownell in the dispute over the Southern
delegations at the 1952 convention. Meanwhile, Coudert's
margin over the Democrats dropped every two years because he was too stiffly conservative for his district. In
1958, Lindsay announced against Coudert for the Republican nomination, scared him into retirement, and then
defeated a substitute candidate chosen by the organization. Coudert had won reelection in 1956 by only twenty-
five hundred votes despite the help of the Eisenhower
landslide; Lindsay in his first race against the same opponent won by almost eight thousand. His pluralities increased sharply every two years until in 1964, he won by

nearly one hundred thousand votes and polled 71 per cent of the vote.

In the House, Lindsay was a member of a small "ginger group" of younger liberal Republicans. He and his friends were effectively isolated by the plodding Midwestern conservatives who dominate the House GOP. His voting record was solidly progressive; he did not hesitate, for example, to vote for the enlargement of the House Rules Committee to dilute the power of the reactionary Republican-Southern Democrat coalition. In addition, he waged a lonely battle on civil liberties issues such as mail censorship, the school prayer amendment, and a proposed wide extension of the government loyalty-security program to employes on government contracts. In these fights, he put to shame the bread-and-butter liberalism of the New York City Democratic delegation, most of whose members are tone deaf on civil liberties.

In early 1965, Lindsay seemed to have reached a political dead end. Javits and Kennedy occupied the two Senate seats and looked unbeatable for the indefinite future. Rockefeller, who then looked a good deal less unbeatable, showed no disposition to yield the governorship. Lindsay ran for mayor because there was no other way out. He was sure to make a good run and even if he were defeated, this show of strength in an overwhelmingly Democratic city might advance his career.

Lindsay made his decision after intensive "skull sessions" with Robert Price, his thirty-two-year-old manager. Lindsay regards Price, who managed all his Congressional races, as a native political genius. There were many during the mayoral campaign who doubted it, but there is no answer to a victory cleanly won. Opinionated, hardworking, serious, sometimes brusque, Price is also extremely bright, witty, and a born political operator. He managed Rockefeller's Oregon primary campaign in 1964 and helped achieve the only victory Rockefeller won in the

presidential primaries. Price is like Lindsay in that both
are driving, relentless, ambitious workers, flogging themselves and everyone else to new peaks of effort. But in
every other respect, they differ. Where Lindsay is tall,
handsome, blond, Price is of medium height, dark-com-
plexioned, and notwithstanding heroic dieting has a tendency to be pudgy. (They have been called "Beauty and the
Beast.") Lindsay talks of ideals; Price of deals. Other New
York City politicians do not quite know what to make of
Lindsay; he is stiff-necked, imperious, idealistic. Price they
regard as one of their own. He is a Jewish boy from the
Bronx who grew up in modest circumstances (his father is
an efficiency expert for a shirt manufacturer), went to law
school and wants to be a millionaire. He is much more
fascinated with the politics of a human situation than
with the formal programs that preoccupy Lindsay; he
also loves the intricacies and organizational details of
politics the way baseball addicts love old batting averages.
Price served during the first year of Lindsay's administration as deputy mayor and then resigned to pursue his
financial ambitions as a vice-president of the Dreyfus
Corporation, an investment and mutual fund group, but
when Lindsay makes his try for national office, Price is
sure to be on the scene.

In planning the mayoral campaign, Price decided, rather
than gamble on a blitz of television spot announcements
and telethons, to invest most of the available money in 117
storefront headquarters, which became the neighborhood
nuclei for the canvassing drives of thousands of Lindsay
volunteers. It amounted to setting up an entire clubhouse
network in three months in a city where the Republican
organization, in the words of one of Price's aides, "has
made a career out of losing to the Democrats. We've got
to get our own people in there and make sure the work
is done." It was a triumph of organization, and it delivered
the votes on Election Day.

From June to Labor Day, Lindsay spent his time touring the city opening these storefronts. On a typical day, he left his headquarters in the Roosevelt Hotel on schedule at 10:30 A.M. The tour stayed almost precisely on time throughout the day. By the sixth stop in mid-afternoon, it had fallen five minutes behind, which caused the staff much concern. A shortwave radio kept Lindsay's car in continuous contact with the Roosevelt and his scheduled stops.

"Come in, Benjamin. Where are you? Over," a staff member queried from the Roosevelt.

Lindsay picked up the microphone: "This is Benjamin" —his code name. "We're five minutes out of the Midtown Tunnel. Over and out."

Whatever those Midwesterners in the House may think, Lindsay is Republican in his efficiency.

His research people had prepared a one-page data sheet about each neighborhood he was to visit, its ethnic makeup, income level, local grievances, and attitudes on issues. Lindsay kept close to these suggested topics in his five-minute, extemporaneous talks.

At each headquarters, he thanked the small shopkeepers who were its neighbors, sometimes adding, "I hope we bring you some business." Then into his local pitch: "I know you have a growing crime problem. You are worried about the lack of streetlights at some corners and have had some accidents. You have a protection problem." Then on to the need for more lights, more police, or a mention of potholes in the street or a junior high school that was overcrowded. And then the finale: "Friends, fellow New Yorkers, we have the possibility of creating something new and exciting and hopeful for New York. If you give me your trust, give me your confidence, together we can make New York the great Empire City again."

He spoke of it as an Empire City, but he campaigned as if New York were a thousand small towns. His campaign never "built" to any climax. Lindsay is one with Robert Kennedy in his disdain for the jargon about campaign peaks and troughs that Richard Nixon once made fashionable. There was enthusiasm for Lindsay at the outset and enthusiasm for him at the end. He, his staff, and his volunteers never expected to lose but were never quite confident of winning. They took the underdog position and stayed with it, straining every nerve and muscle all the way.

An able research staff headed by the candidate's brother George produced position papers on a wide range of problems from narcotics to housing to transportation to recreation. However, Lindsay never made any single issue the dominant theme in the campaign. Many suspected this would be a weakness. Liberal Democrats complained that his campaign was too much image and too little issues. But, at the end, it was clear that his real theme was not an issue but a promise—the hope of change. Like John F. Kennedy in 1960, Lindsay offered not a new program or a new set of answers to the old urban questions but a new perspective and a new source of energy. A stalemated, weary, cynical city decided to give the fresh-faced new boy a chance. As Sky Masterson, the gambler in *Guys and Dolls*, sang:

"You have wished yourself a Scarsdale Galahad
A breakfast-eating Brooks Brothers type."*

New York City, like Sarah Brown, the pretty evangelist, replied:

"Yes!"

Lindsay took office as mayor pledged to make a revolution. Asked a week before his election what he regarded as the central issue of his campaign, he replied, "New York

---

* © 1950 Frank Loesser. Used by permission.

City needs, and must have, a change. It must change completely in all its institutions from top to bottom."

Like other revolutionaries, he has found it easier to conquer power than to put across a program based on this radical premise. His career in City Hall has a checkered pattern of brave beginnings and recurrent frustration, of a lively new spirit and persistent old problems.

His initial period in office was very much like the opening months on the New Frontier in 1961. In terms of new programs, new policies, new people, he has been a success. But measured in big, visible accomplishments, legislative or administrative, the record is much more meager, though not empty. A pointless and costly subway strike was Lindsay's Bay of Pigs; the local Democrats have proved as complaisant as Everett Dirksen; and there has been the same eager wooing of the press and the same uproars over "managed news" and image-making.

A typical criticism of the Lindsay administration at the end of its first year in office would run something like this: "The trouble in New York today is that the mayor has never learned how to be mayor. He thinks he is still running. There is a difference between being a perpetual candidate and being the mayor of the City of New York. . . . The fact that he hasn't been able to get his program through indicates . . . more public relations than substance in the mayor's efforts. If we were treated to less personal image-making, and more concern about basic problems and their sensible solution, we would have better government."

With "New York" substituted for "Washington" and the "mayor" substituted for the "President," this is actually a criticism that Lindsay made about John Kennedy in 1962.[1]

Lindsay, like John Kennedy, had never been executive head of any operation bigger than a Congressional office or a campaign headquarters before assuming his immense responsibilities. Each was accustomed to the Congressional vice of disposing of a complicated problem by making a speech or issuing a press release about it. It is actually somewhat easier to get on-the-job training in the White House than in City Hall because a President is insulated against direct personal pressure and is surrounded by some of "the divinity that doth hedge a king." But a mayor is seldom held in awe for long. He has to preside at public hearings where ordinary citizens and protesting organizations denounce him to his face, and almost every morning as he arrives for work, he has to pass a picket line calling attention to some fresh injustice he has failed to remedy.

Like the Kennedys, Lindsay is a romantic regarding the style of government and the possibilities of leadership. He is forever tilting with the lethargic bureaucracy trying to impart to it some of his own dash and sense of urgency. Just as President Kennedy tried, but soon abandoned, the experiment of sitting in on a State Department staff meeting and often startled middle-echelon officials by telephoning them to ask their opinions, so Lindsay now and then pops up in some neglected corner of the metropolis, holds regular cabinet meetings in a different departmental headquarters each week, including one in the vast new garage of the Sanitation Department, and leads a crew of volunteers to clean up the debris on Welfare Island. (Lindsay, like his avowed hero, Fiorello LaGuardia, also attends fires and has tried his hand at conducting the Sanitation Department Band, but in neither of these efforts does he quite match the gusto of the Little Flower.)

During the interregnum between election and taking office, Lindsay was fond of ruminating aloud, "Why can't service in the city government be made as exciting as a job in the federal government? I want young guys to feel that being a deputy commissioner is as attractive, as big a challenge, as Assistant Secretary of State."[2]

A more sobersided type might have realized that there

are several discouraging differences, a simple one being that after the little flurry of his swearing-in, a deputy commissioner never makes the newspapers again, unless he is indicted. Washington may forget an Assistant Secretary just as easily, but at least ambassadors and other notables come to call and a sub-Cabinet member's wife can, if she chooses, at least be a big figure on the Washington society pages.

If Lindsay has found he cannot compete with Washington on the glamor-and-prestige front, he has nevertheless succeeded in making municipal government less drab and in recruiting a remarkably strong group of top officials. He persuaded Mitchell Ginsberg, the dean of Columbia University's School of Social Work, to accept the thankless job of Welfare Commissioner. The Corporation Counsel, the city's chief lawyer, is J. Lee Rankin, who served as Solicitor General under Eisenhower and who took a steep cut in income by leaving his corporate practice to help make the Lindsay administration a success. Austin Heller was recruited from the Public Health Service to lead an invigorated campaign against air pollution, and George McGrath, the new Corrections Commissioner, formerly headed the prison system in Massachusetts.

Lindsay's most popular appointment was Thomas Hoving, formerly curator of The Cloisters, the medieval collection of the Metropolitan Museum of Art, as Park Commissioner. Hoving proved to be a tireless innovator and an ebullient, imaginative administrator. He had a professional sense of the importance of planning and public design in creating a livable, attractive urban environment, and he made use of the best architects and landscape architects in designing buildings and park projects. Hoving devised festivals and "happenings" in the parks to recreate the sense that New York could be, in Lindsay's words, a "fun city." Under his leadership, the city vetoed proposed garages, restaurants, and other intrusions which park conservationists had protested in vain in the Wagner era. He made a modest start toward reclaiming the city from the automobile by banning cars from Central Park on Sundays, leaving it for cyclists and walkers. When Hoving resigned after fifteen months to become head of the Metropolitan Museum, Lindsay chose the equally capable August Heckscher, head of the Twentieth Century Fund, to replace him.

On one critical front, the Police Department, Lindsay's performance has been impressive. To reassure the public that the bad old days of Tammany manipulation of the police were not coming back, the Democrats, restored to power in 1945 after LaGuardia's retirement, had asserted the principle that even the mayor should not interfere in the department's affairs once he had appointed the commissioner. When Wagner's next-to-last police commissioner retired, he expressed special gratification that Wagner had called him on his direct telephone line from City Hall only twice.

An inadvertent by-product of the no-interference principle was the perpetuation of an Irish establishment in the top levels of the police force. Wagner's police commissioners were either promoted from this establishment—like Stephen Kennedy and Michael Murphy—or were outsiders who did not challenge it, like Vincent Broderick. In a city where the Irish had lost much of their political power, the Police Department remained an Irish barony.

Lindsay challenged the status quo in behalf of the city's two fastest-growing and most disadvantaged minorities, the 1,100,000 Negroes and the 730,000 Puerto Ricans. Out of 27,000 policemen, there were only 300 Puerto Ricans. Negro representation in the lower ranks was much higher, but of 79 precinct commanders only 1 was a Negro. Out of some 400 police captains, only 3 were Negro. Moreover, both minorities assert they are the victims of police brutality and have been clamoring for a civilian board to review such charges. The police, both in the ranks and in the Irish-dominated hierarchy, are united in their opposition to such a board.

In search of a new commissioner, Lindsay went outside the city to pick Howard Leary, the commissioner in Philadelphia, who had worked amicably with the civilian review board there. Leary is of Irish ancestry (some traditions can't be *completely* escaped), but he appointed a Jewish officer as his top deputy and a Negro officer as next highest officer. Lindsay made plain to these new appointees that he wants a more intensive recruitment campaign among minorities. He also wants many more Negro police in Harlem and other ghettos where white policemen, who themselves live far away in Queens or the Bronx, have had the aspect of an occupying colonial force among black natives. These changes prompted a few top officers to retire and aroused much muttering in police ranks. Several ex-commissioners raised the familiar cry of "political interference," but after a few weeks the uproar died away.

The worst and most significant problems for the city, however, do not lie wholly or even principally within the mayor's sphere of decision. Housing, unemployment, and taxes are the city's make-or-break problems.

New York has 35,000 rotting tenements that ought to be torn down but instead house nearly half a million people. Twice that number live in other structures that are salvageable but substandard. Candidate Lindsay promised to launch a $2 billion housing program. "I will build 160,000 new units of low- and middle-income housing," he declared in September 1965.[3] Now that he is mayor, Lindsay has no reason to question this estimate of the need; he just marvels a bit at that other Lindsay's temerity in promising to build "the city of tomorrow." There is little money in sight to redeem the promise. In the same election in which he was chosen, the voters of the state rejected bond issues for low- and middle-income housing. Congress is deeply reluctant to appropriate money for President Johnson's "demonstration cities" program on a scale large enough to do any good. Since the city has no uncommitted financial resources to throw into the struggle against slums, Lindsay has achieved only negligible gains on the housing front.

"Unemployment" is shorthand for poverty, a mismatch of skills and jobs (a surplus of common laborers cannot relieve the shortage of secretaries), and the social disorganization of the slums. The Wagner administration's anti-poverty program was wretchedly run with three rival and overlapping agencies approving programs and supposedly doling out money. Lindsay turned to the Ford Foundation for help. A Ford grant financed a lengthy study by Mitchell "Mike" Sviridoff, the successful chief of New Haven's anti-poverty operations. Sviridoff proposed to centralize all policymaking at the top in a new Human Resources Administration but to decentralize operations through a chain of one-stop employment centers. These centers would seek out the unemployed in each neighborhood and administer a comprehensive manpower program including testing, job counseling, training, work experience programs, and aggressive follow-up once a worker is placed in a job. These and related functions had been scattered among thirty different public and private agencies in the manpower field.

As Lindsay told the Conference of Mayors in Dallas in June 1966, "This is not an academic problem to the man in Harlem. His future may well depend on which of these thirty doors of opportunity he happens to open. Each agency has one or two programs or services. But none offers the full roster. . . . The hard core of our unemployed and underemployed require not merely a single program or isolated service. Different combinations of programs and services must be tailored to the needs of each individual."[4]

Lindsay accepted Sviridoff's recommendations and appointed him to head the new Human Resources Administration. Sviridoff's ideas worked brilliantly in New Haven, a city of 150,000, but New York is forty-five times as big. The difference in size makes for serious differences in kind. There is a defeatism, a sullen apathy, a depth of degradation in Harlem that is unknown in smaller cities. Mayor Richard Lee in New Haven can reach directly and effectively the natural leaders of his city's relatively small Negro community in a way that Mayor Lindsay cannot cut across the Democratic machine and rival power structures in Harlem. Lindsay's reforms of the poverty and welfare programs move in the right direction, but he is engaged in a work of social renovation that will require decades to complete.

The tax fight, the third in Lindsay's trinity of major problems, provided abundant evidence of his stubbornness. He inherited from his predecessor numerous debts and a rising curve of municipal expenditures and obligations. During the previous ten years, although the city's population actually declined slightly, its annual budget climbed 125 per cent to $3.8 billion, second in size only to the federal government. Real estate taxes went up by 75 per cent and business and sales taxes more than doubled.

Lindsay increased the budget by $500 million and asked for the equivalent in additional taxes. He proposed a graduated city income tax covering residents and commuters alike at a rate one-half that of the state's tax and also a 50 per cent jump in the tax on the sale of shares on the New York Stock Exchange. After months of maneuvering, bluffing, and loud cries of outrage by all participants, the tax question was finally resolved at 4 A.M. on June 16, 1966, following three days and nights of a marathon bargaining session of city and state leaders in Albany. Lindsay wound up with only $283 million in new taxes, or somewhat more than half of what he had asked for. In principle if not in disposable cash, however, this settlement was a notable victory for Lindsay. Almost no other city has a graduated personal income tax; most cities which have anything of this type have a flat payroll tax that is regressive. Moreover, the settlement established the principle that commuters have to bear at least some share in the cost of running the "core city" off which they make their living.

By his resistance to the payroll tax (which further endeared him to the Liberal Party) and his cool refusal to be bluffed by Stock Exchange threats to pull out of the city in retaliation for the higher tax on stock transfers, Lindsay amply demonstrated that he is not in guiding strings to the business community, even though its members supplied most of his $2 million campaign fund last year.

Lindsay's biggest failure has been his mismanagement of the 1966 transit strike. Every other year for twenty years, a strike "crisis" on the city-owned subways has been a regular feature of the week between Christmas and New Year's. The late Mike Quill of the Transport Workers was always the star of this adult version of a Christmas pantomime. He made bad faces, shouted ugly threats, waved his Irish blackthorn stick, and generally did his histrionic best to make the city shake and quiver. He held forth the prospect of a paralyzed transit system if his wage demands were not met. The mayor, regardless of his identity, regularly played straight man, pleading municipal poverty and wringing his hands in seeming despair as zero hour approached. But these little dramas always ended with a last-minute, New Year's Eve settlement—at a figure far below what Quill had been publicly seeking. The late president of the Transit Workers Union was, in fact, something of a patsy for the Democratic politicians with whom he was used to doing business.

Although Lindsay's face was unfamiliar and his St. Paul's School accent rather startling to Quill's sensibilities, he could have eased his way into his appointed role in the script if he had chosen. Instead, Lindsay threw away the old script and wrote his own. The result was a show that most New Yorkers wish had closed out of town.

Lindsay was impelled by a complicated mixture of motives and misconceptions: a naiveté about Quill's motives; an underestimate of the narrow-minded obstinacy of the union hierarchy's attitudes; a confidence streaked with self-righteousness that no union would seriously entertain the idea of a long strike that would jeopardize the city's welfare, particularly at the start of a new administration; curiously formal attitudes toward the Transit Authority, the city's nominal bargaining agent, and subsequently toward the judge who irresponsibly delayed a settlement by clapping Quill in jail for contempt; and, finally, a mistaken perception of the power that personal leadership and example could effectively bring to bear in the situation. Lindsay apparently believed that if he were firm, Quill would not dare call a strike and that if Quill did dare, he could overawe and defeat him by rallying the city's populace to get along without a transit system.

He refused to engage Quill in the public posturing and private haggling with which that worthy was familiar. Almost to the moment of his taking office, Lindsay maintained an icy aloofness except for one brief, inconclusive conference with Quill. As the incoming mayor, he observed all the formalities and ignored all the realities, the chief of them being that he alone could set the figure the city was willing to pay the workers in increased wages. As a result, the Lindsay administration made its debut on New Year's Day with the threat of a subway strike turned into a dreary reality.

For two miserable weeks, Lindsay exhorted the citizenry by walking four miles to his City Hall office, by daily pep-talks on television, and by helicopter inspections of the unbelievable traffic jams. It was all very stylish and slightly mad. It ended with the union getting the biggest settlement in history.

During the strike, Lindsay inveighed against unnamed "power brokers" with whom he would not deal. Asked to identify them, he replied only that "they know who they are" and that "they" would be permitted to run the city no longer. The press insisted upon pretending that without Lindsay's help, they could not possibly guess the people he had in mind. New York has several sets of power brokers for different situations, but there is really no mystery who has been making the odds and putting together the combinations in the labor field for a good many years. Indeed, former Mayor Wagner, giving a nostalgic interview on the occasion of Quill's death two weeks after the strike ended, listed most of them.

"One of my favorite stories about Mike concerned the 1959 negotiations," Wagner told the New York *Post*. "It was New Year's Eve and we were at Gracie Mansion— [Transit Authority Chairman] Joe O'Grady, Ted Kheel, Anna Rosenberg, John Coleman, Quill, and his special counsel [now UN Ambassador] Arthur Goldberg—when I suggested that we go down to City Hall.

"Mike was the last one to leave and as he got to the door my wife said to him, 'There's not going to be a strike, is there?' Mike winked and answered, 'Of course not.' They were the only people in New York that night who knew it."[5]

If Wagner had added the names of Harry Van Arsdale of the Central Labor Council and Peter Brennan of the building trades, he would have about completed the roster.

There is little doubt, for example, that Lindsay could have called in labor attorney Theodore Kheel in December 1965 and said something like this: "I want you to be my man in these transit talks. Try to hold the price to the city down as much as possible, but find out Mike's ultimate terms and make a deal. If he wants an all-night bargaining session on New Year's Eve or even a quickie, five-hour strike, I'll go along." If Lindsay had given such instructions to Kheel or some comparable professional, there would have been no transit strike and the final wage package would have been no more and probably less than what the city finally granted. But to Lindsay, this approach was too reminiscent of Wagner; it seemed like political fixing rather than collective bargaining as he envisaged it (having never experienced it). He could not countenance this approach or accommodate it to his ideals of civic virtue, although he did eventually enlist Kheel's services.

Once the strike began, many rank-and-file citizens, and not all of them in the middle or upper class, began to growl demands for a crackdown. Why not put the strikers in jail? Why not mobilize the National Guard to run the subways? Or at least drive the buses? Where is the spirit of Calvin Coolidge who broke the Boston police strike with an epigram? Only Lindsay's innate good sense saved him from this reactionary *cul de sac*.

If there really is a middle way in strikes of public employes between Robert Wagner and Calvin Coolidge, Lindsay has yet to find it. He still talks hopefully of a "more scientific approach" and of "genuine collective bargaining," but as the public health nurses, the garbage collectors, the firemen, and all the other municipal unions come trooping in to bludgeon him with their pay demands, he speaks with less and less optimism.

From the debacle of the subway strike, the trend of the Lindsay administration could only move up. As it has gained in experience and confidence, it has begun to come to grips with the serious, fundamental problems of the metropolis. Lindsay and his associates have evinced energy and enthusiasm and goodwill. Combined with growing political skill, these qualities should bring lasting results.

Lindsay has broken the crust of stale weariness that overlaid municipal government. His administration is a power center that competes with Robert Kennedy's public service projects for the enthusiasm and idealism of young people. One prominent Reform Democrat said, early in 1967: "If you were an energetic young guy wanting to do something in a public service way, would you join the nearest Democratic clubhouse? No, of course not. You would hook up with this new bunch in City Hall and become a Lindsay Republican."

As against the magnetism of his personal leadership, Lindsay has weaknesses in working with his political equals. He is prone to announce complicated or potentially unpopular programs with insufficient political preparation. When the opposition breaks forth, he often has to retreat and then arrange under pressure the compromises that he might better have worked out in advance. Lindsay is testy and impatient and if he could, he would brook no opposition. His impulse is to respond to resistance by saying, "But I am the mayor." He has found it hard to learn that in one sense, he is *only* the mayor. His formal authority is the necessary but not sufficient part of his power; after defining the issue and making up his mind on his policy, he has then to persuade his colleagues on the Board of Estimate and the City Council, his subordinates in the bureaucracy, and the decision makers in other power centers to accept and sustain that policy. Like the President of the United States maneuvering with Congress, a mayor can only intermittently assert his own will and expect to be obeyed; more often, he has to inspire, cajole, induce, and compel support. After much frustration and some defeats, Lindsay is gradually learning this truth about executive leadership.

Lindsay clearly prefers the public and inspirational side of his office to the political and bureaucratic in-fighting.

There his courage in speaking up for what is unpopular, his willingness to experiment, and the grace notes of his personal style are most effective. If Albany and Washington were to shower down an abundance of tax dollars, Lindsay could transform his dreams and ambitions for the city into realities and become unquestionably a great mayor. But even if the dollars are not forthcoming and many of the dreams remain earthbound, his personal attributes are likely to make him a man to be reckoned with in future national politics.

NOTES

1 The original statement is quoted in Daniel E. Button, *Lindsay* (Random House, New York, 1965), p. 106.
2 Private interview.
3 Lindsay's "White Paper" on Housing.
4 Text of Lindsay address, June 12, 1966.
5 New York *Post*, January 30, 1966.

CHAPTER TEN

Toward the Restoration

"In every campaign I've ever been in, they've said I was starting too early—that I would peak too soon or get too much exposure or run out of gas or be too easy a target. I would never have won any race following that advice."
— JOHN F. KENNEDY

"The man coming toward you is marching forward on all fronts." — poem by OSCAR WILLIAMS[1]*

THE KENNEDYS do not care for the waiting game. "Never take second best" was their father's motto, and they have made it their own. They always aim for victory, and they storm their goal by direct assault. John Kennedy was not only the first Catholic President; he was also the youngest President ever elected to the White House. He did not get there by deferring to his elders or waiting his turn.

Robert Kennedy, too, forces the pace. Remembering his older brothers killed before their time and his younger brother invalided for several months by an airplane crash, he is haunted by the harsh fact of human mortality. The fatalism bred by these tragedies would immobilize many men, but it serves only to reinforce his compulsion to compete and his royal sense of family pride. Asked once if his family's misfortunes had shaken his religious faith, he replied in a ruefully jocular vein: "Oh, no, not really. Of

* Used by permission of the Executors of the Estate of Oscar Williams.

course, sometimes we do think that Someone Upstairs is
out to lunch when He ought to be attending to business."

Asked directly about presidential ambitions, he replies:
"There are so many risks in life that long-range plans
don't make much sense to me. Who knows whether any
of us will even be alive then?"[2]

The sentiment is sound and the words are doubtless
sincere. But Kennedy's actions spell in capital letters the
story of a man on the move. It is as if every day he re-
peats to himself those inciting lines of A. E. Housman:

> "Clay lies still, but blood's a rover.
> Breath's a ware that will not keep.
> Up, lad: when the journey's over
> There'll be time enough to sleep." [3]

In these years since his brother's death, Robert Kennedy
has achieved a crucial triumph in transforming his own
reputation. When he ran for the Senate, he discovered that
he had a serious "image problem." In the course of the
campaign, the issue of his sponsorship by the political
bosses slowly faded out. His status as a carpetbagger
(from Massachusetts via Florida and Virginia) was soon
ignored. But the matter of his "ruthlessness" did not fade.
Too many people saw him as a tough cop, a relentless
prosecutor, an arrogant little man a bit too big for his
britches. The early association with Joe McCarthy, the
terrier-like persistence of his cross-examinations in the
Rackets Committee, his long, relentless pursuit of Jimmy
Hoffa, and his occasional rudeness and dourness as the
straw boss and political overseer of his brother's administration—all these memories clung to him.

Kennedy is too shrewd and has too strong a sense of his
own wholeness as a human being to attempt—as Richard
Nixon did during his vice-presidential years—to retool his
image by mere words and superficial gestures. Since the
gains to be made are great, he has the boldness to take the

risks to win them. He has carved out some new ground on basic public policies. On the Vietnam War, he has not been afraid to develop and sustain a major difference of opinion with the President and his former colleagues in the Administration. He interpreted his brother's ambiguous legacy of Latin American policies in a way that enabled him to criticize the Johnson intervention in the Dominican Republic. In controversies as widely separated as a Surrogate judgeship in Manhattan and *apartheid* in South Africa, he has demonstrated that his residual moralism reacts against other evils than Communism or labor corruption. Whether he is in Bedford-Stuyvesant or a *favela* in Brazil or a hearing on auto safety in the Senate, his capacity for involvement and indignation moves him into frontier areas and has earned for him enthusiasm and political support that he did not have as a rackets investigator and as Attorney General.

The most extraordinary aspect of Kennedy's changing reputation in these post-assassination years has been his identification with and glorification of youth. The cult of youth is a natural outgrowth of his brother's legend. If the torch of leadership was passed to a new generation of Americans on Inauguration Day, 1961, it is in Robert Kennedy's interest to identify himself as the spokesman for that generation and to keep asserting its claim to political preferment. This approach also underscores his link to the Peace Corps, the most popular and least controversial accomplishment of his brother's administration.

Hard political reality also suggests the wisdom of courting the young; the proportion of young people in the nation's population is steadily rising, and by the 1972 election, one voter in every three will be under thirty-five. Moreover, advertising's constant stress on the desirability of youthfulness helps condition many middle-aged and older voters in their political attitudes. The defeat of older but mentally alert and competent incumbents by their younger opponents is often due not to any differences on public issues but simply to the desire of voters to see youth and physical vitality in their elected officials.

Kennedy orients himself to youthfulness in small ways and large. A small way is in his physical appearance. He has before him the example of his brother John, who coolly recognized that his handsome thatch of hair and good looks were assets with women voters. Robert, who used to wear his hair cut short, almost in a crew-cut, has adopted the shaggier look now in vogue in high schools and colleges. A reporter who traveled with him in the 1966 campaign offers this vivid description of his haircut: "It is a marvel of the hairdresser's art. It puffs out on the sides over his ears, and it cantilevers down and over his forehead like an awning. Watching Mr. Kennedy comb this incredible tangle is almost like watching an exercise in isometrics. He tugs at the comb so hard that his muscles ripple."[4]

Most politicians like to talk in colleges because it is a means of reaching people, both students and faculty, who are more alert and vocal on political issues than ordinary voters. But Kennedy devotes more attention to college groups than is normal for major politicians. He has also developed a speech format that he uses on campuses and in street rallies elsewhere which is a cross between a class-room quiz and a football pep rally. He keeps his prepared remarks short, and talks from notes in a semi-extemporaneous fashion. Most of his time he devotes to answering questions. But he varies the question-and-answer period by taking impromptu polls of the students. "How many favor stopping the bombing of North Vietnam?" "How many favor complete United States withdrawal from South Vietnam?" "How many want to continue student deferments?"

Away from the campus, Kennedy follows a question-and-answer format but instead of probing for opinions, he works up a partisan dialogue in which he feeds the questions and his listeners, like a thousand straight men, shout back the answers. It is the audience participation show brought into politics.

Kennedy likes to quote Goethe, who said, "The future of a nation is to be found in the opinions of its young men—under the age of twenty-five."

It scarcely seems one of Goethe's wiser remarks. Most people change their opinions after they are twenty-five—fortunately. There is nothing like a wife, children, and a mortgage to alter a man's perspective. Only in Latin America and other parts of the underdeveloped world are students a significant political force because only there are institutions too fragile or too ossified to give direction to society. In the United States and other wealthy, stable societies, student opinions on politics have less importance than their taste in sports cars or popular music. It is also hazardous to forecast tomorrow's political climate from the opinions of today's high school and college students. As columnist Kenneth Crawford wrote in *Newsweek*, "There is a strange mythology about youth in politics. The John Held, Jr., types of the Prohibition '20s earned a reputation for irresponsibility, but they supported and manned the New Deal in the '30s. The Depression so traumatized another generation that it was regarded in its time as revolutionary, yet it won a war in the '40s and elected Eisenhower in the '50s."

The argument in terms of generations is inherently fallacious. As Crawford added: "Youth is an impermanent condition, almost always outgrown; each new generation adopts its own fads, different from its predecessors'; youth's half-formed political opinions are as varied as their elders' more hardened views. Young fogies are almost as common as old fogies."[5]

The examples abound. Campus radicals held sway in the 1930s, yet in their midst young Joseph McCarthy was playing poker at Marquette, Richard Nixon was cracking the lawbooks at Duke, and George Romney was earnestly selling aluminum. In the 1960s, conservative students were saving God and man at Yale and other places by joining Young Americans for Freedom, while liberal students were heading South to help register Negroes to vote in Alabama and Mississippi.

Kennedy, however, persists in attempting to invest the ideologically empty concept of youth with content. Speaking to a dinner of the Americans for Democratic Action in Philadelphia on February 24, 1967, he said that "perhaps the clearest mirror of our performance, the truest measure of whether we live up to our ideals, is our youth. ... And we will learn most, I think, from the minority who most sharply articulate their criticism of our ways. And we may find that we learn most of all from those political and social dissenters whose differences with us are most grave; for among the youth as among adults, the sharpest criticism often goes hand in hand with the deepest idealism and love of country."

This is an agreeable sentiment to set forth to a liberal audience, but it is of doubtful validity. Adults can probably learn as much about America from its young conservatives as its young radicals, and youthful readers of the *National Review* have presumably as much idealism and love of country as the readers of *Ramparts*.

Kennedy went on to draw a gloomy picture of the nation's best young minds: riots on the campus, Peace Corps recruiting falling off, suicide rate rising, and delinquency, drug addiction, and draft dodging also on the increase.

"The gap between generations, always present in the past, is suddenly widening," Kennedy asserted; "the old bridges which span it are falling; we see all around us a terrible alienation of the best and bravest of our young."

And what is causing all this disaffection among the

young? Kennedy listed several explanations, notably the war in Vietnam, the political impotence of the young, the lack of social purpose and idealism on the part of the great corporations in whose service most people have to earn their living, the bureaucratization of trade unions and their consequent loss of crusading spirit, and the swollen size and impersonality of university education.

"We can understand," Kennedy concluded, "why so many of our young people have turned from engagement to disengagement, from politics to passivity, from hope to nihilism, from SDS [Students for a Democratic Society] to LSD.

"But it is not enough to understand, or to see clearly. Whatever their differences with us, whatever the depth of their dissent, it is vital—for us as much as for them—that our young feel that change is possible; that they will be heard; that the cruelties and follies and injustices of the world will yield, however grudgingly, to the sweat and sacrifice they are so ready to give. If we cannot help open to them this sense of possibility, we will have only ourselves to blame for the disillusionment that will surely come. And more than disillusionment, danger; for we rely on these young people more than we know: not just in the Peace Corps, though the Peace Corps has done more for our position around the world than all our armed forces and foreign aid; not just in Civil Rights, though our youth have done more toward a solution of that problem than all the power and panoply of government; we rely on our youth for all our hopes of a better future—and thus, in a real and direct sense, for the very meaning of our own lives. If we would look back with pride at the lives we lead, we know above all that we will judge ourselves by the hope and direction we have left behind."[6]

This speech presents such an astonishing perspective on public affairs that it is hard to say on the basis of it

whether Kennedy is seeking the Presidency or the leadership of a new Children's Crusade.

Valuable as the Peace Corps is, it cannot seriously be
said to have done as much for America's world position as
the armed forces did in the Berlin airlift or the Korean
War or as much as the foreign aid program did through
the Marshall Plan or the billions invested in keeping India's
economy afloat. To judge otherwise is to mistake the popularity of the Peace Corps for the substance of power.
Similarly, the sit-ins of the Southern Negro students re-
vitalized the civil rights movement in 1960 and the subsequent efforts of white students helped sustain the momentum of that movement, but most of what the students
accomplished would have proved ephemeral if the several
Civil Rights Acts approved by Congress had not brought
to bear the "power and panoply of government."

There is scarcely a limit to Kennedy's capacity for
exaggerating and romanticizing youth's role. Elsewhere
in the same speech, he says of the young of the '60s:
"They have struggled and sacrificed alone too long." This
is a rather dramatic way to describe the spiritual travail
of nineteen- and twenty-year-olds. And again, he explains
away youthful lack of support for the Vietnam War: "This
is a war surrounded by rhetoric they do not understand or
accept; these are the children not of the Cold War, but of
the Thaw. Their memories of Communism are not of
Stalin's purges and death camps, not even the terrible
revelations of the Twentieth Party Congress, or the streets
of Hungary." But, one is impelled to ask, have they read
no history? And is not a United States Senator obligated
to try to deepen their understanding rather than to in-
dulge their innocence and confirm their superficialities?

Kennedy does not take account of what is undesirable
in youthful attitudes toward politics. On the one hand,
youth's idealism, spontaneity, and willingness to ask basic

questions are refreshing and attractive. But on the other hand, young people's refusal to recognize complexity, their intolerance, and their emotionalism are unattractive and, where serious public issues are concerned, potentially dangerous. Whether they are young conservatives reared in snug comfort who are prating about "rugged individualism" and denouncing welfare programs whose origins and usefulness they do not comprehend, or whether they are young radicals ridiculing the economics and politics of an America that has done more to advance human freedom and dignity than any other society in the history of the world, the young can only be seen as contributing, not to serious politics, but to their own self-education. Their political slogans and postures are mostly a comment on themselves and their own immaturity, not upon their parents or their society. Rather than a wearisome pretense of "trying to understand" their political opinions, any sophisticated adult should enter a discussion with high school students or college undergraduates with the conviction that although the young are very important, their political opinions are the least important thing about them. Or, as George Bernard Shaw said, "Youth is such a wonderful quality it is a crime to waste it on the young."

Kennedy's preoccupation with the cult of youth goes beyond speeches. He also espouses causes that are fashionable in radical campus circles. Asked in California in 1965 whether he favored donating blood to the Viet Cong, he replied that he did. Giving blood to anyone who needs it is in the American tradition, he added. No one can recall any such tradition when the United States was fighting Hitler in World War II or when it engaged in earlier wars. Nor did Kennedy himself actually contribute blood for the Viet Cong or do anything to facilitate the collection or transmission of blood supplies to North Vietnam. But his endorsement was a symbolic affirmation of sympathy with the radical young who dreamed up this form of dissent. Similarly, when American Communist Robert Thompson was denied burial in Arlington National Cemetery although he was a veteran who had been wounded in World War II, Kennedy made a point of expressing public disagreement with this decision. If anyone doubted that he was no longer a McCarthyite, this expression of tolerance for a dead Communist removed the doubt.

His comments on blood for the Viet Cong and the burial of Thompson are also in line with bolder positions he has taken on more substantial questions such as his criticism of the president of General Motors on auto safety and his endorsement of the strike of the California grape pickers. So pronounced has his reputation become for bold liberalism—much more clearly defined than his late brother's ever was—that when farm laborers in Texas marched to the state capitol in Austin on Labor Day, 1966, to demand a minimum wage, they responded to mention of his name with shouts, "*Viva* Kennedy!"

Yet Kennedy is not a liberal in any coherent, conceptual sense. The appeal to him of the whole "youth bit" may be that he is as uncertain in his groping toward large ideas as many students are. He has his old capacity for indignation; he is fond of quoting an inscription which he says was found on an Egyptian pyramid: "No one was angry enough to speak out." He is at the same time moving away from some of the simplistic ideas he once had, and thus has also developed a budding liberal's agreement with Learned Hand, who praised "the spirit which is not sure it is right." He would like to commit himself to some overarching conception, but cannot discern one that justifies such commitment. His power reflexes and his acute political intelligence continue to work alongside of and independent of this intellectual questing; while he operates as a politician, he also sniffs the intellectual air for fresh currents. And, of course, leaving aside the romantic ideas about youth being the mirror of a society's performance and the justification of adult lives, one has to agree that on campus and among radicals is the best place to seek intellectual trends. As the literary critic Theodore Solotaroff has observed, "Most of the serious intellectual action today has shifted from the centers of orthodoxy and authority to the margins of radical doubt and protest. . . . It is not simply a resurgence of radicalism, since the old distinctions between left and right are themselves being dissolved by the general mood of doubt in our institutions and their executives. The anxious question that emerges from it, found both in the flailing criticism of 'the Establishment' and in our moments of serious reflection about the quality of our daily life, is whether American society, for all its visible affluence and efficiency, is a fit place in which to live, whether indeed we are living in a rational society or in an increasingly absurd one."[7]

Kennedy, if he is to be a candidate for the Presidency in the 1970s and frame a platform in liberal terms, has to project a convincing picture of the future that at least takes account of this "anxious question." Although he does not know the shape of the future and neither do the members of his youthful audiences, he doubtless calculates that he cannot lose much in the adult world by associating himself with their questioning and groping. Some observers, however, explain his fondness for college audiences on the simple basis that he is more at ease with young people than with those his own age and that his very shyness, his "communications hangup," is an intrinsic part of his appeal to young people. Whatever the explanation, the fact of his appeal is evident. He commands a much more respectful and enthusiastic hearing from college audiences than President Johnson or any of his other rivals in either party. Among teen-agers, he evokes shrieks of "Bobby, Bobby" rivaling the acclaim these same youngsters give the Beatles and that their mothers gave Frank Sinatra a quarter-century ago. In short, Robert Kennedy has become not just another big-shot politician but a contemporary culture hero in the fast-moving world of pop heroes and pop art.

"He's not really handsome, and he's not *that* talented. [He] projects a certain contemporariness. He is the man of the moment—surly, tough and cynical, yet somehow very innocent and gentle. . . . He is a shrewd nonconformist who knows exactly what he wants and doesn't mind going oustide established channels to get it. He is impatient, impulsive and not at all humble. He is stubborn, innately distrustful and overly sensitive to real or imagined slights. He is also fiercely loyal to his friends, honest and without guile. . . . Away from the [public], his face resumes its natural expression: a curious mixture of bashfulness and distrust."[8]

The foregoing could stand as a remarkably accurate description of Robert Kennedy. It only happens to be an account of another pop culture hero, screen actor Steve McQueen.

If his forthright opinions on public issues have converted the liberals and his openness to experience and lack of stuffiness have engaged the enthusiasm of youth, Kennedy has employed humor to good effect in winning over both older, sophisticated audiences and the apolitical mass public. Jokes alone are not enough to change an image, but they help a man handicapped by a reputation for toughness and ruthlessness.

Kennedy has tried to adopt a public style as much as possible like that of his late brother. In the 1964 campaign, he hired Gerald Gardner, a gag writer who helped produce the television show "That Was the Week That Was," and paid him ten thousand dollars to supply a steady flow of quips and witticisms in the JFK manner. In recent years he has relied upon several of the same writers who produced material for his brother including Theodore Sorensen, Arthur Schlesinger, Jr., and Richard Goodwin.

By nature, Kennedy is too taut and shy to be humorous in public; it has required conscious effort and practice for him to deliver amusing lines before audiences. But he has always had an authentic vein of dry wit that he previously revealed only to intimates. With a few members of his staff, he was watching one of his brother's press conferences shortly after the Bay of Pigs disaster. When a reporter asked if the President planned to unleash Chiang Kai-shek's troops for an invasion of Communist China, Kennedy cracked: "That will take their minds off Cuba."

Once when a lawyer from the Anti-trust Division was describing a business run downhill by an incompetent son, Kennedy interjected: "That's one mistake our father never made—taking us into business with him."

During an early meeting to organize the 1964 campaign in New York, Fred Papert, who planned the television advertising, said, "The basic aim of all our commercials, Bob, will be to present you as a warm, sincere individual."

Deadpan, Kennedy asked: "You going to use a double?"

Asked privately why he did not run for the Senate in Virginia, where he actually resided, he replied: "Because Charlie Buckley and Adam Clayton Powell couldn't sponsor me in Virginia."

Shortly after his election to the Senate, he began regaling audiences with that self-deprecatory humor that Adlai Stevenson made familiar in contemporary politics and that John Kennedy adapted to his own style. Speaking before the Women's National Press Club in Washington, Robert Kennedy satirized the carpetbagger issue: "I can't tell you how happy I am to be here representing the great state of . . . uh . . . uh . . . uh." He assured them, "I have no presidential aspirations." After a pause, he added, "Nor does my wife—Ethel Bird."

During the 1966 campaign, he and brother Ted both

made use of a fabricated anecdote that gently makes fun of the family's reputation for impatient power seeking. He would say, "I just received this message from Washington. President Johnson is in Manila. Vice-President Humphrey is in Minnesota. You are in Michigan [or wherever he was that day]. I have seized power. [Signed] Ted."

Where once he resented personal questions as an intrusion, he has learned to live in a goldfish bowl of publicity and to make little jokes about his family. When his tenth child was born on March 24, 1967, he told reporters upon leaving the hospital that his mother had said: "If I had known that this was going to be a contest, I would not have stopped at nine."

His climb of Mt. Kennedy in the Yukon two years earlier held a great deal of emotional significance for him, but his concern for the private symbolism did not inhibit him from the public exploitation of it. He permitted color photographs to be taken of every part of the ascent and later wrote an article about it for *Life*. The article and his remarks afterward to reporters were practically a blizzard of witticisms and anecdotes. "I began to climb," he wrote in *Life*. "I remember my mother's last words to me, 'Don't slip, dear,' and the admonition of a friend who had obviously never climbed, 'Don't look down.' . . . And the reporter from a national newspaper covering the climb told me before I began that his paper had just completed my obituary. All of these splendid thoughts raced through my mind."[9]

Kennedy wants to be an existential hero but has also become sophisticated enough to know that others may poke fun at his own heroics, so he beats them to the punch and does it first. Many of the anecdotes may be contrived and the witticisms ghosted, but enough of them are his own to prove his impulse toward sardonic humor.

The liberalism, the accent on youth, the humor, the skillful perpetuation of his brother's legend had by the

summer of 1966 transformed Kennedy into a presidential
possibility of the front rank. The Gallup Poll showed that
Democrats preferred him over President Johnson as their
1968 nominee. Pitted against George Romney, he was
ahead 55 to 39 per cent. Other polls showed him defeating
Richard Nixon by a similar margin. Even in so unlikely
a state as Iowa, either of the leading Republicans would
defeat President Johnson while either would lose to Kennedy. The polls merely confirmed what every reporter
could observe: Robert Kennedy had become the most popular man in his party and probably in the nation. In two
short years, he had transformed the cheers and the sentiment of the Atlantic City convention into a discernible
base of political power.

In the midst of this swelling popularity, there came the
public relations disaster of the Manchester affair. Of the
three principals in this drama—Robert Kennedy, Jacqueline Kennedy, and William Manchester—only Robert
Kennedy was in a position to lose anything, and he lost
heavily. Mrs. Kennedy was the instigator of the public
controversy because she believed that the privacy of herself and her children was at stake. But since she lives in
a continuous stream of publicity, no single book or magazine serialization could seriously affect her privacy or
lack of it. Manchester believed he was defending his book
and the claims of history, but the notoriety served to
stimulate public interest in his writing. Only Robert Kennedy actually suffered since his quest for the Presidency is
heavily dependent upon his receiving the right kind of
publicity. Because of sentimental loyalty to his brother's
widow, his own imperiousness, and a certain failure of
imagination, he emerged from the dispute in the public's
eyes as an arrogant, unattractive bully. No single episode
since he became the heir apparent has done him remotely
as much harm.

From the outset Kennedy's dealings with Manchester were clouded by sentiment and confused by a lack of good judgment. He and Mrs. Kennedy were impelled to commission an authorized version of the events surrounding the President's death only because they wanted to head off writers such as Jim Bishop, the author of *The Day Christ Died, The Day Lincoln Was Shot,* and similar works of popularized history.

If a book was to be written they wanted to do as much as they could to ensure that it was accurate, complete, and in good taste. This was an intrinsically mistaken notion because it was based on an exaggerated conception of their power; even without their permission or co-operation, an experienced writer could still construct a salable book about the assassination.

Having decided to try to control the writing of the account, they made a second mistake in the choice of a writer. They first proposed the idea to Theodore H. White, but he was deeply involved in writing his 1964 installment of *The Making of a President.* Walter Lord, the author of *A Night to Remember,* was likewise reluctant to undertake the assignment. They then settled upon Manchester, whom neither of them knew. He was selected because he wrote *Portrait of a President,* a sensitive and literate but unpenetrating account of President Kennedy, and one which *The New York Times* reviewer accurately characterized as "adoring." (In the concluding pages of that book there is a passage which is poignant now. Discussing whether Kennedy was as well loved as some earlier Presidents such as Lincoln, Manchester wrote: "Certainly John Kennedy is not as lovable as Abe. He has a weaker grip on the nation's heartstrings, and the reason isn't that he hasn't been shot.")[10]

Pierre Salinger, who as White House Press Secretary had become acquainted with Manchester while he was writing *Portrait of a President,* was instrumental in recommending him to do the story of the assassination. Robert Kennedy recalled later, "We just didn't want to go through it [the assassination] over and over again. I suppose we were naive, because we're going to have to live with this thing the rest of our lives. But in January of '64, we thought we could have one man do it, and have it done with. Most of this reasoning came from Pierre, and it was Pierre who suggested Manchester. I had never met Manchester before."[11]

In strictly professional terms, Manchester was well qualified to undertake the assignment, but the Kennedys had no way of knowing whether he was a man in whom they could repose special trust or develop the unique relationship necessary between a family and an authorized biographer. Under the circumstances, one might have expected that Robert Kennedy, as an experienced lawyer, would have made up for that lack of personal acquaintance by drawing a detailed contract covering all contingencies. Instead, although book contracts are highly specialized documents, he did not consult a publishing industry lawyer, and the contract which he and Manchester signed was vague and loosely worded at almost every critical point. It did not, for example, spell out whether the Kennedys were to have a right of veto over the publication of Manchester's manuscript in perpetuity and if that veto were exercised, what compensation, if any, Manchester would receive for all his time and work. The contract likewise failed to define what would constitute a legally binding statement from the Kennedys releasing the manuscript for publication. Robert Kennedy was Attorney General but he still needed a lawyer. Manchester, from his own viewpoint, was equally ill protected.

Rather than pay attention to these vital matters, Kennedy was most preoccupied with money, a subject which scarcely ought to have concerned him. The moral aspect of it troubled him: "I don't want anybody to make a killing out of my brother's death," he told Manchester in their first conversation. To which Manchester grandly replied: "I'm not going to negotiate about your brother's death—you dictate your terms." But in addition to the moral aspect, Kennedy was obsessed with the idea that every project had to be bent somehow to contribute to the fund-raising campaign for the Kennedy Library. Some of old Joe Kennedy's conviction that money is the ultimate measure of all value seems to have passed to his son. In any event, the contract was drawn to provide that Manchester and the publisher would share only in the profits of the first printing and that the profits from all subsequent printings would go to the Kennedy Library, an institution which the members of the Kennedy family could, of course, easily endow out of their private fortune.

To keep the book under friendly auspices, and for the sake of sentiment, the Kennedys requested Manchester to switch from his regular publisher, Little, Brown, to Harper & Row, the publisher of *Profiles in Courage* and of Robert Kennedy's own books. Manchester agreed, but the ambiguity of the publisher's position—was he on the side of the author or the patron?—was to prove another fruitful source of confusion and misunderstanding.

On March 26, 1964, Kennedy announced that "the Kennedy family has authorized William Manchester to write an extensive account describing the events of and surrounding the death of President Kennedy on November 22, 1963. These arrangements were made with Mr. Manchester in the interest of historical accuracy and to prevent distortion and sensationalism."

For his part, Manchester declared that he would regard the writing of the book as a "sacred trust."

Nothing more was heard of the project for two years. Manchester was later to complain that Mrs. Kennedy had helped him gain access to only three people, none of them vital. But the truth is that many busy and important people made themselves available to him for extensive and exclusive interviews only because he had the Kennedy *imprimatur*. Manchester writing in *Look* asserts, "I believe most of them would have received me anyhow. I was, after all, no newcomer to national reporting. I had my own sources, and my relationship with President Kennedy had been rather well known in Washington before I ever met his widow."[12] This assertion of confidence in his own reportorial powers is understandable inasmuch as the Kennedys bruised his ego badly during the book quarrel. But it is still a fantasy. The Kennedy endorsement opened many doors for him and the withdrawal of that endorsement would have closed them just as quickly.

Moreover, Manchester had the unique privilege of ten hours of tape-recorded interviews with Jacqueline Kennedy. Like the diversion of the book's royalties to the library fund, the character of these interviews was clouded by the effort to serve a double purpose. Soon after the assassination, Robert Kennedy organized an interview project in which all the late President's friends and all the senior officials of his administration were to be interviewed on their recollections of him while those memories were still fresh. The tapes of the interviews are to be deposited in the Kennedy Library. The question naturally arose who was to interview Mrs. Kennedy. Arthur Schlesinger, Jr., agreed to question her for the period up to November 22, 1963, but he had no desire to relive the traumatic emotions of that day and the weekend that followed. Since Manchester would have to question her in doing his book and since it seemed pointless to interview her twice on this painful material, it was agreed that he would do the taping for his own purposes and for the library as well. Mrs. Kennedy talked with complete freedom and in remarkably intimate detail because she assumed that she was talking primarily for the library—"for some scholar in the year 2000" as she later expressed it—and that none of it would be used in Manchester's book without her express permission. She used the interviews as a kind of therapy and relieved her anguish by pouring out her innermost thoughts and feelings. On his own volition, Manchester did not use a great deal of this material, but some of it he did use. When she objected, he refused to give way and contended that she was attempting to compromise his integrity as a writer and his duty to history.

The controversy over the book began to develop shortly after Manchester submitted his completed manuscript to Harper & Row in late March 1966. His contract with the family provided: "The complete manuscript shall be reviewed by Mrs. John F. Kennedy and Robert F. Kennedy, and the final text shall not be published unless and until approved by them." Instead of reading the book, Mrs. Kennedy deferred to Robert Kennedy. He, in turn, delegated the task to two trusted former aides, Edwin O. Guthman, his press secretary in the Justice Department and now the national news editor of the Los Angeles *Times* and John Seigenthaler, once his special assistant and now editor of the Nashville *Tennessean*. They suggested deletions and revisions, some to correct factual errors, some to cut out personal material about Mrs. Kennedy, and still others to tone down some of the descriptions of Lyndon Johnson, the other Texas politicians, and the animosity between the Kennedy and Johnson staffs immediately after the assassination. They sent their recommended changes to Evan Thomas (the son of socialist leader Norman Thomas), who is the top editor at Harper & Row.

Thomas agreed with Guthman and Seigenthaler on most of their suggested changes. In a letter to them on May 16, 1966, he wrote: "The book was in part tasteless and gratuitously insulting to President Johnson and even to the memory of the late President Kennedy." This was because Manchester was unable to resist turning the story into "a magic fairy tale."

"The marvelous Irish politician who became one of the world's great statesmen is almost deprived of his miraculous self, seen as the child of Arthur and Guinevere, while Black Jack Bouvier's daughter is somehow deprived of her hard-won stature by being born of elves in a fairy glade, by being dressed in magic cloth of gold.

"The Texans in their polka dot dresses and bow ties are seen as newly arrived scum plucked from the dung heap by magical Jack. . . . The fact that Manchester wants so badly to present Oswald as a product of the Dallas-Birch sickness intrudes to the point of suspicion."

But Thomas added, "This is such a good book, I can't see any publisher leaving any stone unturned, no matter what the consequences, and there will be bloody consequences when truly dedicated Manchester comes across my markings."

This letter clearly suggests that Thomas thought of himself at that time as being as much the Kennedys' publisher as Manchester's. It had the unintended consequence of making the Kennedys and their intermediaries overconfident in their subsequent dealings with the author because they incorrectly assumed that they had Thomas in their pocket and that he would act as their representative and ally in bringing Manchester around. But in a crisis, a publisher of integrity who believes in a book ultimately sides with the author. Within a very few weeks, Thomas had moved unmistakably to Manchester's defense and had ceased in any sense to be a Kennedy partisan, although he was still eager to make peace.

Manchester at first proved more tractable than had been feared. He accepted most of the changes proposed by Guthman and Seigenthaler as well as additional revisions urged by Thomas and other editors at Harper &

Row. "Most were wise," Manchester later recalled, explaining that their common aim as well as his own was to eliminate the problem of overwriting—"for this had been an easy book to overwrite."[13]

At Manchester's own request, two mutual friends of his and of Robert Kennedy—Arthur Schlesinger, Jr., and Richard N. Goodwin—also read the manuscript. Goodwin made only three specific suggestions. They were to change the title from *Death of Lancer* ("Lancer" was the Secret Service code word for JFK), shorten the closing section by five pages, and omit one quote by Jacqueline Kennedy. Manchester accepted all three. But Goodwin, like Guthman and Seigenthaler, was disturbed by what he regarded as the "venomous" anti-Johnson tone of the book and uneasy over the damage that might be done to Robert Kennedy's political career by airing the ill will between him and President Johnson.

On May 24, Schlesinger wrote Kennedy a six-page memorandum about the book with copies to Thomas and Manchester. "I think that this is a remarkable and potentially a great book. The research, the feeling, the narrative power, the evocation of personality and atmosphere, much of the writing—all are superb."

Schlesinger, however, criticized Manchester's depiction of both President Kennedy and President Johnson. In his original draft, Manchester in the opening section harked back to the earlier trip that JFK had made to Texas in late 1960 as a guest at the LBJ Ranch. Johnson had insisted that Kennedy go deer hunting, which he did although he had little enthusiasm for hunting. Schlesinger objected that by tying this unrelated hunting episode to the ugly, right-wing mood of Dallas three years later, Manchester unfairly presented Johnson as a symbol of "the forces of violence and irrationality." He suggested that instead the book open with an account of the public issues and the political infighting at the time of the assassination. Manchester accepted this advice, writing in new material in the opening chapter and shifting the nine pages about the hunting episode to later in the book.

Manchester in his draft also made much of the fact that JFK was worried about whether Mrs. Kennedy would pick the right clothes for the weather in Texas and of the fact that his White House office was being redecorated while he was on the trip. Schlesinger complained that the overemphasis on this trivia created a picture of a man "who is not the Kennedy we knew." Manchester was less amenable to these criticisms, and this trivia retains its prominent place in his account.

Schlesinger's memo, as Manchester later wrote in *Look*, "was peppered with such tart remarks as '92–3: keep this paragraph—it consists of facts, not opinions'; '398: restore passage marked for deletion; it sums up the point'; '821–2: restore deletions. An essential part of the story'; '871: restore deleted passage. This is perceptive and important'; '876: restore deleted passage at bottom of page. True and important'; and '1111: of course LBJ had more confidence in Rusk than Kennedy had had. Why delete?' "[14]

This memorandum brought to Manchester his first realization that there was a divergence in viewpoint among Robert Kennedy's several manuscript readers and that some of them wanted to edit his manuscript not only for what he was coming to regard as legitimate reasons—accuracy, literary taste, and Jacqueline Kennedy's feelings—but also for what he was coming to regard as an illegitimate reason—the protection of Robert Kennedy's reputation and political interests. What Manchester refused to recognize then or later, however, was that the memorandum of agreement that he had signed in March 1964, gave him no right to distinguish between legitimate and illegitimate editing. He had granted the Kennedys total control over his manuscript, and they could prevent its publication in whole or in part for any reason whatsoever. He had anticipated no difficulty getting clearance because he had romanticized Jacqueline Kennedy and Robert Kennedy as beautiful people, perfect people. They were treated as adoringly in this manuscript as he had treated JFK in *Portrait of a President*. How could the widow and the brother of his martyred hero do him any wrong? Only in the early summer of 1966 did it begin to dawn upon him that however splendid their personal qualities might be, the surviving Kennedys had interests of their own that ran counter to his as a writer. Realizing how dependent he was upon their favorable judgment of the book, he gave way to panic. His nerves were already strained and exhausted as those of writers sometimes are at the conclusion of a long creative task, and now his fear that his book would be killed or emasculated began to obsess him. He bombarded Robert Kennedy and his intermediaries with pleas for early approval. He pressured Evan Thomas to get the matter resolved.

At a meeting with Kennedy's representatives in Washington in mid-July, Thomas asked: "Do you think Bob would write a letter to Manchester saying the book will be published—in 1968 or whenever? He's going to be despondent over all these changes."

When several days passed and the letter was not forthcoming, Thomas tried again. He explained to Seigenthaler that he was leaving on a cruise and wanted the letter sent before he departed. "Manchester is making changes. I think we're going to get ninety-nine per cent of them. Can you get him [Kennedy] to do it? I'd hate to leave Manchester behind without it."

Thomas and Seigenthaler then discussed the wording of a possible letter of reassurance. But another week passed without Kennedy doing anything.

Kennedy at this point entered the scene actively for

the first time and made what proved to be his crucial mistake. He was busy with his work in the Senate and with his pre-convention maneuvering over the governorship nomination in New York. He still had not read the manuscript. (As far as can be determined, he never has.) All he had to go on were the somewhat contradictory opinions and impressions of several advisers. The consensus was that Manchester had written the book well but that it needed editing, which it was now receiving, that it was highly favorable to the Kennedys but might be embarrassing to him in his relations with President Johnson because of the detail and emphasis given to their distrust of one another, and that Manchester was in a distraught condition.

"They told me the man was sick, that he might jump out of a building or something," Kennedy said afterward.

The disagreement among his advisers was whether he should give Manchester any assurances of publication until they had the manuscript before them in its final, revised form. There was the further problem of whether he should disengage himself from any responsibility for the book and thereby escape the political onus of the author's anti-Johnson sentiments. In retrospect, it seems strange that anyone believed Kennedy could escape political embarrassment from a book that he had publicly authorized, but at the time complete disavowal of all responsibility looked like one feasible course.

Ethel Kennedy was influential in making up her husband's mind. This was an unexpected role for her since as a totally devoted wife, she normally reflects his opinions rather than influences them. But she had read Manchester's manuscript and liked it, although she made minor suggestions for revision to Seigenthaler. If his wife liked the book, Kennedy naturally felt there could not be much wrong with it. (Manchester was later to say: "Ethel is a kind girl.") As for the political consequences, he could live with them just as he had survived the uproar the previous year on the publication of the books by Schlesinger and Theodore Sorensen. But still Kennedy held off.

At 8 A.M. on July 28, Manchester telephoned Angela Novello, Kennedy's personable and highly efficient secretary, at her home. Manchester had come to know her during his research on his book. He now told her that he had not slept for three nights because he was worried over his failure to hear anything from the Senator. She passed this information to Kennedy and that afternoon, he sent Manchester a telegram:

"Should any inquiries arise *re* the manuscript of your book, I would like to state the following: 'While I have not read William Manchester's account of the death of President Kennedy, I know of the President's respect for Mr. Manchester as a historian and a reporter. I understand others have plans to publish books regarding the events of November 22, 1963.

" 'As this is going to be the subject matter of a book and since Mr. Manchester in his research had access to more information than any other writer, members of the Kennedy family will place no obstacle in the way of publication of his work.

" 'However, if Mr. Manchester's account is published in segments or excerpts, I would expect that incidents would not be taken out of context or summarized in any way which might distort the facts of or the events relating to President Kennedy's death.' "

This remarkably unlawyerlike document is as soft and vague in its wording as the original memorandum of agreement with Manchester. Its language reflects the conflicting advice Kennedy was receiving. He begins by avowing that he had not read the book and in that way suggests that no one can blame him for anything that Manchester wrote. He carries the disassociation further by blandly referring only to the possibility that other books may be published on the assassination and that Manchester had access to more information than any other writer. There is no reference to the fact that Kennedy had selected Manchester, had seen to it that he had access to information, and had assigned trusted advisers to read every word of the manuscript.

In what on the surface seems a non-sequitur, Kennedy then abruptly says, "members of the Kennedy family will place no obstacle in the way of publication of his work." On the basis of the telegram up to that point, a reader who did not remember the 1964 announcement of Manchester's selection would have had no reason to expect that the Kennedys had any right or opportunity to block publication. To Manchester and his publisher, this wording suggested—but did not actually state—that they were free to publish the manuscript. Does "members of the Kennedy family" specifically include Mrs. Jacqueline Kennedy as the contract required? Is "place no obstacle" the same as final approval of a manuscript for publication? Evan Thomas had good reason to question the precise meaning of this murky passage. But Manchester himself had no doubts or was perhaps too relieved to quibble. He wrote Kennedy an ecstatic note: "Your telegram to me was superb. It covered everything and was airtight."

It was as airtight as a bowl of fog. What Kennedy intended to do was to calm Manchester down and give what might be termed his provisional approval to publish but not make it so specific that he would lose his leverage over whatever final editing still needed to be done. He could not know the exact state of the editing since no fewer than five people—Guthman, Seigenthaler, Schlesinger, Goodwin, and Ethel Kennedy—had sent in suggestions, not to mention the editors at Harper & Row, and it was impossible to determine yet how many Manchester had actually incorporated in his final draft, particularly inasmuch as some of the suggestions were in conflict.

Manchester and his literary agent, Don Congdon, meanwhile immensely complicated an already tangled affair. They submitted copies of the manuscript to leading magazines and invited bidding on the prepublication serialization rights. The editors of *Look* and *Life,* the two chief bidders, immediately realized that Kennedy's telegram provided less than a clear go-ahead. *Life* asked author Theodore White to make a personal inquiry of Mrs. Kennedy and ascertain that she had no objection. *Look* sent Warren Rogers, its Washington representative, to see Kennedy on a similar mission. Kennedy did not conceal from Rogers his hope that *Look* would win the bidding.

"*Look* has been very good to the Kennedy family over the past two and one-half years and even in the years before that," Kennedy told him.

On July 30, *Look* purchased the rights for $665,000.

Manchester telephoned the Senator and told him of the sale and the price. According to Manchester, Kennedy replied: "Great, isn't that a record? *Look* has been so nice to the family and Henry Luce has been such a bastard."

Kennedy's animus toward Luce was based on the publisher's well-known Republican leanings and also on the belief that in serializing Schlesinger's *A Thousand Days* in 1965, *Life's* editors had cut and arranged it to embarrass Kennedy.

The contract with *Look* provided that if the Kennedys wanted to review the installments in the magazine they would have to submit their request through Manchester and *Look* would deal only with the author.

Mrs. Kennedy, who had been vacationing with her children in Hawaii, returned home in late July as these arrangements were being worked out but before the *Look* contract was signed. Before going to Hawaii, she had written Manchester that she did not intend to read the book and that she had complete faith in him. But upon hearing about the plans for serialization, she had second thoughts. Although the 1964 contract specifically permitted Manchester to arrange for magazine serialization, she had apparently not kept this in mind. The *Look* deal startled her; she was opposed to any of the book appearing in any magazine on the grounds that this would, *per se,* entail sensationalism. She expressed the rather astonishing opinion, "I thought that it [the book] would be bound in black and put away on dark library shelves."

The intensity of her feelings disconcerted Robert Kennedy. From that time forward there was a sharp turn in his attitude. He would obviously not have sent Manchester a telegram granting even qualified approval and would not have encouraged *Look* to bid for the rights if he had anticipated blocking the path to publication. He now had no alternative except to reverse his field and either halt publication or delay it for an indefinite time. He had no alternative, that is, since he is the kind of man that he is; his personal code commands him to appear always in his own mind as a knight on a white charger defending fair ladies, and most particularly his brother's widow. Her wish might not be reasonable, but her wish was still his command. The fiercely held family loyalty which sustains his drive for the Presidency is also the only commitment that takes precedence over that ambition. Mrs. Kennedy, who has intelligence but not always the best judgment, did him a deep disservice by making this heavy draft on his loyalty.

On August 10, Kennedy wired Evan Thomas at Harper & Row:

"Under the present circumstances, with the situation as difficult as it is, I feel the book on President Kennedy's death should neither be published nor serialized. I would appreciate it if you would inform Bill Manchester.

"As you know only too well, this has been a trying situation for everyone and I understand the problems this situation has caused you and the author. It just seems to me that rather than struggling with this any longer we should take our chances with Jim Bishop."

Manchester and his agent and his publisher were now in a roughly analogous position to that of President Kennedy and his advisers in the Cuban missile crisis. Since Khrushchev had sent several messages taking different positions with regard to the missiles, President Kennedy and the National Security Council decided to reply to the most favorable one and ignore the others. Since Robert Kennedy had seemingly authorized publication on July 28 and forbidden it on August 10, Manchester decided to treat the first telegram as definitive and ignore the second. In this way, he would not only be free to sell the pre-publication rights to *Look* but also and more important to publish the book. He could not accede to the demand to cancel the serialization without also implicitly conceding that Kennedy still had the right to veto the publishing of the book itself. If he held firmly to the line that the first telegram was a waiver of the Kennedys' rights, he was free of his contract restriction and in the clear to do whatever he wanted.

On August 12, he signed the contract with *Look* and then flew to Washington and confronted Kennedy with a *fait accompli*. He was prepared to yield some of the *Look* money to the Kennedy Library if that would quiet Mrs. Kennedy's concern about "commercialization" and "exploitation," but during a hectic three-hour conference in Kennedy's office, it became apparent that the money was only a symbol. Mrs. Kennedy was adamant against any serialization, and Kennedy was determined to bludgeon Manchester into yielding to her views—as he himself had yielded.

Kennedy asked Manchester to join with him in preventing the serialization and lost his temper when Manchester refused. At one point in the argument, Manchester inquired how many other authors of Kennedy books had provided that royalties be paid to the Kennedy Library. This was an irrelevancy since the other books were memoirs written by insiders; Manchester was the only outsider who had been commissioned to write a specific book. But Kennedy, unable to keep the main issue in perspective, became entangled in this money question and finally asked with heavy sarcasm: "How much do you want? Three hundred thousand? Four hundred thousand?"

The imputation was clear. Kennedy was now accusing Manchester of "making a killing" out of the President's death, the very concern he had voiced in their original interview in 1964. This was exactly the wrong approach to Manchester. However conflicting his motives, his picture of himself clearly depended upon his conviction that he was laboring solely to do justice to his fallen hero, JFK.

Subsequently, Manchester cried out, truthfully enough: "I didn't come to you, you came to me. I was perfectly happy writing a book I was interested in doing. . . . This book has ruined my life, my family life is not the same. I've been under a doctor's care."

After this tortured confrontation between Kennedy and Manchester, both driven by emotional imperatives and not wholly in control of themselves, the two men were to meet once more in the autumn, but after that climactic interview on August 12, their relationship was never to be restored. The opportunity for diplomacy was lost. Kennedy had already moved to threats of lawsuits. During that interview, Kennedy telephoned John F. Harding, the general counsel for *Look*, in New York and said he had never approved the manuscript for publication and requested Harding to cancel the series. When Harding refused, Kennedy asked for a postponement. Harding said he would take it up with Gardner Cowles, the publisher of *Look*.

Cowles and his editors proved much tougher to deal with than Evan Thomas and Harper & Row. They had a valid contract covering the manuscript and were determined to publish it as they saw fit without yielding any editorial powers to the Kennedys. There were numerous telephone calls from Mrs. Kennedy to Cowles which started out on a "Jackie" and "Mike" basis and ended up on a "Mrs. Kennedy" and "Mr. Cowles" basis. In late August, Cowles and his lawyer, Harding, visited her in Hyannis Port. Her attorney, former Federal Judge Simon Rifkind, was present as was Robert Kennedy. During the course of this lengthy, inconclusive conference, it was unmistakably clear that she rather than Robert Kennedy was the aggressive protagonist in the dispute. She stated that she wanted both the book and the serialization halted.

"No, not the book," Kennedy interjected.

Harding asked her if Kennedy had been speaking in her behalf on July 28 when he sent Manchester the telegram stating that "members of the Kennedy family" would place no obstacles in the way of the book.

"Bob doesn't represent me, he sort of protects me," she replied.

Mrs. Kennedy asked Cowles if he were determined to publish installments in *Look*.

"First, let me ask a question," Cowles said. "I sense an undercurrent that *Look* didn't act in good faith."

"*Look* acted in good faith," Senator Kennedy replied.

Cowles then said yes, he was determined to publish the serialization.

On the flight back to New York, Kennedy and Cowles sat together, spending much of their time discussing an article, "Suppose God is Black," which *Look* had just published by Kennedy about his trip to South Africa. Saying good-by in New York, the Senator, reverting to the Manchester book, said, "Mike, you're a publisher, see what you can do about this."

In an effort to compromise the dispute, Cowles two days later informed Rifkind that *Look* would postpone serialization from the issue of October 18 to that of January 12 (so that it would not be on the newsstands during the anniversary of the assassination) and would reduce the number of installments from seven to four. *Look* kept to this schedule, but the compromise did not really mollify Mrs. Kennedy. She was determined to prevent any serialization whatever.

A week later, on September 6, she invited Manchester to Hyannis Port in an attempt to win him to her side. This only resulted in another long, inconclusive afternoon.

"It's us against them," she said.

By then, Manchester was no longer as sure as he once had been that the Kennedy "us" included him.

"Your whole life proves that you are a man of honor," she said.

But Manchester was by then in the grip of an obsession of his own: that his honor would be destroyed if he compromised any further.

During the course of this conversation, Mrs. Kennedy, according to Manchester, made the now famous remark, "Anyone who is against me will look like a rat unless I run off with Eddie Fisher."

Mrs. Kennedy, however, had unwittingly alienated Manchester in the course of the summer by permitting Mrs. Pamela Turnure Timmins, her press secretary, to read the manuscript. Before taking the job of Mrs. Kennedy's buffer against the press, Mrs. Timmins had been the receptionist in John F. Kennedy's Senate office. She is pretty and charming, but Manchester understandably felt that she had no professional credentials to edit his manuscript. She suggested seventy-seven changes, some minor and some serious, and Manchester refused to consider any of them. At the rate intermediaries were getting into the act, he feared that soon Mrs. Kennedy would be turning his manuscript over to her hairdresser for his comments.

Having failed to convert Cowles or Manchester, Mrs. Kennedy had only two alternatives by mid-September: to sue to prevent publication or to hope that, working through Manchester, she could achieve the elimination of the offending passages that various of her advisers complained about. (At this point, she herself had not read the entire manuscript.) She chose the second course and, on Kennedy's advice, settled upon Richard Goodwin as her representative in dealing with *Look* and Manchester. *Look* reluctantly agreed to accept changes proposed through Goodwin if they were questions of accuracy. Robert Kennedy, although busy campaigning across the country for Democratic Congressional candidates, took time to hold conferences in New York with Sorensen, Schlesinger, Seigenthaler, Guthman, and others. All the doubts of the previous spring about the political wisdom of permitting a book to appear with the Kennedy stamp of approval which said so many bitter words about Texas and Texans and which reported so much antagonism between the Johnsons and the Kennedys now resurfaced. Kennedy, who had been willing to risk the political consequences in the spring and early summer, now shifted ground. He decided that not only the personal material that was offensive to Mrs. Kennedy but also the political material that some of his advisers felt was risky to him should be deleted. His growing antagonism toward Manchester and his deepening conviction that the writer had double-crossed him by signing the contract with *Look* were important factors in his decision, which evolved over a series of meetings.

This decision, however, made Goodwin's task much more difficult. Manchester was by then in a highly agitated state of mind; the revision of a word or a phrase presented itself to him not as a minor problem but as a crisis of conscience. He was simultaneously editing the final version of his book and, under his contract with *Look*, editing the four installments. He would make some changes requested of him and not make others, although an outside observer would be hard put to see why one was more objectionable than the other.

As the weeks and months of haggling and conferring passed, Mrs. Kennedy's objections centered on six episodes —two describing her actions and thoughts as she stood by her husband's coffin, two concerning her and her husband as they prepared to retire on the night before his assassination, and two that quoted letters that she and her daughter Caroline had written to her husband and which she had made available to Manchester.

But the political changes that Robert Kennedy sought were much more extensive. Some of them involved Mrs. Kennedy, and some did not. There was, for example, her observation about Governor John Connally of Texas: "I can't stand him." Another typical change involved the following passage in which Manchester described a request she made of Mac Kilduff, the assistant White House Press Secretary, as the plane bearing her husband's body prepared to land in Washington. The words which the Kennedys wished to delete are italicized:

"During her three years in the White House, she had learned much about Lyndon Johnson. Their rapport had been excellent, *but she knew how skillful he was at manipulating people. She intended to make certain she was not manipulated now.* A great deal depended upon what the press was told when they landed.

"She sent for Kilduff and said, 'You make sure, Mac— *you go and tell the President—don't let Lyndon Johnson say that I sat with him and Lady Bird and they comforted* *me all during the trip. You say—*you say that I came back here and sat with Jack.' "

Other changes would have greatly toned down Manchester's account of President Johnson's first Cabinet meeting, which Robert Kennedy did not want to attend and for which he arrived late.

In the end, Manchester would make very few of the revisions, either personal or political. He had become convinced that any concession he made would only lead to demands for further concessions. In late October, while the proofs of the *Look* articles were still under consideration, Robert Kennedy made another attempt to resolve matters on a man-to-man basis with Manchester. It was their first meeting since their confrontation in the Senator's office two months earlier and it was almost as disastrous. Manchester agreed to visit Kennedy's home in Virginia and discuss the proofs with him and Goodwin. It was a mistake on Manchester's part to agree to go since he really did not want to make any concessions to Kennedy. Their conversation was polite but strained, and the two kept marching up verbal dead-end streets.

"Bill, you have the vagueness of a genius," Kennedy remarked.

The day was cool, but Kennedy suggested a dip in the swimming pool. Manchester found the swim "unnerving." "Kennedy would ask me a question, then duck under water and I would wait for him to surface in the pool before answering. His head was under water most of the time." By this rude behavior, Kennedy acted out the anger he felt toward his guest but was struggling to keep under control.

When no accommodation could be reached, Mrs. Kennedy, after prolonged vacillation, sued Manchester, *Look*, and Harper & Row in December. Robert Kennedy did not join her in the suit because he wanted to limit his own public involvement and because her case was legally stronger if she acted alone and maintained that his telegram of July 28 did not speak for her.

The suit was pointless. By the time it was filed, so many copies of the manuscript were in existence and had passed through so many hands that even if the defendants had agreed to suppress every disputed passage, the original text would soon be circulating in bootlegged copies. But the suit brought the long-simmering controversy to the boiling point. There followed several days of intense negotiations. The Kennedys had originally asked *Look* and Manchester to delete a total of about six thousand words from the four installments, roughly ten per cent of the sixty thousand words. Both sides now arrived at an out-of-court settlement deleting only sixteen hundred words. The Kennedys had wanted other cuts from the book itself, but the separate agreement provided for deleting only another two thousand words. The principal deletions were the same as in the magazine since the most sensitive passages were there. In addition, Manchester agreed to disassociate the Kennedys from the book by not mentioning them in the foreword and— money again—to turn over to the Kennedy Library certain ancillary sources of income from the book that had been scheduled to go to him.

Notwithstanding this final provision, Robert Kennedy at the conclusion of "the Battle of the Book" was justified in observing: "They've got the money and we've got the public relations problem."

The actual rights and wrongs were closely balanced. On the basic issue of whether the book could be published if it contained material of which they did not approve, the Kennedys were in the right. Manchester had signed a contract giving them the absolute right of review, and he violated the contract. Until Mrs. Kennedy sued and the out-of-court settlement was reached, Manchester was pre-

pared to publish a book and a serialization both of which
he knew did not meet with the Kennedys' approval. Even
if it is conceded that Robert Kennedy's telegram of July
28 constituted a waiver of his right of review, Manchester
still did not abide by the spirit of the agreement. By early
August, it was clear to him that Mrs. Kennedy was not
pleased with the idea of serialization or with everything
that was in the book manuscript, but instead of holding
off until he had her approval, he went ahead and sold
the manuscript to *Look*.

These facts are all irrefutable. Nothing Manchester
subsequently said in his own defense about his honor as
a writer, the integrity of his book, and the claims of history alters those facts. The belief that history is a blind
goddess who speaks through the writer and must be
heard is a romantic but false idea. It carries the implica-
tion that there has to be total exposure instantly after
the event or else the writer is corrupt. In reality, history
is the work of many hands adding and rearranging bits
and pieces of the evidence, never definitive and always
in the making, as various writers work at different times
and under different conditions. What matters is what
might be termed intellectual truth-in-labeling. A writer is
free to write or not write under certain conditions. If he
chooses to accept conditions, he should state in his book
what these conditions were and to what extent they limited him. Throughout the controversy, Manchester talked
as if he were being subjected to some unprecedented
restraints and as if he were the first person ever commissioned to write an authorized biography or an official
history. The contemporary historian, he argued, has to be
tough: "better bruises than history without flesh." In his
apologia in *Look*, he suggested that only a hack would
have done otherwise: "Had the Kennedys chosen a pedes-
trian talent, the resulting chronicle would have been
bland and flat, yet there would have been no row. My

offense was that I was determined to give this generation a living history." But great writers from ancient times to the present have written worthwhile books under one kind of restraint or another. To take a modern example, Sir Harold Nicolson's authorized biographies of Dwight Morrow and King George V in no way impaired his high reputation; both books are well regarded although no one seriously supposes that Nicolson wrote the last word or even everything he personally knew about either of his subjects. As far as serving history is concerned, Manchester could have told this generation all that his contract permitted him to tell and left his unedited manuscript in the archives for future historians to read.

But if the Kennedys were right in principle, they did everything wrong in practice. Mrs. Kennedy was more to blame inasmuch as she delegated all responsibility to her brother-in-law and then contradicted him and intervened when the situation was far advanced and already complicated. But in judging her adversely, one has to recognize the context in which she makes most of her decisions. It is a mistake to see her, as Manchester and others have, opposing him in her role as Mrs. Kennedy, the widow and former First Lady. She was learning to function as a politician's wife in 1963, and her decision to accompany her husband to Texas was an expression of a new determination to play her public part. If the President had not been assassinated, she would have grown into that role and become a somewhat different woman. But since November 1963, she has largely reverted to the intensely private person she always was; she has become once again Jackie Bouvier. Only at intervals of her own choosing does she act once again as a public figure.

As a private person, she is a member of "the very rich" in the F. Scott Fitzgerald sense. She is part of that small group of moneyed families who have had wealth and social status for five generations or more. The Bouviers and, on her mother's side, the Lees of Maryland and Virginia are among this group as is her stepfather's family, the Auchinclosses. Novelist Stephen Birmingham writing about the Auchinclosses observed that they have been "called 'the most marvelously connected family in the United States,' a family whose members occupy nearly two full pages of the New York *Social Register,* some forty-seven separate listings, compared with forty-two for Rockefellers, eight for Vanderbilts, and a mere two for Astors. Through what society terms 'brilliant' marriages, the Auchinclosses are kin to such formidable families as the Saltonstalls, Winthrops, Sloans, Jenningses and Rockefellers—and to their respective fortunes—as well as to those of the Frelinghuysens, the Van Rensselaers and more than a dozen others. One in-law remarked, "The Auchinclosses aren't a *family.* They're a land mass."[15]

The members of this small world of the very rich, and particularly its women, live sheltered, privileged, ordered lives modeled on the standards and decorum of the British landed aristocracy of a century ago. They unself-consciously behave, make the claims and exact the deference that royalty and aristocracy did in Britain in the bygone era before democracy and inheritance taxes. In fighting Manchester, Jacqueline Kennedy was asserting the standards of her own upbringing and her own parents as to what is private, what is in good taste, what is owed a lady. This personal hierarchy of values can sometimes sustain her brilliantly as it did during the weekend of her husband's funeral, but at other times it undercuts her political role as a Kennedy and it can make her appear arbitrary and imperious.

If she had been performing her public role as a great man's widow, she would have recognized that her privacy had already been breached and that public persons have to make accommodations that are not demanded of those in private life. Because at critical moments in the

Manchester affair she lapsed into being Jackie Bouvier rather than Mrs. John Kennedy, she stumbled badly in her role as queen regent of an ambitious political dynasty.

Robert Kennedy was well aware from the outset of the political and public relations risks of a quarrel with Manchester, but his rigid code of personal loyalty impelled him to try to carry out the wishes of his brother's widow. He failed in the attempt because he misjudged Manchester and hopelessly mismanaged his dealings with him. When they met on August 12, it should already have been clear to Kennedy that his own telegram, his encouragement to *Look* to pursue the bidding, and Manchester's signing of the contract had almost foreclosed the situation from his and Mrs. Kennedy's standpoint. His only hope was to win Manchester's cooperation and through him get deleted whatever material was essential to delete. But he tried pressure instead of charm.

In this context, it is intriguing to speculate how John Kennedy would have handled a comparable situation. He would probably have had the courage to read the manuscript, painful though that would have been, and to take personal charge of the problem. It is certain that he would have kept his temper under strict control and avoided the distracting issue of the money. John Kennedy was always fascinated as to how much money writers earned from their books and articles and would jokingly advise them to hold out for the highest price. However strong his private feelings for a dead brother, he would not have taken the position that any writer was getting overpaid for his labor. Since he cherished his own Pulitzer prize and profoundly admired men who have what Lord Morley called "the glory of words," he would have been able to establish an empathy with almost any writer, particularly one as susceptible to the appeal of ideals and romantic ideas as Manchester. One can well imagine how John

Kennedy would have taken Manchester aside and virtually swept him off his feet.

Robert Kennedy was simply unable to enter imaginatively into a writer's mind. President Kennedy, a writer himself, understood that a writer will accept almost anything if he is treated as a kind of magician and will forgive almost nothing if he is condescended to as a technician.

Manchester, reacting against Robert Kennedy's pressure and condescension, went all out to win the battle of reputations and easily succeeded. He overdid it a bit when he compared himself to a victim of Nazi tyranny: "As a scholar of Germany under National Socialism, I perceived a kind of American *Nacht und Nebel Erlass* [a Hitler decree]. It was as though the First and Fourteenth Amendments had been struck from the U.S. Constitution." Nevertheless, he successfully established the picture of himself as an honest man persecuted by an implacable, power-mad Kennedy surrounded and served by "a great many gifted men [who] were staking their careers on an RFK administration. . . . The Kennedy court was . . . active. Trumpets were sounded, courtiers assembled, proclamations read, long knives sharpened."

Kennedy is indeed seeking his family's restoration to power. It is for him a bitter irony that the court historian he selected has provided the worst moments in his career as heir apparent.

The Manchester episode was a setback, but the long march goes on. And 1968 remains the first target date.

Kennedy is determined to be prepared for the unexpected, and the first unexpected development could be Lyndon Johnson's voluntary retirement in 1968. Mr. Johnson is not likely to withdraw by choice; politics are his whole life, and he has no desire to sit on the LBJ Ranch all week and count his cows. Nor is he likely to be scared out of running by public opinion polls forecasting his defeat; no President ever really believes in the likelihood of his own defeat, and Harry Truman's upset victory in 1948 shows that incumbents have good reasons for confidence. But if his health failed, Mr. Johnson would have no alternative except to step down. If that should occur, Kennedy intends to make certain that he is the new nominee, not Vice-President Humphrey. Conceivably, Kennedy could be so well positioned that he would obtain the nomination even if Mr. Johnson died shortly before the convention and Humphrey had already succeeded to the office.

Speaking at Princeton University on March 7, 1967, Theodore Sorensen pointed out that the three other Vice-Presidents in the twentieth century who inherited the Presidency—Theodore Roosevelt, Calvin Coolidge, and Harry Truman—were content to retire after winning only one election. The four Vice-Presidents who reached the White House the same way in the nineteenth century did not obtain a nomination for even one full term on their own. Observers quickly pointed out that both Theodore Roosevelt and Truman served almost a full eight years since they completed all but a few months of their predecessor's term. Only Coolidge provides an exact precedent in the modern period for a Johnson withdrawal in 1968. But for a politician, historical parallels are what one makes them; Sorensen speaking for the Kennedy wing of the party has provided Mr. Johnson with a rationale for retirement if he wants one. In his words, "If Mr. Johnson of his own accord chooses [to retire], no one can call that a retreat from the historical pattern when it would in reality be fidelity to it."

On the assumption that Mr. Johnson seeks reelection, the Vice-Presidency is an interim goal for Kennedy in 1968. As late as the autumn of 1966, Kennedy avowed to intimates that he would take second place on the ticket if it were offered to him. The dropping of Humphrey and the substitution of Kennedy could, with skillful publicity, be made to appear not as an act of bold usurpation by Kennedy but a reluctant rescue mission to prop up an aging, wartime President whose popularity is sagging.

Many observers believe that Kennedy would be foolish to accept the Vice-Presidency, and they note how stultifying the office has been for Humphrey. But that is only because Humphrey is almost totally dependent on Mr. Johnson for his political future. The office during Mr. Johnson's second term would be far less confining for Kennedy, who, unlike Humphrey, has his own independent power base and is a more aggressive and freewheeling operator.

Replacing Humphrey on the ticket in 1968 would accomplish two important objectives. It would eliminate Kennedy's only visible rival for the presidential succession, thereby consolidating his position as the most powerful man in the Democratic Party next to Mr. Johnson. Second, it would place him one heartbeat from the White House. As matters now stand, if the Johnson-Humphrey combination is reelected in 1968 and the President were subsequently to die, Humphrey's elevation would block Kennedy's path in 1972, when Humphrey would presumably seek reelection in his own right, and conceivably in 1976 as well. Kennedy has no intention of hanging around the Senate until 1980.

But the prospects of Kennedy joining the Johnson ticket were sharply reduced early in 1967 when he and the President again disagreed openly over the course of the war in Vietnam. As if to foreclose this possibility for Kennedy, the President gave Humphrey a strong public endorsement for renomination. At news conferences in August and September 1966, he had evaded questions about Humphrey's future. But on March 9, 1967, he praised Humphrey to a news conference in the strongest terms and made it clear that he regarded him as the ideal running mate.

Yet, as Sorensen had earlier observed to a reporter after his Princeton speech, "Politics is one of the most uncertain areas and the situation could change radically by next year."

One contingency is that Humphrey, too, is mortal. Another is that Mr. Johnson if he found himself in a really desperate fight for reelection might change his mind and decide he needed Kennedy on the ticket, much as he disliked him. He would regard taking Kennedy aboard as rather like signing up Long John Silver as his first mate. But the President is an old professional, and old pros who find themselves in a tight corner have been known to make equally strange and distasteful alliances. Moreover, Mr. Johnson has an emotional vested interest in not downgrading the political importance of the vice-presidential candidate in a campaign: he firmly believes that his own presence on the ticket in 1960 carried the South and elected John Kennedy.

Kennedy's power drive is such that there is even the possibility he may fight President Johnson for the top of the ticket in 1968. The odds are against his doing this since, if he did, his chances of success seem so poor. No incumbent President who wanted renomination has been denied it in the past seventy-five years.

Since the possibilities of Kennedy's being nominated for President or Vice-President in 1968 are marginal, they would merit little discussion were it not for the fact that Kennedy's relentless round of activities establishes him as a leader bidding for national support. He could scarcely have been more active on all fronts in 1966–67 if the nomination were wide open. He is staffed and organized like a presidential candidate; his speaking schedule takes him to every corner of the nation; he has interested himself in the complete range of issues, domestic and foreign.

Sound political logic argues for Kennedy making his bid in 1968, if he can get the nomination, rather than waiting four years. If he is right that a bloody stalemate in Vietnam will lead to a Johnson-Humphrey defeat in 1968, then four years later he would be running against a Republican incumbent. Barring a special circumstance such as an unpopular war, it is always more difficult to defeat an incumbent. Kennedy would much prefer to be the Democratic peace candidate in 1968, running on even terms with a Republican opponent, than be the challenger against a new President in 1972.

Although he is impatient, he is not reckless. He pushes as hard as he can but he is careful not to tear apart the party he hopes to lead.

Kennedy's boldest ploy against Johnson has been to cast subtle doubt on the latter's political legitimacy. On the morning of Johnson's inaugural on January 20, 1965, Kennedy visited his brother's grave in Arlington. When photographers wanted a picture he revisited the grave early in the afternoon. No one seeing that picture the next day was in any doubt as to whose inaugural day it should have been.

Normally, Kennedy does not have to be so direct in challenging Johnson. His every action as keeper of the flame of his brother's legend is challenge enough. In the spring of 1965, he climbed Mt. Kennedy in the Yukon. (Has jowly, paunchy LBJ climbed any mountains recently?) In the fall of 1965, he toured Latin America: "I want to see if the Alliance for Progress is doing as well as it was in President Kennedy's time." (If it is now failing, who is to blame?) In June of 1966, he visited South Africa and spoke up for freedom there as his brother once spoke up for Algerian independence. (What stodgy officeholder is maintaining the status quo in relations with South Africa's tyrannical and exploitative government?)

Kennedy's problem is to project himself as a viable and

convincing liberal alternative to President Johnson and to Johnson's chosen heir, Hubert Humphrey, but yet not go so far as to make impossible an eventual accommodation between himself and his party rivals. He wishes to supplant them but also to hold at least their nominal support once he has done so. Thus it is that every criticism is coupled with a compliment. He attacks Johnson for stiffening the negotiation terms in Vietnam and then praises him as "a man of peace." He deplores the failure to expand the war on poverty and then lauds Johnson as "a man of compassion." There is no more hypocrisy in all this than is strictly necessary. It is merely the gentle oscillation between rebellion and conformity of a political leader moving toward power in rather heavy weather.

What kind of President would Robert Kennedy make?

He would try to live up to the activist, innovative concept of the Presidency that his brother had. Speaking to the National Press Club in 1960, the then Senator John Kennedy articulated a view of the office that he frequently expounded to college audiences. Asking himself what do the times and the people demand for the next four years in the White House, he answered: "They demand a vigorous proponent of the national interest—not a passive broker for conflicting private interests. They demand a man capable of acting as the Commander-in-Chief of the Grand Alliance. . . . They demand that he be the head of a responsible party, not rise so far above politics as to be invisible—a man who will formulate and fight for legislative policies, not be a casual bystander to the legislative process."

Robert Kennedy would be a President with a broad national view, a lively interest in international affairs, and an unflagging concern with many small details as well as the large problems. He would, it goes without saying, be the leader of his party and alert to political advantage. In dealing with Congress on behalf of his legislative program, he might show less deference to committee chairmen than his brother and a somewhat greater disposition to wage open combat.

If he were elected, he would meet three criteria his brother also outlined for a chief executive: "He must master complex problems as well as receive one-page memoranda. He must originate action as well as study groups. He must reopen the channels of communication between the world of thought and the seat of power."[16]

Kennedy has the intelligence and energy to master complex problems. Since he is open to new ideas and likes to experiment, he would originate action on problems rather than shelve them for study. He has great respect for brains and has developed as large a coterie of academics as his brother had; he would have no difficulty making use of professors and keeping open the channels of communication with the world of thought.

The most famous definition of the Presidency was offered by Harry Truman: "The buck stops here." Robert Kennedy not only accepts responsibility; he covets it. But equally important to what stops at the President's desk is what starts there. The kinds of programs and policies that Kennedy would initiate or continue, if he were elected in the near future, are foreseeable; he is interested in stepping up the pace of racial integration, in breaking down the slum ghettos, and in putting an end to the hard-core poverty and degradation of the worst-off Negroes. He is interested in improving education and in reducing juvenile delinquency. His mind is practical rather than doctrinaire. He also places a high value on cleaning up old problems and finding some solutions, even if less than entirely satisfactory. As he demonstrated as Attorney General in approving the New York Central-Pennsylvania Railroad merger, in working out the details of the mixed public-and-private Communications Satellite Corporation, in raising private funds to ransom from Castro the Bay of Pigs captives, in dickering with racist governors in the Southern school crises, and in settling the long disputed General Aniline and Film alien property case, he is flexible and pragmatic. He has few preconceived intellectual commitments that inhibit him in arriving at compromises.

In this skepticism and fluidity, he resembles his late brother; he, too, is "an idealist without illusions." What Henry Pachter, an editor of the radical magazine *Dissent,* once wrote of President Kennedy is almost equally true of his brother: "The terms 'liberal' and 'conservative' had no meaning for Kennedy, a disciple of Castlereagh and Talleyrand for whom ideologies were right if and when they worked. . . . What distinguished Kennedy from the New Dealers was his conviction that the problems of modern society are not so much based on conflicts of interests as on questions of management. . . . To ideologies or 'myths' he opposed 'reality,' which meant the technological, administrative means to attain accepted ends."[17]

Robert Kennedy is more passionate, more openly aggressive, more impulsive, and more capable of commitment than was his brother, but fundamentally, he also is neither liberal nor conservative; he is an ideologically uncommitted man. If once he saw the world as a struggle of "the black hats vs. the white hats," he no longer believes in this Hollywood Western scenario. His youthful enthusiasm for Joe McCarthy's adventure soon flickered out; the long, wearying pursuit of James Hoffa diminished his zeal for chasing crooks; and his experience near the summit of power both as Attorney General and as an adviser to his brother on foreign affairs brought him a more complicated, sophisticated view of the world.

Kennedy has identified himself with the concerns and

aspirations of the young because it is good politics to be
associated with the future rather than the past and because he is admiring of their commitment and receptive
to their enthusiasm. But he has a tougher, more complex,
more worldly-wise understanding of power and political
realities than his youthful admirers. When the public
controversy developed in February 1967 over the Central
Intelligence Agency's clandestine financing of student
groups, labor unions, and other private organizations to
fight the political and intellectual cold war against the
Communists, Kennedy held a not-for-attribution press
luncheon with several reporters. He told them that it was
unfair for Vice-President Humphrey and other top officials
of the Johnson administration to let the CIA "take the
rap" alone for this policy of secretly financing private
groups.

"Top officials in the executive branch in the Eisenhower, Kennedy, and Johnson administrations knew about
this policy. All the relevant government agencies were
approached for approval. If the policy was wrong, it was
not the product of the CIA but of each administration,"
Kennedy explained.

Since he had been chairman of the committee super-
vising the CIA in his brother's administration, Kennedy
was intimately familiar with the subsidies. He made no
effort to defend them at length, but he did tell the
reporters, "We must not forget that we are not dealing
with a dream world, but with a very tough adversary."

A week later, when columnists Drew Pearson and Jack
Anderson, who had not attended the luncheon, printed
a story about it, Kennedy allowed the reporters who had
been present to publish his remarks.[18]

Kennedy tries to avoid the moralizing, self-righteous
overtones that brought so much criticism upon the late
John Foster Dulles and other cold warriors, but as a
realist, he recognizes that "the thaw" in relations with

the Soviet Union is not the same as an unending summer. President Kennedy once characterized the Russian attitude concisely: "They do not wish us well." And what is true of Russia is equally true of Communist China and Castro's Cuba. The Communist countries are training political agents and guerrilla fighters, dispensing propaganda, giving arms, bribing politicians, and infiltrating student groups, trade unions, and political parties in an effort to win the underdeveloped countries of Asia, Africa, and Latin America to their side. In his visits to these countries, Kennedy tries to combat these Communist efforts. His numerous talks with foreign students, his concern over the effectiveness of the Voice of America, and his fascination with counter-insurgency are all part of this central preoccupation.

"If we do not do more in Africa to show that we are concerned, then we can expect Communism to fill the void," he said after his trip there in 1966. "A revolution is coming in Latin America," he prophesied a year earlier, and pointing to the efforts of Chile's reform government, he warned that if it failed, the country might go Communist.

Kennedy's peace proposals in Vietnam and his call for rethinking of U.S. relations with Communist China are, therefore, not a complete guide to the foreign policies he would pursue if he becomes President. He is a hero to many liberals and radicals, but he is not a captive of the mythology of the New Left, or the Old. He remains a hardheaded pragmatist intent upon exercising power in the best national interests of the United States and the cause of freedom.

The Presidency if it comes to him is a future chapter in an unfolding story, but whatever that future holds, Robert Kennedy's extraordinary political accomplishment is already secure. In less than four years after his brother's assassination, he has raised himself to a position of independent national political power. He is not only a leading contender for his party's presidential nomination; he has made himself almost its inevitable choice. His family's reputation and accomplishments helped him, and so did the nation's guilt over the crime in Dallas. If Abraham Lincoln had had a younger brother, he might have gone far in national politics. But Robert Kennedy has done more than perpetuate a legend. He has established himself in his own right, successfully confronted new issues, and developed new sources of political strength. No dynasty could ask more of its heir apparent.

NOTES

1 John F. Kennedy, quoted in Sorensen, *Kennedy.*, p. 77; Oscar Williams, ed., *A Little Treasury of Modern Poetry*, "The Man Coming Toward You," (Charles Scribner's Sons, New York, 1946) p. 381.

2 Personal interviews.

3 A. E. Housman, "Reveille," *A Shropshire Lad.*

4 James M. Perry, The *National Observer*, October 17, 1966.

5 Kenneth Crawford, "The Youth Myth," *Newsweek*, November 7, 1966.

6 Part of the speech is reprinted in *The New Republic*, March 11, 1967, p. 11.

7 Theodore Solotaroff, "The Pursuit of Paradise," *Book Week, World Journal Tribune*, March 5, 1967. For an interesting discussion of Kennedy's intellectual interests see also Andrew Kopkind, "He's a Happening," *The New Republic*, April 2, 1966.

8 Trevor Armbrister, "A Loser Makes It Big," *Saturday Evening Post*, January 14, 1967.

9 Robert F. Kennedy, "Our Climb Up Mt. Kennedy," *Life*, April 9, 1965.

10 William Manchester, *Portrait of a President* (Little, Brown, Boston, 1963) p. 217.

[11] Interview in New York *Post*, January 31, 1967, p. 33.

[12] William Manchester, "Manchester's Own Story," *Look*, April 4, 1967, p. 72.

[13] *Ibid.*

[14] *Ibid.*

[15] Stephen Birmingham, "How the Remarkable Auchincloss Family Shaped the Jacqueline Kennedy Style," *Ladies Home Journal*, March 1967.

[16] Address to the National Press Club, January 14, 1960.

[17] Henry Pachter, "JFK as an Equestrian Statue," *Salmagundi*, Vol. 1, No. 3, p. 3.

[18] Pearson and Anderson, Washington *Post*, February 21, 1967; *The New York Times*, February 22, 1967.

Index

Index